THE FIFTH *TIMES*
BOOK OF BEST SERMONS

The Fifth *Times*
Book of Best Sermons

Edited and Introduced by

Ruth Gledhill

Foreword by

Dr Margaret Brearley

CASSELL
London and New York

Cassell
Wellington House
125 Strand
London WC2R 0BB

370 Lexington Avenue
New York
NY 10017-6550

First published 1999

British Library Cataloguing-in-Publication Data
A catalogue record for this book is available from the British Library.

ISBN 0-304-70656-6 (paperback)

Typeset by BookEns Ltd, Royston, Hertfordshire
Printed and bound in Great Britain by
Martins the Printers Ltd, Berwick upon Tweed

Contents

CONTENTS

Foreword

Dr Margaret Brearley
*Writer and academic specializing in
Jewish–Christian relations*

From a worm's eye view: a few *aperçus*

'It is become an impertinent Vein among People of all Sorts to hunt
after what they call a good Sermon, as if it were a Matter of Pastime
and Diversion. Our Business, alas, is quite another Thing, either to
learn, or at least be reminded of our Duty' (Jonathan Swift, 'Upon
sleeping in church').

The *Times* annual Good Sermon hunt: diversion, duty – or even,
as some have suggested, an impertinence? 'Impertinence indeed!',
Martin Luther might well have cried, for in his view: 'A poor speaker
may speak the Word of God just as well as he who is endowed with
eloquence. A father speaks the Word of God as well as God does, and
your neighbour speaks it as well as the angel Gabriel. There is no
difference between the Word when uttered by a schoolboy and when
uttered by the angel Gabriel; they vary only in rhetorical ability.'

This is debatable. There have always been bad preachers as well as
good, and to encourage good preaching is to nurture a potent force
for spiritual awakening and ethical change, as an English friar noted
in the early fifteenth century: 'By preaching folk be stirred to
contrition, and to forsake sin and the fiend, and to love God and
goodness; and be illumined to know their God, and virtues from vice,
truth from falsehood, and to forsake errors and heresies.' The
Anglican poet-priest George Herbert urged parsons to remind their
listeners that 'sermons are dangerous things, that none goes out of
church as he came in, but either better or worse'. Why? Because, for
Herbert, the preacher stands 'in God's stead'. 'Who is speaking? The
pastor? By no means. You do not hear the pastor. Of course the voice
is his, but the words he employs are really spoken by God' (Luther).

The Christian preacher as mouthpiece of God, a bridge between
God and man: a lofty and difficult ideal. St Gregory wrote in his
Pastoral Rule: 'True preachers both aspire in contemplation to the
holy Head of the Church, that is the Lord, above; they also ...
descend in commiseration downwards to His members ... Within,

they consider the secret things of God; without, they carry the burdens of the worldly.'

Preaching can change lives. It inspires contrition, comforts the bereaved and offers hope for despair. At its best, it can excite audiences 'to the practice of virtue' (Pascal) and 'enflame the hearts of the auditors from the burning heart of the preacher' (Guibert de Nogent). It can be as powerful as the greatest music. A twelfth-century homily likened a sermon to David's harp, the preacher's words and deeds the strings for the music of God's word. The preacher 'should be as Orpheus playing the cithara, attracting people through his sweet notes of warning and gentle invitation to penitence' (Pepin, fifteenth-century France), whereas John Knox's preaching had more power to awaken hearers than a blast 'from 500 trumpets'. Little wonder, then, that Bishop Hensley Henson argued that 'of all the actions of the Christian ministry preaching is the highest, and the test of our reverence for our profession is our performance of the preacher's duty'.

Bad sermons, however, can be, as one foreigner described mid-eighteenth-century English preaching, 'most tedious monotony'. Worse still, they are soporific. Latimer told of a London gentle-woman whose neighbour asked her where she was going. 'Marry', she said, 'I am going to St Thomas of Acres to the sermon. I could not sleep all this last night, and I am now going thither; I never failed of a good nap there.' Worst of all, they can induce anger, as St Ambrose of Milan recognized: 'A tedious sermon arouses wrath.'

'But who are you to be judging?', you might well be thinking by now. 'Have you preached 42,500 sermons like John Wesley, or Whitefield's 18,000, or the average Anglican vicar's 6,000–10,000? Have you preached even ... one?' Well ... no! pulpit lectures and talks, indeed, but sermons? ... Afraid not. 'Then why on earth, Dr Brearley, did Ruth Gledhill invite you to judge this competition?'

Perhaps I am here to offer a worm's eye view, so to speak, a hearer's ideas, having listened over the years to more than 4,000 sermons, mostly Christian, some Jewish. More to the point, I have read thousands of mediaeval and post-Reformation sermons and many *artes praedicandi* (preaching manuals). Ruth Gledhill suggested that it might be a interesting exercise to compare some of today's preaching practices both with mediaeval Christian preaching and with Jewish preaching traditions. For while outstanding sermons are preached today, and some are included in this book, the general level of preaching is arguably considerably lower than at some other times in Church history. It is possible, therefore, that modern preachers might glean one or two ideas from earlier patterns and practices. For although preaching is a pastoral duty and should be divinely inspired, it is also a craft with techniques to cherish and hone. 'There is a particular art of Preaching, to which if Ministers did more seriously apply themselves, it would extremely facilitate that service, making it both more easie to us, & more profitable to others' (Bishop Wilkins in *Ecclesiastes, or the gift of Preaching*, 1646).

Self versus congregation

In mediaeval sermons the focus was generally on the congregation and on God, never on the preacher. Occasionally a preacher would introduce a story or quotation by saying 'I have heard/read/seen', but he was otherwise self-effacing. The ideal was to be, as a vehicle for God's word, both humble and bold. Today's ubiquitous trend towards subjectivity and 'authenticity' based on individual experience encourages many preachers to begin sermons with personal anecdotes, often of surprising banality and perhaps less riveting to audiences than they imagine. As long ago as 1939 Charles Smyth, noting that 'the Christian religion is objective to the core', lamented this trend towards subjectivity among preachers: 'The *exempla* of the modern pulpit have become desperately egocentric, and in consequence they are limited in range and lacking in variety.'

Mediaeval preachers commonly addressed congregations in warm, affectionate terms: 'my great dears', 'dear brothers and sisters', 'very dear ones'. Post-mediaeval preachers as commonly addressed God, apostrophizing him in such terms as: 'O Lord, bless my people and teach them this point.' George Herbert praised this practice for making the congregation more conscious of God's presence, and commented, 'some such irradiations scatteringly in the sermon, carry great holiness in them'.

One of the most important considerations in framing a sermon was to make it utterly appropriate to the specific audience. (Some manuals identified no fewer than 120 varieties of possible congregation, from kings to nuns and sailors, from peasants to harlots; so successful were some preachers in moving harlots to desire virtue that many sanctuary-hostels had to be constructed to house reformed prostitutes. Indeed, one of the most popular sermon *exempla* for centuries was the story of the repentant harlot.)

Unlike most preachers today, many mediaeval preachers took trouble to address parts of sermons to individual groups within the congregation. This served to provide ethical teaching for their specific needs, and, as George Herbert pointed out, to procure their attention 'with particularising of ... speech – now to the younger folk, then to the elder; now to the poor, and now to the rich: "This is for you, and this is for you;" for particulars ever touch and awake more than generals'.

The role of intellect

Perhaps the most striking difference between mediaeval and modern sermons is the relative lack of objective knowledge transmitted by the latter. Today there is a marked paucity of references to any biblical passages, other than the chosen passage or lectionary reading. By contrast, pre-Reformation sermons had on average some 28 references to other biblical passages relevant to the theme. It was common for twelfth-century homilies to make valuable reference to as many as seven biblical books in 50 lines, and Cistercian sermons of that time indicate that their preachers must have known the Bible intimately, the Psalms and much else by heart.

Few sermons today show anything like this depth of biblical knowledge. In his recent book *Evangelicalism in Britain: 1965–1995* (InterVarsity Press, 1997), Oliver Barclay lamented precisely this (recent) loss of knowledge of the Scriptures among Evangelicals. Many current sermons bear out his assertion, and they are the poorer for it. For, as George Herbert urged, for the regular preacher – whose pulpit is his 'joy and throne' and whose every word is to be 'heart-deep' – 'the chief and top of his knowledge consists in the Book of books, the storehouse and magazine of life and comfort – the Holy Scriptures. There he sucks and lives.'

Equally disturbingly, few contemporary sermons show familiarity with the Church Fathers, with mediaeval or Reformation theologians, or even with many modern commentaries. Yet even mediaeval vernacular sermons, clearly written for relatively uneducated audiences, offer numerous insights drawn explicitly from Jerome, Augustine, Bernard of Clairvaux and other commentators. It was not unusual for one single seven-minute homily to draw apt wisdom from Chrysostom, Ambrose, Gregory the Great and several other theologians. For mediaeval preachers, these writers were part of their living heritage, a rich well of holiness, a constant source of inspiration for congregations.

It is rare today to hear a sermon revealing such capacious knowledge of the greatest of past biblical commentators – and virtually unheard-of to learn anything factual about Church history. Is this because preachers have too little time to read deeply or to prepare sermons? Is it because they have had little opportunity in seminary or theological college to immerse themselves in the Fathers and in Church history?

Or is it perhaps because they expect too little of their congregations? Typically, D. Martyn Lloyd-Jones urged preachers to 'beware of too much intellect', instructing them to remember, as he had been told in his youth by an old preacher, that 'Only one in twelve in your congregation is really intelligent. Remember that as long as you live: only one in twelve.'

Artes praedicandi, on the other hand, taught that even sermons for a largely unlettered audience should include some material to delight and teach those of greater education, and that sermons should not only edify but also instruct. Alan of Lille, one of the greatest twelfth-century theologians, wrote: 'A sermon is an open and public instruction in ethics and faith; a sermon is dedicated to in-forming man and issues out of the narrow path of reason and the fountain of learned authorities.'

Preaching manuals taught that God has provided three mirrors which the preacher may offer to the congregation: the mirror of Scripture, the mirror of Nature, and the mirror of creatures, both human and animal. All three mirrors reflect God's light, all three contain in-built God-given messages about morality and ethics, about the Church, about eternal verities. One of the preacher's tasks was to learn not only the Scriptures but also the book of nature and the book of humanity in order to transmit faithfully these messages or inner meanings. Thus the more he knew about, say, geometry or astronomy or gems or the habits of bees or the minutiae of agriculture, the better equipped he was to extract from their various attributes their deeper significance *sub specie aeternitatis*. Encyclopaedias, scientific writings, bestiaries and fables: all were grist to a preacher's mill and his weekly grind.

For this reason, pre- and post-Reformation sermons commonly showed familiarity with secular authors – Livy, Cicero, Plato, Suetonius, Valerius Maximus and others – on whom they drew particularly in order to reinforce ethical teaching. Today, in my experience at least, it is fairly rare to encounter such breadth of reference in Anglican sermons. Yet Hugh of St Victor recommended the preacher to 'learn everything: thou shalt find in the end that nothing is superfluous' and George Herbert anticipated that 'the Country Parson is full of all knowledge'. (Readers whose appetites have been whetted by these hors d'oeuvres of Herbert's wisdom and common sense will find the main course in *A Priest to the Temple: or The Country Parson. his Character, and Rule of Holy Life*, 1652. Donald Demaray, a contemporary writer on preaching (*An Introduction to Homiletics*, Grand Rapids, Michigan, 1990), agrees: 'A universal mark of the called preacher is an insatiable thirst for knowledge, and [wide] reading defines one sure path to spiritual and intellectual growth.'

Sacred eloquence

Alan of Lille argued that sermons should move congregations by means of 'rousing words, which mollify minds and bring forth tears'. He recommended a style which was neither boorish and colloquial nor over-eloquent, but which found a golden mean in a gentle but skilful artistry. One twelfth-century homily described preachers as 'adorning the bare words of the Gospel with a fair interpretation to be pleasing as instruction'. To move and to please, to balance spiritual power and verbal beauty – this was and is part of the craft of preaching. Preaching manuals described preachers as church bells summoning, by harmony and beauty, congregations to their devotions; as craftsmen skilled in the appropriate tools; as painters choosing the right colours; as master carpenters building the city of God with the people as living stones.

Stories *exampla* were, and remain, a key means of moving and pleasing congregations: 'men heed them better than exhortations' (George Herbert). (Ian Sweeney's final story in last year's winning sermon was unforgettable in its harrowing detail and utter appropriateness to his theme.) They could be witty, even ribald, but always pointed.

But ultimately the preacher's choice of words was more important than his choice of story. 'In the beginning was the Word', and to employ 'sacred eloquence' in God's service was to make God's Word doubly potent: 'if the words be old, be a physician and rejuvenate them' – by unusual imagery, by striking simile or metaphor, by cadences which please the ear and remain in the memory. At times even new language was coined in the attempt to express the ineffable nature of spiritual experience. The late mediaeval German mystics, for example, minted in their sermons and writings utterly new German words to convey the wonder of God's presence and the dynamic power of the Holy Spirit. (It was precisely these new coinings which resulted in German being the best European language for the expression of abstract philosophical thought.)

Today homiletics is little taught in theological colleges, and rhetoric is unknown. But virtually all pre- and many post-Reformation preachers did study the art of classical rhetoric. Oratory used in God's service – 'divine rhetoric' – gave preachers invaluable tools. It taught them the skill of using three distinctive styles: firstly, a colloquial, vivid, racy style, full of idioms, stories, picaresque diversions; secondly, a plain style, simple and unadorned, used generally in expository homilies; thirdly, an elaborate, ornate style, with rich use of rhetorical devices such as anaphora, wordplay, antithesis and alliteration and piling-up of images: lusts as robbers, for example, and the Virgin Mary as dawn, moon, dew and sunrise, jewel and burning bush and Aaron's rod. Some sermons used one single style. Others used a mixture of two or all three, in order to keep the audience awake and interested. (The proof of the padding is in the heeding, so to speak!)

Prolixity could be used, especially when robustly attacking vices or extolling virtues, but brevity was always the ideal. To use language peeled, pared of superfluity, as does the Welsh poet-priest R. S. Thomas today, is to startle hearers into listening intently. For listening, like fine preaching, is an acquired art, just as being bored, like waffling, is an acquired vice.

Our predecessors were better at listening than we are. For centuries hour-long sermons were the norm, and, when the hourglass was empty, it was not unknown for the congregation to beg the preacher to continue for another hour. Puritan preachers often preached for two hours on Sunday mornings (on the Hebrew Scriptures), another two hours in the afternoon (on the New Testament) and a final hour in the evening (on more general themes), followed by debates on the sermons with the listeners. French sermons in the same period could even last four or five hours (and France has arguably the finest preaching tradition in Western Europe).

Entertaining, sometimes humorous, profound: such sermons were crafted with verbal skill enough to wrap spiritual medicine in pills of delicious sweetness to both ear and heart.

Some clergy nowadays have bought the notion that congregations have only a three-minute attention span. Ten-minute sermons are common, and 25-minute sermons considered long. And, to be sure, ten minutes of meat is worth 30 of mash. But give a congregation a sermon with variety of pace and style, delivered with *élan* and panache, and they will be, so to speak, all ears.

'Feed my sheep', said Jesus. 'Meat rather than milk', urged Paul. Given the widespread loss of liturgy today, with congregations consequently deprived of both beauty and doctrine; given the widespread ousting of meaty hymns by *da capo* choruses, often milked for emotion, the sermon now has greater importance than ever. Yet the preacher now has arguably less time than ever to prepare each sermon. So how can preachers ensure that sermons remain nourishing? How can they ensure that their morsels of time are miraculously transformed into food for thought and more than crumbs of comfort and wisdom?

Firstly: of course by prayer, by more prayer and, on occasion, by prayer and fasting. (Some Orthodox Jews fast each Monday and Thursday until after sundown, and many Orthodox Christians fast for six hours before Communion.)

Secondly: by reading omnivorously, in the Bible and biblical commentaries and concordances above all. Donald Demaray, citing Alexander Whyte's dictum 'Sell your shirt and buy books', urges preachers both to set aside blocks of time for their (well-stocked) study room and also to have books of all kinds – spiritual, non-fiction, classical and modern novels, poetry, detective stories – with them at all times.

Thirdly, and lastly (Luther's sermons could have as many as twenty points), by reading aloud regularly, the preacher's equivalent to playing scales or weight training. In comparison to earlier generations we are deprived of the living spoken word. Telephone calls, e-mails, radio and television inundate us with floods of verbiage. Yet most of us have far less face-to-face conversation than our predecessors. We rarely hear words hand-picked for freshness or penned with painstaking care.

To read aloud – even for only ten minutes a day – is to instil cadence and rhythm, style and sonority into the memory's ear. Whether Beatrix Potter or Edward Lear, Shakespeare's sonnets or Dickens or Lewis Carroll or the five-star hot-shot Prefaces to the 1611 Authorized Version of the Bible: any sparkling poetry or prose can help to kindle a scintillating sermon, So, too, will masterly sermons of the past. (When did you last see your Bishop Lancelot Andrewes or Bossuet or St John Chrysostom or Ephraim of Syria?) And, of course, a quick dip into the treatises on rhetoric by Cicero or Quintilian will crisp even the most limp sermon style.

Finally, a brief plunge into Jewish preaching traditions: biblical, the original wellspring of Christian preaching, and still of interest today.

For the annual *Times* Preacher of the Year Award has demonstrated what good sermons are preached within synagogues. This is nothing new. In the ninth century Archbishop Agobard of Lyons, a notable anti-Jewish polemicist, protested to Emperor Louis the Pious that many Christians in the region regarded Jewish preachers as better than Christian ones. They had had long practice! The Jewish sermon, like the synagogue, probably developed as an institution during the Babylonian exile and was fostered by Ezra and his successors and later by the Pharisees and scribes. Beginning as simple Bible translation from Hebrew to the vernacular Aramaic, it found a regular place within synagogue liturgy as Bible exposition and interpretation. By the first century CE preachers used parables, striking images, boldly juxtaposed biblical texts to delight and educate worshippers and to deepen their understanding of God's Word. One famous mediaeval rabbi ruled that 'one must preach in words more precious than gold on the Sabbath'. Earlier rabbis had urged that preaching on the Torah (Pentateuch) should be as pleasant to the hearers as honey from the comb, even as pleasant as a bride in the bridal chamber is pleasant to her husband. Today the teaching of homiletics is taken seriously, with departments of homiletics in all major rabbinical seminaries, and leading scholarly preachers teaching within them.

There are fascinating differences historically between Jewish and Christian preaching. By and large, Jewish preachers were more heterogeneous, since theoretically any knowledgeable and skilled layman accepted by the local community could preach, whereas until long after the Reformation all formal Christian preachers had to be ordained. Early Jewish audiences, too, tended to be more hetero-geneous than their Christian counterparts; most synagogue congrega-tions, which contained many women and children and all social groupings, had sermons on all festivals and commonly each Shabbat, whereas only in 1215 did it become compulsory for every church to have at least one sermon preached in it each year.

Even today there are intriguing differences. One lies in the role of the preacher. The New Year liturgy contains a long prayer asking God 'to inspire the lips of those' deputed by the congregation 'to stand in prayer before thee, to beseech ... thy presence for them. ... Guard their lips from uttering any word that is not according to thy will. ... The preparations of the heart belong to man, but the answer of the tongue is from the Lord.' Jewish preachers traditionally ended sermons with glorious prayers blessing God and the congregation. But since rabbis have no priestly function, their preaching is simply understood as 'teaching, inspiring and uplifting the congregation' (Abraham Milgram, *Jewish Worship*, Philadelphia: Jewish Publica-tion Society of America, 1971). They are transmitting the long Jewish legacy of *derashah*, 'searching' the Bible for its innumerable meanings, emphasizing the need for ethical guidance and values, the practice of holiness. In giving spiritual and practical guidance 'for conformity to the will of God and communion with God', they are preaching biblical truths rather than proclaiming, as Martyn Lloyd-Jones put it, 'the Truth itself'. They preach from love of God, proclaim and praise God, point the congregation to 'Our Father, Our King', but never claim to speak 'in God's stead'.

A second difference may lie in the attitude to the congregation. Every rabbi will have learnt a healthy respect for the critical faculties of his congregation and know that, however extensive his training, there may well be members as learned as himself. Some will have been studying that Shabbat's Bible portion of several chapters throughout the previous week. A well-known Jewish story is of Aaron the tanner, who constantly criticized a famed Jerusalem rabbi's decisions and picked up errors or inconsistencies in his sermons. When Aaron suddenly died, some assumed that it was God's judgement upon him. He had been old and alone, and few mourned him except for the rabbi, who showed genuine grief. 'Why do you weep?' asked the rabbi's disciples. 'He was your enemy, your chief critic.' 'Ah, but he was my truest friend', replied the rabbi. 'He forced me to think clearly and reason carefully. Who is there now to show me my faults?'

Traditionally, sermons were robust, strongly ethical in tone and unstinting in appropriate rebuke, though the preacher took care to please the congregation with ingenious and thoughtful interpretation before any rebuke and to include himself among the rebuked. Such sermons could evoke a robust response. In pre-modern times preachers were sometimes interrupted or publicly opposed. While this now virtually never happens, sermons can be vigorously discussed ('Two Jews, three opinions!', as the saying goes). Public castigation from the pulpit of perceived faults within the community is not uncommon and can be forceful, though often with humour. This has a long tradition; in the twelfth century Maimonides ruled that 'each Jewish congregation must arrange to have a respected and wise elder who has been known for his piety from his youth and who is beloved by the people, who will publicly admonish the community and cause them to repent'. Yet such preachers also brought comfort in sorrow, hope in persecution, and warm reminders of God's mercy and love.

Another difference from current Christian sermon practice is frequent reference to Talmudic and later Bible commentators, of whom many in the congregation will have more than passing knowledge (as they will, too, of Jewish history). The differing opinions of Rabbis Shammai, Akiva and Hillel, the ideas of Maimonides and Rabbi Nahman and Rashi and the Vilna Gaon and dozens of others are discussed in sermons and study sessions, at times passionately and as though they were still alive. If only the Church Fathers were as well known as they used to be!

The entertainment value of sermons has always been appreciated, with preachers modulating their voice to imitate different characters in dialogues and using other dramatic techniques and rhetorical techniques, fables, stories, exaggerations and the element of surprise to maintain interest in biblical exegesis. Even today it is common for a preacher to begin with a dramatic story or a biblical passage far removed in theme from the weekly Torah portion, in order to intrigue and interest the listeners. Or they begin with a joke. I shall end with a couple.

It was announced in Tel Aviv that God was soon to send a tidal wave thirty-feet high over the city because of its sins. Muslims went to their mosques and prayed for a speedy translation to the paradise of Muhammad. Christians went to their churches and prayed for the intercession of the saints. Jews went to their synagogues and prayed

'Lord God, it's going to be very hard living under 30 feet of water' (Lionel Blue, A. Roy Eckardt, *Sitting in the Earth and Laughing: A Handbook of Humour*, New Brunswick: Transaction Publishers, 1992)

As a tribute to the excellent preachers included in this volume and to their many fellow servants of God, who sustain their congregations with nutritious sermons, here is a definition of an ideal preacher made by the Jews of Cracow in 1717: 'In his pleasant utterances [he] gives joy to both God and man, and quenches the spiritual thirst of every class of people according to the depth and breadth of their understanding. Sometimes he teaches the Law in depth ... Yet he can still clarify, instil his hearers with a sense of reverence, sweeten the bitterness of life through his pleasant manner of speaking with straightforwardness ... in sermons open and understood by all, including those whose minds cannot fathom the depth of his words.'

For excellent studies of late mediaeval and early modern preaching, see H. Leith Spencer, *English Preaching in the Late Middle Ages* (Oxford University Press, 1993); Larissa Taylor, *Soldiers of Christ: Preaching in Late Medieval and Reformation France* (Oxford University Press, 1992). Charles Smyth, *The Art of Preaching: A Practical Survey of Preaching in the Church of England 747–1939* (SPCK, London, 1940): Israel Bettan, *Studies in Jewish Preaching: Middle Ages* (Hebrew Union College Press, Cincinnati, 1939); Marc Saperstein, *Jewish Preaching 1200–1800: An Anthology* (Yale University Press, New Haven and London, 1989).

Introduction

RUTH GLEDHILL

My generation is not just the churches' 'missing generation'. We are missed by everyone. We are not the 1960s 'baby boomers', many of whom are currently returning to church, even if only for the sake of securing a Christian education for their children. Nor are we the deeply fashionable 'Generation X', the young adults being assiduously courted by church leaders in desperate attempts to woo them back to church. We fit neither into the under-30s nor the over-40s categories. We appear in few surveys into contemporary *angst* because we don't even have a name within which to categorize ourselves. Occasionally, when flares and platform shoes or other iconic items of the 1970s come back into fashion, we feel we have a public identity, but such moments are rare, because the 1970s were, by and large, so abysmal in terms of style, music, liturgy and belief. My own experience of visiting a different church each week, for my 'At Your Service' column that appears on the faith page of *The Times Weekend* section on Saturdays, suggests that few of us are in church – and who can blame us? Being a teenager with an interest in religion in the aftermath of *Honest to God* was bad enough – spirituality cannot flower when any attempt to express it provokes howls of laughter, mockery and jokes about unbelieving bishops from those supposedly older and wiser. The liturgical reforms of that era were simply death blows on top of injuries already done to the language of the spirit. The decline in church attendance now appears unstoppable. Although it is of course 'politically incorrect' to suggest that there could be any link between the malaise currently affecting contemporary youth – teenage pregnancies, drugs, the crisis of identity among young boys – and the decline in religious practice and church attendance, this is a decline which has surely been brought on partly at least by the churches themselves, however much they might publicly bewail it.

In spite of being a traditionalist at heart, however, I do accept that it is impossible to go back. It is necessary to go forward. Preaching must have a future, even if some of this future should be outside the traditional environment of a church service. What is unclear is what shape this future will take. A Preacher of the Year competition certainly puts preaching in a more public and secular environment than it is habitually associated with. Some in the churches (the *declining* churches) have anathematized our competition as something unsacred, because a competition is not an appropriate arena for the word of God to be spoken in. I was deeply shocked when the original organizers of the competition, the College of Preachers, refused to have anything further to do with it after we invited Jewish preachers to enter. But in an era when there is so much bad news around, something which is fundamentally good deserves to survive. In spite of the almost insuperable difficulties involved in organizing it alone, and in spite of an unclear future, the competition *has* survived at least another year without the College.

Some preachers have entered year after year, and to them I owe eternal gratitude. To one former shortlisted preacher, the Reverend Mervyn Roberts, Team Vicar of Warwick, must go a special acknowledgement. Here is a man who is unafraid of change, or of trying something different. A few months after preaching in last year's final, Mervyn tried to set the record for the world's longest sermon. He succeeded in staying in the pulpit for nearly 36 hours, preaching non-stop, in the seventeenth-century chapel at Warwick Castle. He had planned to give a 48-hour sermon, but illness cut him short at 35 hours and 57 minutes. His sermon, a fund-raising marathon for the British Diabetic Association, is being evaluated for possible inclusion in the *Guinness Book of Records*.

But, outside competitions such as ours, or record-breaking stunts, does preaching have a real future? This year I surveyed our 30 preachers selected from all those entered for inclusion in this book. Not surprisingly, given their profession, all agreed it does have a future. But most were also able to supply useful ideas for change – ideas which any who care about not just the future of preaching, but the future of religious belief and thereby of our wider society, might do well to note. Their comments are reported fully in the individual biographies preceding each sermon, but there was a wide concern about how to get God's message across in an increasingly secular, material society. According to Rabbi Shmuley Boteach, runner-up in last year's competition and a finalist in the top ten this year, preaching is becoming more fashionable, but needs to change. 'Religion has assumed a moral and pious manner and it is as if we are teaching people why they are doing bad things and why the world has so many flaws. Religion should be offering guidance. Preaching should show people how to be better parents and how to forgive their family for any wrongs that they may have done to them. Preaching can also teach us how to succeed in business but also how to remain ethical and moral as well. Religion should be the next self-help wave after the secular self-help wave which led to the sale of so many millions of books.'

Rabbi Albert Friedlander, a leading Reform rabbi in London, would like to see more preachers open to debate and dialogue from the floor – even allowing members of the congregation into the pulpit to make a point. 'I believe that many of the sermons in the next century must be *open*. They should include a question period which must be more than a period for information. It must be a time for congregants to challenge the preacher, to give their own views – even to come up to the pulpit.'

The Reverend Mike Starkey, another finalist from last year who is back in the top 30 this year, believes preaching can restore the sense of wonder to life. 'It can point people to realities beyond the mundane details of daily life. It can bring alive biblical scenes, so that people are enabled to stand face to face with the wonder of Christ, as the early Christians did ... Preaching can be the bridge between the profound questions people are asking and the answers offered by the historic Christian faith.'

In tandem with this book, another *Times* sermons book is being published this autumn, by HarperCollins. *The Times Greatest Sermons of the Last 2000 Years*, edited by John F. Thornton and Katherine Washburn, includes Jesus' own Sermon on the Mount, as well as sermons from St Peter and St Paul – sermons which have at various times been entered into our competition by *Times* readers with a sense of humour. It goes on to include sermons from throughout subsequent ages – including St Basil the Great, St Augustine, St Thomas Aquinas, John Calvin, John Donne, Rabbi Nahman of Bratzlav, Samuel Johnson, John Henry Newman, Karl Barth, Billy Graham and Pope John Paul II. But as Jonathan Swift said in his sermon 'Upon sleeping in church', included in the book, there is one serious disadvantage to which all preaching is subject: 'That those who, by the Wickedness of their Lives, stand in the greatest need, have usually the smallest Share.' It is positive and encouraging, and probably as close to proof as any of us can get that God is not dead, that so many volumes of sermons are still being published, even at the dawn of a third millennium. And maybe it is even possible that, unlike Swift's view of those who hear them in church, those who have gone to the time, trouble and expense of buying and reading these collections of sermons, are not just those who are least in need of what they say.

Ruth Gledhill is the Religion Correspondent of *The Times*.

Acknowledgements

Thanks to Dr William Beaver without whom this book would not have been possible; former *Times* secretary Karen Wright and her successor Katie Clayton; *Times* News Editor Ben Preston for his patience; *Times* Editor Peter Stothard for his support; *Times* publicist Jessie Hewitson of THP; and all the *Times* work-experience students who helped with various stages of the competition.

Thanks also to Ruth McCurry of Cassell publishers and all those involved in the book's production – Diana Smallshaw, Alan Worth, Fiona McKenzie, Father David White and Ian Sherratt.

Stories in the sermon by Christine Scott (see p. 60) were taken from Anthony P. Castle, *Quotes and Anecdotes* (Rattlesden: Kevin Mayhew Ltd).

Permission to reproduce copyright material from the following publishers is gratefully acknowledged: Carcanet Press Ltd, for Edmund Blunden's 'Report on Experience', from *Near and Far* (1929), reprinted in *Poems 1914–30* (see sermon by David Hatton, p. 79); Hodder and Stoughton, for Steve Turner's 'Mikhail Suslov', from *Up to Date Steve Turner* (1983) (see sermon by Andrew Sails, p. 171); Macmillan Publishers Ltd, for R.S. Thomas' 'The Musician' (see sermon by Clare Herbert, p. 69); Boosey & Hawkes Music Publishers Ltd, for Helen Taylor's 'Bless This House' (see sermon by Ian Sweeney, p. 201).

Christmas Is Cancelled

SERMON PREACHED BY JOHN ALDRIDGE AT TRINITY
METHODIST CHURCH, OADBY, LEICESTER, ON 13
DECEMBER 1998

*John Aldridge, 61, with his wife June, a former schoolteacher, has
two children and one grandchild. He attends Oadby Trinity
Methodist Church and preaches every three weeks on the Leicester
Trinity Circuit, where the superintendent is the Reverend Martin
Smithson.*

*Mr Aldridge has worked in the newspaper industry all his life,
with the Northcliffe Newspaper Group, the regional division of the
Daily Mail. After fifteen years as Chairman and Managing Director
of the Leicester Mercury Group, he has just retired. His first job at 16
was clearing out printing blocks that were surplus to requirements
and taking them for scrap. He progressed to being tea boy in the
advertisement department of the* Grimsby Evening Telegraph. *'That
was my big break because it got me into mainstream publishing
where I have had a very enjoyable, and some might say successful,
career.'*

*He was converted to Christianity when he was nearly 17. 'I had
not even been baptized. There was an evangelical campaign very
much like a Billy Graham crusade, run by the Methodist Church, in a
wonderful town called Cleethorpes. It was a life-changing moment.
My parents were surprised, and initially I think a little disappointed.
But as they saw it was the real thing, they came to be great supporters
of me.' While at school he worked for his father, the local wholesaler
for the* News of the World. *After working early Sunday mornings, he
would go home, put a suit on and go to church. 'That was quite a
major step to take. Sunday had been a working day, and it became a
working and worship day.*

*'I began to give epilogues to a Methodist youth club. I progressed
from that to a mission band. From that I felt a calling to be a
preacher. I was asked if I felt the call to be ordained, but I strongly
did not. I felt, and have felt so all my life, that God had called me to
be a Christian in the secular world. Given that for 23 years I was the
Managing Director of two different regional newspapers, I felt this
was no accident.'*

He is currently Chairman of the Methodist Recorder *and has been on the board for many years. He is also Chairman of Leicester Sound, part of the GWR group of commercial radio stations. He is past President of the Rotary Club of Leicester and has also been President of the Newspaper Society.*

'I remember when I started work as a local preacher I went to preach in a little village called Cottager's Plot near Grimsby. It was the first time I had preached on my own without another preacher being with me. It was rainy night, and I had cycled about five miles. I put my bike outside this little church and began the service soaking wet. I was in the middle of the opening prayers when, all of sudden, a loud voice said: "Stop this prayer!" I looked up in astonishment and so did the congregation of about eight people. The man said that much more important than the prayer was that it was going to rain again. Everything stopped while he went to bring my bike inside the church! This made me recognize that preaching, in which I passionately believe, is a very down-to-earth operation.'

He believes preaching is here to stay. 'Millennium or no millennium, the word of God will continue to be proclaimed. Preaching a hundred years ago in Victorian times had its own particular style. "Hellfire and damnation" sermons were the norm. Congregations were intimidated into making a response.' But he says such an approach is completely unacceptable today. 'Sermons are shorter, better illustrated, persuasive rather than threatening and generally better delivered.' And in the new millennium, he says, sermons are likely to be shorter still. 'They will appeal to a "sound bite" generation. They will be more Bible-based. They will home in to their target more swiftly. But the word of God will continue to be preached.'

He says worship not only needs to change, but indeed does change all the time. 'Worship patterns have evolved and developed over the years, and I believe will continue to do so. We need different styles of worship, options to suite worshippers' particular needs. On the one hand, open, relaxed, informal worship in the "Spring Harvest" style. On the other, contemplative worship including communion. Fewer church buildings, with large professional staff, will be able to provide this variety of worship, in much the same way as contemporary multiplex cinemas have become a feature of the film-going world.'

Not only worship, but congregations also have changed in this country. 'Generally they have become more elderly. Early retirement, better worshipping environments, improved PA systems, the use of electronic visuals, the awareness of the need to be more user-friendly in our approach to worship, some modern hymns, new Bible translations, all these elements have generally changed the atmo-

sphere in worship for the better.' For many families, he says, Sunday has become a day out, often a day to go shopping together. 'For single-parent families it is a day to be together, and for divorced families a chance to share time with estranged children. There are so many distractions today and the Church has to be innovative in making its worship relevant against these competing demands.'

Text: Luke 1:13

Your wife will bear you a son.

C hristmas is cancelled!
Those of you who haven't written cards, bought the socks, perfume and outrageously expensive gift wrap, will be mightily relieved!

Millions of turkeys will be equally relieved, evergreen forests will be saved and, sadly, retailers will face bankruptcy.

Children by the score will be disappointed that there won't be a pile of computer software beneath the Christmas tree, and chubby men with white beards and red coats face premature redundancy!

Christmas is cancelled!

Who says so? *The Times* newspaper! In a story a few days ago they said: 'Birmingham will celebrate the festive season as usual this year with carol singing, fairy lights and street entertainment, but they won't call it Christmas!'

Council officials have re-named it 'Winterval!'

'Winterval' – what a crass, insulting way to describe the time of Christ's birth. You suspect a strong and misguided element of political correctness in the decision, and yet a Muslim friend of mine cheerfully celebrates both Eid and Christmas!

In the *Times* story, a Muslim called Abdul Hamid said 'If I want to be a true Muslim I have to love Jesus Christ as much as any Christian does'.

Needless to say, the city fathers in Birmingham have been roundly criticized by churchfolk, politicians, other religions and by ordinary people 'in the street' who, to paraphrase a popular Christmas hymn, 'will have winter but no Christmas'.

The time of Advent in 'Winterval' city has been a controversial time. I hope for us the days before Christmas – despite the frenetic preparation which besets us all – will be a time when we can prepare ourselves to meet Jesus in a wonderful way.

I hope, for each of us, those magical, spiritual, expectant moments as Christmas day begins, will be a time for genuine celebration. God has intervened in our world! Lives can be changed. There is hope in our

3

world. All because, as Johnny Mathis famously sang, 'A child is born'. Or, as George Macdonald so memorably put it:

> Thou camest, a little baby thing,
> That made a woman cry.

In this time of preparation an elderly couple, who made headlines in their day and would have made enormous sums of money from selling their story to a tabloid newspaper had they lived today, are very much in our minds: Zechariah and Elizabeth. It is their news that brings me to the first of three points. As we prepare for Christmas, we must try to:

1. Make sense of the past

Zechariah was a priest who had demanding duties in the Temple. He and Elizabeth were old people. They had no children and Elizabeth, rather unkindly, gets the blame: The Bible says bluntly: 'Elizabeth was barren.'

But God had different ideas! He had plans. He needed someone to prepare the way. As ever, he planned ahead. He sent an angel. Poor Zechariah, he must have been terrified by what he saw and heard in the Temple that day.

When he learned that he and Elizabeth were going to be parents, he asked the angel in his disbelief 'Are you absolutely sure? Elizabeth and I having a baby at our age – you must be joking!' But the angel wasn't joking. Elizabeth was pregnant!

And which man, if he has been fortunate enough to discover that he's going to be a father, hasn't phoned his nearest and dearest with the news 'We're pregnant!'

Zechariah was a good and committed Jew; he knew that God's faithfulness shone through the wonderful history of his people.

He knew that the prophets had spoken about a Messiah who would lead the Jews out of their oppression. What he didn't know was he and Elizabeth were to have a major part in Jesus' arrival. That he found impossible to believe – but God had other ideas!

For nine months poor Zechariah was struck dumb. In that time he began to see that everything that had happened in the past, good or bad, was leading to the present moment.

It was all part of God's plan for the salvation of His people. Zechariah was able to say, with such perception: 'God has come and received His people.'

People like us.

Against that background we should:

2. Face the present

Everyone of us has gazed on a new-born child and has known they were looking upon a miracle.

It's immaterial whether the child is our own or someone else's. The sheer perfection of the creation before us is awesome. It is hard not to see God in the child. (Although, I guess, in later life frustrated parents might confess that it is impossible to see God in that same child!)

Every new-born child is a sign of hope. A new, as yet unspoilt, life. A life of vast potential.

Someone else has said: 'For many, having a child is the only way of sending a message to the future.'

But Zechariah knew his child was a unique messenger – the final stepping stone in the old order from which the Messiah would burst into His mission.

And he was right. The child grew to be John the Baptist, who preached of salvation to a clamouring, oppressed people, who baptized for forgiveness and prepared, as we do now, for the arrival of Jesus.

Jesus arrives in our contemporary world amidst huge distractions. He arrives in the present where a largely indifferent people will enter fully into 'Winterval' but not, I fear, into Christmas.

Part of our preparation has to be rejoicing in the present, enjoying the anticipation of His arrival whilst communicating, as we have the opportunity, the fact that Jesus was born into our world to save souls, not to wear out credit cards.

And finally we must:

3. Prepare for the Future

For soon, the millennium will dawn. The 2,000th birthday of Jesus. However diminished by commercial opportunism, it remains His birthday. However much the Faith Zone of the gigantic millennium Dome may be diminished in its impact month by month – it's still His birthday! And however indifferent we are to all the countdown clocks and the questions about what we're doing over New Year's Eve 1999, we know it's still His birthday!

We Christians must hold on to that, make sure our celebrations centre around the Christ child and never lose the opportunity to remind those around us that the millennium is about Jesus and about the wonderfully different future He offers us all.

Zechariah called on his knowledge of the prophet Malachi to describe what the Messiah would bring to the world. He spoke of the night – the haunt of darkness, bad dreams, fear and evil – being driven away by the sunrise. What a marvellous image of what Jesus has done for our world, what He does for it still, and what He will continue to do in the future!

For the gift Jesus brings us all this Christmas time is tender mercy. The babe who made a woman cry is able to end our separation from God ...

There is light to take away the fear of death ...
There is forgiveness to take away the fear of sin ...
There is hope to take away the fear of the future ...
There is guidance to show us how to live rightly and peaceably ...
This surely is the true message of Christmas.

'Winterval' may represent fun, bright lights, jolly TV jingles, pantos and the rest – let's enjoy them. But they won't last. By 26 December they'll look pretty tardy.

Christmas, by comparison, represents, as it always does, our unorthodox God stooping down and touching our lives. If we accept His gift it will last. We will be forgiven. We can start again. The darkness will disappear, the Light has come!

In his Christmas broadcast in 1939 made as Europe plunged into war, King George VI, quoting from words written by Minnie Louise Haskins, concluded with these words:

'I said to the man who stood at the gate of the year: "Give me light that I may tread safely into the unknown."

And he replied: "Go into the darkness and put your hand into the hand of Christ. That shall be to you better than a light and safer than a known way." '

Don't celebrate Winterval, celebrate Christmas!

Amen.

Comments

Ian Sweeney: *'Why in a so-called Christian country do many undermine its Christian tradition? John Aldridge takes on "political correctness" and argues that we should celebrate the Christ behind Christmas.'*

Jonathan Romain: *'Lively, engaging, a strong opening paragraph that holds our attention. He develops his theme well and has good use of quotes. There is a powerful end and a definite message.'*

The Word of God

SERMON PREACHED BY JOYCE CRITCHLOW AT LITTON,
DERBYSHIRE, ON 6 DECEMBER 1998, THE SECOND
SUNDAY OF ADVENT

Dr Joyce Critchlow, an Anglican Reader, lives in the Derbyshire Peak District, and preaches three or four times every Sunday, covering around 40 churches in the Derby diocese. Dr Critchlow, who was also shortlisted for the 1997 Preacher of the Year Award, edits the Church Pulpit Year Book *(SCM Canterbury Press) and is a member of the Buxton Deanery Synod, and churchwarden at Christ Church, King Sterndale, which she has attended since 1944.*

A member of the College of Preachers, the Walsingham Association, the Prayer Book Society and the Hymn Society, Dr Critchlow has composed many hymns for her Derbyshire congregations; among her published works are Derbyshire Churchyards *and* Derbyshire Stained Glass.

She believes firmly that the Ministry of the Word is as vital in the new millennium as it has ever been. 'How can they hear without a preacher?' St Paul is still asking (Romans 10:14). There may be more Bible versions in the vernacular than ever before, but the sermon reaches out to those who may not readily search for God's truths in the written word. Sermons at baptisms, marriages and funerals can be the means of bringing God to those who do not even own a Bible.

In preaching, she maintains, we are following in the steps of Jesus Himself (Luke 4:20f.), which is surely ample justification for not excising the sermon from public worship. People in the new millennium have souls to be saved for eternity; they may reject our message, but that is not our problem. While God gives us life and breath, we are committed to preaching His Word. If we fail to do this, we shall have to answer to our Maker. 'Woe is me if I do not preach the Gospel!' St Paul, again, is declaring (1 Corinthians 9:16).

Does preaching need to change to survive? Dr Critchlow considers that it does, to some extent. Tempora mutantur, et nos mutamur in illis *('Times change, and we change with them'). Changes in the language: new words, new ways of using words, need to form a part of our preaching in the modern world. Illustrations from contemporary life, Bible truths impacting on current situations – in all this, we are not only adapting to changing times, but also following in the footsteps of St Paul and his ministry team. If in doubt, check it out in the apostle's sermons in Acts! Yet the essential 'sermon slot' – be it ten, fifteen, twenty minutes or longer, in the context of worship – should remain unchanged. 'A service without a sermon', declares Dr Critchlow, 'is like a sandwich without the filling.'*

Statistics can be made to show whatever their compilers wish them to show, and the figures can be so misleading as to do more harm than good. Have congregations dwindled in recent years? Yes, in some churches, but in others they have grown, and continue to grow – and the reasons for decline or growth are difficult to quantify. There will always be those who attend because they like the preacher – or stay away because the reverse is the case! But birth rate, housing and development, communications – all these and many other factors play a part and each church has its own benefits and drawbacks.

Serving such a wide range of churches makes it difficult for Dr Critchlow to assess the changes in any particular congregation in recent years, but as a general observation she has noted a small but sustained return to liturgical worship, after a period in the late 1980s and early 1990s when 'Family Services' of a non-liturgical pattern (or little pattern at all) had a brief popularity.

In the new millennium, the pendulum may again swing back from the established liturgy. Who knows? But in any case, the Ministry of the Word will continue! And Dr Critchlow unhesitatingly reiterates her declaration after being shortlisted for this award in 1997: 'If God called me to preach 20 out of 24 hours, I would do it.'

May the words of my mouth, and the meditations of our hearts, be now and always acceptable in Thy sight, O Lord our Strength and our Redeemer. Amen.

O ne of our greatest twentieth-century Christian scholars, Karl Barth (1886–1968), saw in the Bible 'a strange new world' which spoke of God, and the 'otherness' of God – a world which is totally different from our world. Barth maintained that 'Christianity' is not a religion at all: it is God's sovereign and revealing WORD, to which we can only respond.

Barth argued that God's word stands against man, and judges him. Christianity is a matter of revelation. All of man's religious aspirations, any point of contact between God and man, lies solely in God's revealing word.

This eminent theologian, lecturer and pastor was once asked 'What do you think is the most profound Christian truth you have ever heard?' And Barth replied:

'Jesus loves me, this I know –
for the Bible tells me so.'

Today is Bible Sunday. However much or little time we normally
spend each day with the Bible in our hands, today Christians the
world over are encouraged to give some extra thought, some extra
time, to reading the Bible, seeking God's will through the Bible,
sharing the Bible, and generally re-evaluating the importance of the
Bible, in their lives and in the lives of others.

The Bible – the world's no. 1 bestseller – is like no other book. It
clams to be the very Word of God, as mediated through godly men
and women over a period of around 4,000 years. It claims also, in the
witness of Jesus, to be the only way in which believers can come to a
knowledge of God, and salvation and eternal life.

And, even in the 2,000 years of Christian history, the Bible has not
only been the means of bringing millions of folk to God, but it has
also been at the centre of many wars, controversies and disagreements
– and for the Bible, many, many people have lost their lives.

In the sixteenth century, William Tyndale was disgusted at the
bigotry, immorality, ignorance and selfishness of many of our clergy.
He told one vicar: 'By God's grace, I'll live to see the boy who drives
the plough knowing more of God's Word than you know!'

But the clergy, taking their cue from the bishops who were
supposed to be shepherds of their flocks, were more concerned about
keeping England's Catholic Church untainted by Lutheran influences,
and were implacably against the lay-people being exposed to the
Word of God in anything but the Latin which 99.9 per cent of them
couldn't understand anyway. Can you credit it? Men of the cloth,
invested with Holy Orders to lead people to God, were denying those
people the very Scriptures which could point them to God!

So Tyndale left England for the Continent. He was never to return.
But across the Channel he set to work. The Lollards' Bible had been
translated from the old Latin Vulgate, and was full of errors. So
Tyndale worked from the older, Hebrew and Greek, texts, and
eventually his New Testament in English was printed in Cologne, in
1525. It was a super translation – and it was to stand the test of time:
90 per cent of our King James Bible is Tyndale's translation.

He then began the mammoth task of translating the Old
Testament. But he had only done the first five books, and a few
other portions, before he was betrayed by a sixteenth-century Judas
and arrested near Brussels in 1535. In October the following year, he
was strangled and burnt. His last words were: 'Lord, open the King of
England's eyes.'

Today, the wheel has turned full circle. With the encyclicals following the Second Vatican Council, everyone in the vast Roman Catholic Church is now permitted to own and read and study the Bible.

Who can say that William Tyndale's life was anything but a magnificent leap forward for the whole of Christendom?

And yet, there are still so many parts of the world where the Bible is a closed book, a forbidden book. The William Tyndales of the twentieth century are still giving their lives – still being betrayed, arrested and martyred – simply because they want to share the Word of God with those people who don't yet have it.

I've been involved for some time now with a Bible College in Siberia, very close to the border with Mongolia. We take in Russian and Chinese students, give them a thorough training in discipleship, prayer and evangelism – and then on they go, back to their respective countries, as pastors, teachers and evangelists.

In February last year, Deng Xiaoping died. Suddenly, the Chinese–Russian border bristled with nervous tension. Gun boats sailed up the river that forms the boundary, and moored all along the banks. Great arc lights were set up, which cut giant yellow swathes across the water, all through the hours of darkness.

It was at this very time, that the latest cargo of Bibles and Christian literature, donated by believers over here in the West, had to be got across the water, from Duldurga, Siberia, to Mongolia. But with the tension, the gun boats, the arc lights, the sudden proliferation of soldiers and personnel on the river and its banks, how were the little cargo-boats to make the crossing without being arrested?

Christians in many countries were alerted to pray for the mission – and the strangest thing happened: as they prayed, it became increasingly clear that God was – inexplicably – telling them not to try dodging the arc lights at night, but to sail across in broad daylight, with no attempt at concealment.

In faith, then, one sunny morning, the team of Christians loaded the precious boxes of Scriptures; and then the little boats set out across the water.

Not a shout was heard.

Not a gun was fired.

Every one of the Bible boats made the crossing safely to the Mongolian bank, and within minutes the boxes of books were off-loaded, and on their way to communities in that land which for so long had been deprived of the light of the gospel. It was a case of:' "Not by might, nor by power, but by my Spirit", says the Lord of hosts' (Zechariah 4:6).

Against all the odds, God had safeguarded the passage of His

Word. He alone knows how He made those little boats invisible to hostile eyes and weapons of destruction.

The Psalmist, in that long, long 119th Psalm, rejoiced that God's Holy Word was a lantern unto his feet, and a light to his path (verse 105). That was around eleven centuries before Christ – but it's no less true today. There are those who will tell us the Bible is past history. So it is – but it's also present and future history. Jesus Christ is 'the same yesterday, today and forever'; so the word of Jesus Christ can be no less for 'yesterday, today and forever'.

There are also those who will tell us that there are other ways of coming to God. Don't we live in a multi-racial, multi-faith society? Is it not simply bigotry to say that we have all the answers – the only answers to life and living, and dying, resurrection and eternity?

But the Son of God continues to tell us, as He told His first disciples: 'No man comes to the Father, but by me.'

That's not a verse you hear too often today, when there are so many folk out there trying to 'water down' the truths of the Bible – trying to sound very wise and intellectual and making out Jesus really meant something else.

If we believe God is 'the same yesterday, today and forever', we are saying we believe he is consistent. And, since Jesus told us to 'be perfect, even as your Father in heaven is perfect', Jesus is telling us to be consistent. And if we are to be consistent, and to believe Jesus when He says: 'I am the Way, the Truth and the Life', we are to believe him also when he says 'No one comes to the father but by Me' (John 14:6).

Jesus taught his disciples that the 'end of the world' would come only when 'the Gospel has been preached to all nations' (Matthew 24:14; Mark 13:10). If we are seriously expecting that Last Day, if we can get really thrilled at the prospect of Christ's Second Coming, we could do worse than pray that more – many more – translators and Bible printers, publishers and couriers will be raised up, to get the work of worldwide evangelism completed.

God gives us plenty of encouragement in the Bible. We're well on the way to fulfilling the Great Commission.

'But sanctify the Lord God in your hearts: and be ready
always to give an answer to every man that asketh you
a reason of the hope that is in you with meekness and fear.'
(1 Peter 3:15)

It may be someone in the check-out queue at Safeway; it may be a fellow worshipper one Sunday at church; it may be a couple of Jehovah's Witnesses on your doorstep: whoever, whenever, wherever,

St Peter, in that Second Lesson Dinah shared with us this morning, tells us we've to be so 'genned-up' on the Bible – faith and gospel – that we can share with anyone the fullness of the love of Jesus that's inside us. The sharing will not impoverish us, and it will, by the grace of God, enrich those with whom we share.

Look what one man called William Tyndale achieved, by the grace of God. Like the very Christ foretold in our reading this morning from Isaiah 53, Tyndale suffered for the faith, but his sufferings, and much more the sufferings of Christ, were seeds from which sprang hundreds, thousands, millions of Christian souls.

When will Satan realize that, as often as he throws a spanner in the works, God uses the chaos to cleanse, to re-vitalize, to increase his Church?

When will Satan realize that the more he attacks the very Word of God, the more that Word will spread outwards, north, south, east and west, into the wider world?

Well, if Satan hasn't the brains to see the ultimate futility of what he is doing, who are we to tell him?

When you're having one of those days when everything seems to go wrong, when you're worried, down-hearted, or feel like death warmed-up, when the apathy that's so often seen nowadays towards the Bible threatens to get you down, remember those little Bible boats, sailing bravely out past the guns, taking their precious cargo to a country starved of the light of the gospel.

And thank God that so long as there's a job of evangelism to be done, He'll give someone the grace to do it ...

... and that someone may even be ourselves.

In the name of the Father, the Son and the Holy Ghost. Amen.

Comments

Jonathan Romain: '*A wonderful example of a no-holds-barred evangelical sermon – with a passionate message of mission built around two strong stories and rammed home. I did not agree with much of it, but it was still hard not to be swept along by her fervour.*'

Peter Graves: *Interesting affirmation of the importance of the Bible.*

Hope and the New Millennium

SERMON PREACHED BY GORDON WENHAM ON THE
GOSPEL READING OF THE DAY AT ST MARY'S,
CHARLTON KINGS ON 7 MARCH 1999, THE THIRD
SUNDAY IN LENT

*Dr Gordon Wenham, 56, a lay Reader in the Church of England, is
married to Lynne and they have four children. For seven years he led
the teenage youth group at St Mary's, Charlton Kings, his parish
church, where he preaches about once a month.*

*Dr Wenham was brought up in a Christian family. He had a
period of serious doubt in his teens, but after reading a book written
by an agnostic which examined different possible interpretations of
the resurrection (F. Morison,* Who Moved the Stone?*), he found his
faith was restored and he has been a regular churchgoer ever since.
He took his first degree at Cambridge and subsequently studied at the
École Biblique in Jerusalem, and at London and Harvard Universities.
He also taught at Queen's University, Belfast. He gained his PhD on
the Book of Deuteronomy and now lectures in Old Testament at the
Cheltenham and Gloucester College of Higher Education, which
attracts students from around the world to undertake research on the
Bible.*

*'The purpose of preaching is basically to encourage people to live
in a Christ-like way', he says. 'My aim is to show how the ancient
text of the Bible applies to the modern world. As a preacher you never
really know if you have been successful. You only ever get feedback
from those who like it. I do think that a lot of what I say in sermons
goes in one ear and out the other. Educationally, preaching is not a
very good way of getting ideas across. It is said the people remember
10 per cent of what they hear, 30 per cent of what they see and 70 per
cent of what they do.'*

*However, he still believes the sermon is important, even if people
rarely remember what they hear. 'If you go to a liturgical church,
much of the service is expected and known in advance. The sermon is
then the icing on the solid cake of worship and prayer. If the sermon
is a good one, people will therefore go away with the idea that the
service was a good one. Although they may forget the specifics of the
sermon, it will still flavour their memory of the service.'*

*He believes preaching will continue well into the third millennium.
'At least it will as long as the Church survives, which our Lord has
promised it will', he says. 'The gates of hell shell not prevail against
it.' He says testimony about the faith is essential to evangelism and
the growth of the Church. 'Though such testimony is often most
effective on a one-to-one individual basis, it is also appropriate that
church leaders publicly and powerfully proclaim the faith to
encourage the faithful and persuade outsiders. This is why preaching
must continue.'*

*He finds that preaching is changing in response to the fast-moving
style of the mass media. 'People expect to be engaged and amused even
when serious topics are being discussed. In response sermons have
become shorter, more anecdotal and experience-centred. The great
danger is that preaching will just echo the fashions of the age rather
than draw out the truths of Scripture and Christian tradition. The task
of the preacher is to link the faith given to the saints of old to the world
of today's worshippers in a way that is both relevant and authentic.'*

*His church of St Mary's, Charlton Kings, is a fairly traditional
Anglican church, most of whose worshippers are retired; so changes
in secular society have had relatively little impact there. The
congregation has declined in line with the national trend or a little
faster. The most obvious feature is the loss of local families with
children, who, if they go to church, prefer the brighter, lighter
worship of city-centre churches which expressly cater for young
people and their tastes.*

Text: John 4:5–42

Bible: Revised Standard Version

Just 300 days to go – to the greatest party the world has ever seen.
Yes, it's 300 days to 1 January 2000, which, if all the media hype
is to be believed, will be like no other New Year's Day the world has
ever seen.

But what will most people be celebrating? What is there about the
prospect of a new century and new millennium to cheer them up?

This last century has hardly been one of the most glorious in
human history. Environmentalists tell us that in this century man has
done more damage to the environment than in any previous one.
There have been more forests cut down. More plants and animals
made extinct. More fish stocks depleted. More of the ozone layer
destroyed. More global warning. More pollution of the atmosphere,
and so on, and so on.

If man's treatment of the environment has been abysmal, his
treatment of his fellow man has been even worse.

George Steiner is recognized as one of the greatest literary critics of our age. After holding professorships in several European universities, he is now a Fellow of Churchill College, Cambridge. Though a Jew by birth, religiously he is quite a sceptic. In his recent book *Errata: An Examined Life* (London: Weidenfeld and Nicholson, 1997, pp. 103–7) he says this century is 'the most bestial in recorded history ... Conservative estimates put at *circa* 75 million the total of men, women and children gunned, bombed, gassed, starved to death', since 1914. He reminds us of the horrors of the First World War, of the Holocaust in the Second World War, and of the millions who died in Stalin's labour camps. He continues: 'Nor has the sequence of mass-murder on tribal, ideological or political grounds ceased. Half a million in Indonesia, as many in Burundi ... As I write, mass-graves of the clubbed to death, of the raped are turning up in Bosnia and Croatia. The systematic economic and sexual abuse of children is thought, by qualified observers, to be at its highest level in human history ... Thus the inventory of the inhuman continues without end.'

If this is how the twentieth century has behaved, what is there to celebrate at its close? More disturbingly, what is there to look forward to in the next?

George Steiner points out that for more than two centuries, from the enlightenment in the eighteenth century, Western thinkers have believed man is essentially rational and good. Kant believed universal peace was possible. The French revolution promised equality, liberty and brotherhood. Karl Marx thought socialism could deliver economic freedom and peace. All this century secular social theorists have been assuring us that more education and better political structures will make a better world.

But they have not.

And Christians should not be surprised. Jesus said: 'Out of the heart of man come evil thoughts, fornication, theft, murder, adultery, coveting, wickedness, deceit, licentiousness, envy, slander, pride, foolishness' (Mark 7:21–2). That is why the twentieth century has been such a brutal century. That is why he promised the Samaritan woman in our Gospel 'living water', a spring of water welling up to eternal life (John 4:14).

Later on in John's Gospel he says: 'If anyone thirst, let him come to me and drink. He who believes in me, as the Scripture has said, "Out of his heart shall flow rivers of living water"' (John 7:38).

What did Jesus mean by 'living water' flowing out of our hearts? Naturally, out of our hearts, that is, out of our minds, flow all sorts of evils, murder, adultery, pride, foolishness and so on. But Jesus offers to transform our hearts by filling them with living water, that is, by the Holy Spirit. Then our hearts will be filled with the fruits of the Spirit: love, joy, peace, patience, kindness, goodness, faithfulness, gentleness, self-control (Galatians 5:22–3).

This is what the woman of Samaria needed. She thought she needed a higher standard of living. A tap in her own home would be nice, so she did not have to come to the well to draw water. 'Sir, give me this water, that I may not thirst, nor come here to draw' (John 4:15).

She was your typical consumer. Like her modern counterparts, she believed in novelty and change. Throw-away goods and fresh relationships. She was on her sixth husband, which even by our standards is a bit extreme, and by the standards of her era quite beyond the pale! Perhaps that's why she had come to the well at a most unusual time, at midday when the sun was hottest and most sensible people would stay indoors. But she was a social outcast and therefore to escape abuse went to the well when no-one else would be there. But on this day she found this Jewish man sitting there. And much to her surprise, because she was both a Samaritan and a woman, this Jewish man started chatting to her. And because of his friendliness she did not take offence, when he raised the question of her many marriages. Instead she exclaims: 'Sir, I perceive you are a prophet' (John 4:19). Prophets can read your mind; so that's why she decides Jesus is a prophet.

But Jesus says he is more: he is the Messiah, the great redeemer that both Jews and Samaritans were longing for. The woman said 'I know that the Messiah is coming'. Jesus said to her 'I who speak to you am he' (John 4:42).

So she immediately rushes back to the village without her water pot and invites the villagers to meet Jesus, because 'he told me all that I ever did'. They come out. They persuade Jesus to stay a couple of nights and then they are themselves persuaded. 'We have heard for ourselves and we know that this is indeed the Saviour of the world.'

This is still true. Like the Samaritan woman, we should be inviting our friends and neighbours to meet Jesus, to drink of his living water. So that they will never thirst again. God's Spirit in our own lives can change us. It can change others. We should invite them to share the living water with us.

Novelty, change, greater affluence, political innovation or more education will not alter the heart of man. But Christ's living water can. He is the Saviour of the world. If we can help people see this, there will be something to celebrate on New Year's Day. There will be hope for the new millennium.

Comments

Ian Sweeney: 'Gordon Wenham portrays the Christ at the centre of the millennial celebrations soon to be upon us. He also asks, in the

*light of our past, "Have we really got anything to celebrate?" A
sobering sermon.'*

Jonathan Romain: *'The preacher holds up a mirror to our century
that makes us squirm, and then offers a path forward. I was sorry
that he did not suggest why that path should work now when it had
not succeeded for the past twenty centuries – maybe that is another
sermon – and sometimes one just has to be positive in the face of
adversity.'*

Only God Can Satisfy

SERMON PREACHED BY BISHOP MICHAEL MARSHALL
AT HOLY TRINITY, SLOANE STREET ON SUNDAY 15
NOVEMBER 1998

Right Reverend Michael Marshall is presently Assistant Bishop in the diocese of London and is based for this work at Holy Trinity, Sloane Street, in London, a magnificent example of the architecture of the Arts and Crafts Movement. He was consecrated bishop in 1975, the youngest priest ever to be made a bishop in the Church of England. He had previously been a chaplain at London University and then Vicar of All Saints, Margaret Street in the central West End of London. From 1975 until 1984 he served as Bishop of Woolwich. In 1984 he went to America to found and direct the newly formed Anglican Institute, based in St Louis, Missouri. The Institute was a resource centre for renewal in the Anglican Communion offering a ministry of retreats, lectures, missions as well as written programmes. In 1992 Dr George Carey, the Archbishop of Canterbury, invited Bishop Marshall to return to England as Advisor in Evangelism to both the Archbishops, of York and Canterbury. This work involved him in preaching and lecturing extensively throughout the Church of England as well as throughout the worldwide Anglican Communion. He travelled extensively at that time, and is the published author of some sixteen books, largely on spirituality and evangelism as well as on Church history.

There are marked signs of impressive renewal at Holy Trinity, Sloane Street, which is now a living church, open all day and every day for prayer and worship as well as for exhibitions and lectures associated with the newly formed Arts and Crafts Guild which seeks to explore the relationship between spirituality and the arts.

Bishop Marshall comments: 'Although God is speaking to us on the eve of the millennium, through many different media – not least through art, music, poetry and literature – there is no substitute for the preached word through preachers with a passion for the gospel of Jesus Christ.'

Text: John 6:26ff.

> Jesus said: 'Truly, truly I say to you, you seek me, not because you saw signs but because you ate your fill of the loaf ... I am the bread of life; he who comes to me shall not hunger, and he who believes in me shall never thirst.'

Bible: Revised Standard Version

It is very hard to imagine more presumptuous or preposterous claims than those made about himself by Jesus Christ in the New Testament! What an outrageous claim in those words, which we have allowed to clatter around this church this morning – presumably without batting an eyelid. So perhaps we had better listen to them again. Jesus said: 'I am the bread of life; he who comes to me shall not hunger and he who believes in me shall never thirst.'

In other words, I am the one who can truly and fully satisfy all your needs. As C. S. Lewis so rightly said, 'there really are only three possibilities about this Jesus. Either he is mad: bad: or what he said he was' (*Mere Christianity*).

Mad: megalomania on a scale unequalled before or since. Bad: a liar, making claims which were simply not true. Or, neither more nor less than he actually claimed to be, namely all and more than we can ever imagine is meant by the word 'God'.

In John's Gospel, you see, when we come to chapter 6 it really does sort out the men from the boys and the girls from the women. For by the end of chapter 6, some 65 verses of these kinds of outrageous claims, we are told that many people who had been following Jesus decided from then on no longer to follow him. They voted with their feet, as we say, walking away in the opposite direction. Even the inner ring of the twelve were on the edge of giving it all up.

Perhaps they felt as many people still feel today about this Jesus. If only he had settled for, and indeed the subsequent teaching of the Church had settled for, Jesus the law-giver and greatest moral teacher the world had ever seen – an update of Plato and Moses rolled all into one, giving us the supreme laws of the universe. Or possibly even a great prophet – a mega spiritual guru along with the other spiritual heroes of our world – who had just, perhaps, written a book which could subsequently be translated into all the languages of the world. That would have been reasonable enough. And yes, by all means a wonder-worker, clearly with knowledge both in advance of his years and centuries ahead of his time. Yes, then perhaps we could swallow most of this stuff, and then good sensible Matins would be the typical church service that many would find unobjectionable – a pleasant way of passing a harmless Sunday morning.

But no. Jesus insisted on such absurd claims as: 'Before Abraham was, I am.' 'Come unto me all that travail and are heavy laden and I will give you rest.' 'Your sins are forgiven.' And, perhaps to top it all, the words of my text this morning: 'I am the bread of life; he who comes to me shall not hunger, and he who believes in me shall never thirst.'

Yes, there really are only about three alternatives: megalomania; pathological liar and religious con man; or he is what he says and therefore says what he is in words of one syllable – in a word, GOD.

And if that is the case then the response in Christian worship will be something as mysterious and transcendent as a Eucharistic service is – full of symbolism and mystery – rather than a nice sensible service before cocktails and brunch on a Sunday morning.

Oh, but be careful, because did you notice how I slipped in that word 'mystery'? It's a word which intellectuals are surely and rightly suspicious of, for so often in the history of thought it has covered up a sleight of hand – either intellectually, philosophically, or religiously – or, worse still, is dragged into the argument as an excuse for intellectual laziness.

So just listen to this. When a UFO was sighted over Alaska in 1986, official reports in our newspapers spoke of it as a 'mystery' and, as such, decided (I quote) 'to close the file on all further investigations'.

Now that's the very opposite of course to what Christians mean by a mystery. When we say some doctrine or teaching is a mystery, then we declare a file to be opened and for it to remain opened for indefinite and ongoing investigation, but in the sure and certain knowledge (and here's the rub) that in this world the file will never be closed and the investigations never exhausted, precisely because they are inexhaustible. We call it the journey of faith and that's what we are all about as disciples and followers of Jesus Christ as we meet week by week to explore together the height and length, the breadth and depth of the mystery of truth and love revealed to us in Jesus who said and continues to say: 'I am the bread of life; he who comes to me shall not hunger and he who believes in me shall never thirst.'

Yes, Christianity is not so much a matter of something to swallow, rather someone to follow!

And the language on that journey of exploration into mystery is often more frequently the language of signs and symbols or sacraments, as we call them in the Christian Church, more frequently signs and symbols than words, speaking not so much to the cerebral processes of intellect as to the heart. Signs and symbols have a great capacity to go to the heart of the matter and get beneath the superficial and under our skins, as we say. Thomas Carlyle said: 'It is in and through symbols that man consciously or unconsciously lives, works and has his being; those ages, moreover are accounted the noblest, which can the best recognise symbolic worth and prize it the highest. For is not a symbol ever to him who has eyes for it, some dimmer or clearer revelation of the God-like?' (*Sartor Resartus*).

The universe around us, as well as the mystery of the world within us, is littered with signs and signposts for travellers and explorers, pointing us from the immediate to the ultimate, from the world of facts to the world of faith, meaning and purpose – or, to use the definition of a sacrament, 'outward and visible signs with a spiritual, inner meaning and significance'. But the language of science and symbols speaks only to those with eyes to see and ears to hear. Jesus had just come from the miracle of the feeding of the 5,000 and he had intended that miracle as a sign, pointing to the God who not only feeds our stomachs but seeks also to feed our souls and if, as we say, the fastest way to a man's heart is through his stomach, then that sign should have spoken eloquently to the spiritual hunger that God longs to satisfy, as he will shortly feed us with that same bread of life that alone can satisfy in the Eucharist this morning. He alone can satisfy the deep spiritual hunger which all of us experience from time to time in our lives, a hunger which nothing less than the love and truth of God can satisfy. For, truth to tell, we all have a hole in our hearts which is, as the trite saying goes, 'a hole in our hearts which is God-shaped'. And I profoundly believe that every man, woman and child – whether they come to church or never darken its doors – I believe that every man, woman and child experiences a spiritual hunger for God, whether they know it or not. It does not express itself like that on the surface of course. It is expressed in many different outward forms: loneliness, restlessness, sexual needs and drives, blatant materialism, and so on. But they are only the outward, visible signs of that inner spiritual hunger that only God can fully satisfy. Or, as St Augustine said: 'We were made by God and for God and our hearts are restless until they rest in God.' In a real sense we are all homesick for heaven in some way, longing to belong in the only place we can ever truly and fully belong – namely, in the heart of God himself, broken open for the love of you and me on the cross of Calvary. And I am sad to say, that in many parts of our Church today – a Church which has lost its nerve – there is a conspicuous failing to feed that spiritual hunger, preferring to give stones in place of bread or, worse still, serving up bread and circuses, as the saying goes, offering therapy or, worse still, mindless entertainment instead of transcendent worship.

I want to read you part of a letter, addressed to one of our parishioners only this past week, to serve as a reminder to all of us at Holy Trinity why we are primarily here and still in business.

'It so happened that I was in London on Monday ... and decided to visit Holy Trinity, Sloane Street. I was deeply rewarded. The church was open and I was able to view its treasures at leisure especially the Morris east window, which was of particular interest to me. This time of year, for Christmas, they have a huge range of charity cards for sale. I bought almost my whole supply. Despite that commercial activity at the west end, the atmosphere of the church itself was utterly peaceful and prayerful and I was able to light a candle and say prayers for departed family and friends in the south aisle. A complete package of the 1890s; yes, certainly, for scholars and interested visitors, but also now an active community of worship.'

Everything in this church building, as well as everything we do when we gather for worship, like all true signs and symbols, points us beyond the external and outward appearance to an inner substantial spiritual reality and draws us, beckoning us – for that is what the word 'numinous' of course really means. Yes, *everything*, from the lighting of a candle drawing us into prayer to Jesus who is the light of the world; to the rising of the incense, evocative of our prayers rising before God with the angels and the saints; from the colour and light streaming in through the east window, *bonding* us with the communion of the saints beyond the sunrise; the lines of the architecture of the building, raising our eyes and hearts to heaven so that we can say with Jacob of old, week by week in our worship, prayer and adoration; ' "Surely, the Lord is in this place and I did not know it." And he was afraid and said, "How awesome is this place! This is none other than the house of God, and this is the gate of heaven" ' (Genesis 28:16–17).

Comment

Peter Graves: '*Challenge to explore reality of faith, especially through sacraments and symbol.*'

By Faith

A SERMON PREACHED BY FREDERICK NORTON AT ST
MARGARET OF ANTIOCH, CRICK, ON 26 APRIL 1998

*Fred and Anne Norton have been married 42 years and have three
grown-up daughters, a grandson and a grand-daughter. Since being
introduced to boxer dogs by Anne early in their married life, Fred has
been particularly devoted to them; the most famous of his dogs,
Bendigo, was named after the nineteenth-century bare-knuckle fighter
who later became a noted lay preacher. Fred taught mathematics, first
at Bedford School, then at Rugby School, finally in semi-retirement at
Eton College. He has written numerous mathematics textbooks
ranging from* Secondary Mathematics Books 1–6 *for West Africa to*
Advanced Level Applied Mathematics. *At Rugby he was a house-
master for twelve years, when he was in constant contact with young
people.*

*Fred was licensed as a lay Reader 35 years ago. Although he has
often preached in schools, much of his preaching has been in village
churches, first in Bedfordshire, then Warwickshire, now Northamptonshire. This sermon was preached in a village church and was
received with interest, except by one lady who said she loathed
anything to do with cricket!*

*Preaching offers an ideal opportunity for teaching and encourage-
ment, he says. People go to church expecting to have instruction, to
learn something from a sermon, to go back home with renewed
enthusiasm. Sermons can be augmented by discussion groups, Bible
study groups, courses like Alpha and so on, but these reach few
people compared with the large numbers who on Sunday listen to a
sermon which can, and often should, point out to listeners how they
can find out more about their faith. For the great majority of
churchgoers, the Sunday sermon is their only instruction and
exhortation. 'A kindly nun once described the Sunday sermon to
me as my "spiritual food for the week". This may have been a mild
rebuke, for I had to admit on Monday morning that I had forgotten
the message of the previous day's sermon!'*

*In some ways preaching does not need to change. 'I, together, with
all my schoolfriends will remember to the end of our days our
headmaster proclaiming "Jesus Christ, the same yesterday, the same*

today, the same forever". Much of the Christian message is eternal and unchanging: the creative and redeeming love of God, the selfishness and sinfulness of man, the relation of men and women to each other. Even a topical event, like the campaign to end the debt of the poorer countries at the millennium, appeals to the Law of Jubilee, thousands of years ago. Some new challenges do arise, such as abortion and euthanasia, which all churches should face openly and honestly, and perhaps we should look anew at the Christian's attitude to usury. Compared with 100 years ago, congregations expect shorter sermons – sometimes they are disappointed! – they find visual aids at times helpful, and today's preacher can use many more "effects" than his predecessors. Discussion groups can be useful, but I doubt the value of contributions during a sermon.'

He thinks of his 'congregation' as the inhabitants of Northamptonshire villages, especially Crick. 'In many villages we have seen some expansion of new houses and this new housing has brought in some younger families and children', he says. 'All the churches which are flourishing have regular visiting, often clergy-led, but some led by a lay man or woman. It is a sign of a vibrant, living community that it welcomes newcomers, and where that welcome is provided, people are often willing to become attached, some more firmly than others. Sadly, of course, there are some parishes where there has been little spiritual growth and where there is little life, but that was true 35 years ago, and I doubt whether much has changed overall.'

In his sermon he refers to Archbishop William Laud, who was Rector of Crick for a few years in the seventeenth-century before he was translated to Canterbury and executed in 1645 on a charge of Popery, which he repudiated. A portrait of him hangs in the church.

Text: Hebrews 11

By faith Abraham offered up Isaac ...

Bible: Authorized Version

B y faith Abraham offered up Isaac ... a verse from the letter to the Hebrews, but I could just as easily have chosen almost any other verse from that marvellous chapter 11, for almost all contain the words 'by faith', and it is on faith that I want to think today. By faith ...

One of the joys of Paradise, I am told, though I admit not on very good authority, is watching Lyttleton bat on Upper Club. Now 'batting' obviously refers to cricket, and anyone who saw Denis Compton feathering that late cut on television on Wednesday night will agree that some of the strokes by a first-class batsman, male or female, are amongst the most gracious and elegant movements known to mankind. Upper Club is also obvious: it must be one of the many lovely cricket grounds in England, and indeed it is. One of the grounds at Eton, almost completely surrounded by trees, with the mellow red brick of the fifteenth-century College buildings and the whitish-grey mass of Henry VI's Chapel behind them. But Lyttleton? Lyttleton, who was he? If we rack our brains we can recall Humphrey Lyttleton, the great jazz player, we can recall Oliver Lyttleton, a minor politician, Arthur Lyttleton, a promising politician who died young – all relatives – but of my Lyttleton we can look in only a very few places to find any record of a man who 100 years ago was in his day as famous as, say, Michael Atherton is today.

This Lyttleton was born in 1855 and died as recently as 1942 (though that date will, I suppose, seem to many as far buried in the mists of time as the earlier one). A good scholar, a fine musician, an outstanding sportsman, he captained a Cambridge cricket XI that won all its matches, beating the Australian touring side which included Spofforth, the 'demon bowler' who mesmerized all the batsmen who faced him. In the vacation, Lyttleton played for Middlesex, scoring a century off these Australians. Spofforth had never been demolished before, and he was so impressed that he gave Lyttleton a walking stick mounted with a silver plaque commemorating the feat. Lyttleton played football for England, and, like Compton, played in the losing side in an FA Cup Final.

Like many of his contemporaries, Lyttleton became a schoolmaster, and had to restrict the amount of sport he played. Like many of his contemporaries, Lyttleton was ordained a priest, for he saw his teaching as an essentially Christian work. Unlike most of his contemporaries, he rose to the top of his profession, becoming Headmaster of Eton when he was 50. He was, by his own admission, not a good administrator, which earned him many critics amongst the staff, some of whom anyway were irked at having been passed over in his favour, but he was admired and respected by the boys for what one of his severest critics described as 'innate Christian goodness', which says a lot in favour of the boys, and quite a lot in favour of that critic.

In 1915, the First World War was raging. Hundreds of thousands of young men had already been slaughtered in the war. Anti-German feeling was at its highest, shops bearing German names were looted and set on fire by mobs. The Rector of St Margaret's, Westminster, a fashionable London church which is also the parish church of the Houses of Parliament, arranged a series of sermons on important moral issues and asked Lyttleton to preach on the morality of war. In his sermon, Lyttleton said that it was impossible to justify the fanatical anti-German feeling of that time, that we must remember there were good Germans as well as bad ones, that we should work for a negotiated peace, in the terms of which we, as victors, should be generous to the vanquished foe. There was an uproar in the newspapers, which spread throughout the country. Lyttleton was accused of being anti-patriotic, even of being a traitor. The boys at Eton were solidly behind him. The three most senior boys wrote to *The Times* saying that they were perfectly willing to fight, and if necessary to die, in the trenches, as their older brothers and friends were doing, but that no boy in the school doubted the patriotism of their headmaster.

Nevertheless, Lyttleton was forced to resign, and within a few months moved from being Headmaster of Eton to being an assistant curate at St Martin-in-the-Fields, his stipend being paid by a generous parishioner, Lyttleton having special responsibility for working amongst the prostitutes and tramps which abounded in that parish.

After a few years, the war ground to its conclusion. The countries of Europe, and indeed beyond, had been bled white, and the terms of the Treaty of Versailles, far from reflecting Christian generosity, 'squeezed the Germans until the pips squeaked', as the newspapers joyously proclaimed, and formed the conditions that led to the rise of Nazi Germany and thence to the Second World War. Lyttleton moved on, to work with people less well paid than prostitutes, less highly esteemed than vagrants – to work with schoolteachers. Not the talented and often aristocratic young men amongst whom his life had been spent, but young women, training to teach in what were then called 'elementary schools', often in very tough areas. These young women – for the term 'girls' had not then been stretched to include any female this side of the grave, and they would not have recognized themselves as young ladies, had anyone thought so to describe them – these young women got from Lyttleton his profound Christian faith and his joy of living, which was to sustain many of them in their testing careers. 'Father Ted' they called him, an unbelievable degree of familiarity in those days (I cannot find any of his friends or relatives who were more intimate than 'Edward'), and he became and remained a friend of many. After about ten years, at the age of 75, he took a parish in Norfolk. At 85 he moved to Lincoln, and asked the Bishop there if there was any unpaid work he could usefully do. The Bishop quickly gave him the oversight of a parish in an interregnum, an arrangement which gave so much satisfaction to all that it continued until, at the age of 87, he was 'promoted to glory', to use the Salvation Army phrase.

Lyttleton's life falls into two parts. The first 60 years, in which every worldly honour was his, and a wife to whom he was devoted. The last 27 years, despised, hated even by many who had formerly been his friends, his wife's health broken by the stress, yet regarded by many who knew him as a saint, for through him shone the love of God to mankind.

Lyttleton was often asked if he regretted preaching that sermon. His reply was always the same: that once he had been asked to preach on that topic, he could not refuse, and, having accepted, there was no other message he, as a Christian, could give.

Lyttleton the musician is dead and gone; there are no recordings of his playing, as far as I know. Lyttleton the sportsman is dead and gone, though I have high hopes of Paradise. Lyttleton the Christian saint lives on, partly in the lives of the few remaining people who knew him, but more in his writings. 'Faith,' he wrote, 'is not what the schoolboy said, "the power to believe what you know is not true!" It is the quiet resolve to act on what you hope to be true, before you know that it is true.'

It is the quiet resolve to act on what you hope to be true, before you know that it is true. Here is a man who knows what he is talking about, whose life was characterized by this quiet resolve, who handed on this quiet resolve to so many others, whether they were boys at Eton about to be slaughtered in the trenches, or young women facing a difficult life under harsh conditions.

Abraham preparing Isaac for sacrifice has always been prominent in Christian and Jewish thought and art. It is the most poignant of all the acts of faith recorded in that eleventh chapter to the Hebrews. God told Abraham to take his only son, whom he loved, and offer him as a burnt-offering on Mount Moriah. What did Abraham think? God had promised Abraham a baby by Sarah when that had seemed impossible. Indeed, the faith of Sarah is given as another example of faith in this chapter. This child, the only legitimate child Abraham was likely to have, was to be sacrificed to God. Yet this same God had promised that Abraham was to be the father of a great nation, who were to come presumably through Isaac. How could this happen, if Isaac was sacrificed? The writer to the Hebrews says that Abraham believed that God would raise Isaac from the dead, but, with the greatest of all respect to that writer, I don't think that is so. Abraham did not believe in any resurrection. When Abraham set out on that journey to Mount Moriah, I think that he had not the faintest idea what would happen, but I do think that he knew what the outcome would be, though he could not see how that outcome could be achieved. Isaac would not die, though how that would happen, Abraham did not know. Abraham had faith, and with quiet resolve did exactly as God had commanded him, and what he hoped would be true in fact was true, and his son Isaac survived, and through Isaac Abraham indeed became a father of a mighty nation.

We need this faith today. At the easy level we need faith in God to work through the parish reorganization which may well be ahead of us. Steps may have to be taken that are difficult and challenging; that is the easy part. The hard part is that we have to be a missionary church, we have to show forth to all the love of God, and we have to show to men and women not just what they want to hear, but the truth of God.

The past 30 years have seen changes that would have been unbelievable only a few years before that time. Just 30 years ago, the life of the unborn child was devalued, indeed made of no value, and the Church of England kept silent. For 2,000 years, Christian marriage has been the union before God of a man and a woman, normally hoping that marriage will be blessed with children; that should be the only way that children will be born and the human race, God's people, continued. That's too narrow, we are now told, we have to accept alternative lifestyles. What sudden revelation justifies that view? In matters of belief, we have endured Church leaders sniping at or even denying the articles of our Creeds, even the very Resurrection of Our Lord. Archbishop Laud valued bishops as a means of ensuring that only orthodox views were taught in the Church and that strange heresies were stopped at source. Little did he know what some twentieth-century bishops and ex-bishops would be like! One of the joys, one of the many joys, of coming to live in Crick was to have a bishop who fearlessly and plainly stated his own belief in the Creeds he said each day, and our new Bishop, Ian, is as plain-spoken as his predecessor. It hurts our cause, and wounds us, that the very people who should be on the Lord's side appear not to be, but we must remember that it was one of the Twelve, chosen by Jesus, who betrayed Him, and we, as servants, cannot expect to be better favoured than our Master.

In quiet resolve, let us press on, acting on what we hope to be true even before we know that it is true. Homework has suddenly come back into fashion. Homework today is to take a few minutes to read that eleventh chapter, all 40 verses of it, of the letter to the Hebrews. Note the quiet resolve of each character. Rahab the harlot did not *know* that she was doing God's will letting in the spies; she hoped that was so, and felt sufficiently confident to act on that hope. Moses did not *know* what was in store when he led the Israelites out of Egypt into a barren desert, leaving the lush fields by the Nile and going into country where hardly a blade of grass, hardly a weed of any kind, grows. If the heroes and heroines of faith daunt us, take courage from that hero of doubt, Thomas. It will have taken a lot of courage to eat his own words in front of his friends, yet he did that, and, by tradition, spent his life as a missionary in India.

Faith is the quiet resolve to act on what we hope to be true, before we know that it is true, for that final and complete knowledge only comes when we, with all redeemed creation, appear before our Lord and Saviour.

Comments

Peter Graves: '*Interesting story of Lyttleton of Eton as model of faith.*'

Ian Sweeney: '*While religion continually debates the nature of faith, Frederick Norton illustrates what faith is through the experiences of twentieth-century men and biblical heroes.*'

Margaret Brearley: '*Eccentric but intriguing exploration of "faith", two-thirds of the sermon is (appropriately) a biography of the fascinating early twentieth-century Eton headmaster, Lyttleton.*'

A Conversion of Hearts?
Reflections on the Stephen Lawrence Inquiry

Sermon preached by Chris Chivers at St John's Church, Friern Barnet, London, on 24 January 1999, on the Feast of the Conversion of St Paul

Chris Chivers, 32, who with his wife Mary has a baby son, Dominic, is at present assistant curate of the parish of Friern Barnet, London. Born and brought up in Bristol, where his father is a non-stipendiary priest and his mother a retired charity worker, he is a graduate in music from Magdalen College, Oxford, and in theology from Selwyn College, Cambridge. He spent five years (before preparation for ordination at Westcott House) as lay chaplain of King's College School, Cambridge, where, among other duties, he was tutor to the choristers of its world-famous choir. Ordination training saw him spend a six-month period on the staff of St George's Cathedral, Cape Town, South Africa, working with street children, AIDS sufferers and homeless adults. There he helped to co-ordinate the enthronement of a new Archbishop and the installation of a new Dean and, co-authored a children's project for the Truth and Reconciliation Commission. A book of meditations, Echoes of a Rainbow Song, *published earlier this year and enthusiastically received by the critics, resulted from this formative period. In September 1999 he returns to St George's Cathedral as Canon Precentor.*

Fr Chris believes that preachers easily underestimate the import-ance of what they do. 'I learnt to preach among the liveliest and most openly critical of audiences', he says, 'a group of 8 to 13-year-old children. Their home lives – like many of ours – were often dominated almost exclusively by the television and by video games. Many of them read very little', he continues, 'and when they did read it was purely to magazines or comics that they tended to turn. With this went an experience of life which was often either pretty episodic – a few moments of this, a few moments of that – or chaotically multi-layered – a meal eaten, Neighbours *watched and a family conversation attempted, all at one and the same time.*

'What I sensed was a loss of focus on story and narrative –

*traditionally such a prime medium for the educational development
of children – and a consequent surrender to a rather dilettante mode
of existence. So the opportunity to tell stories and to provide
frameworks for their interpretation was there for the taking. I seized
it and the children did the rest, telling me what worked and what
didn't with honesty and candour. There was a mutuality about this
experience, a relationality which is essential to all effective preaching.
We went on a journey together, a journey which helped us to
understand our own stories by setting them within the overarching
story of the Bible, the Qur'an, the Bhagavad Gita – a whole range of
sacred texts which have been and are life-changing and life-enhancing
for human beings.'*

From this experience came the strong conviction for Fr Chris that
preaching is at the heart of community-building. 'People have always
told stories', he says. 'Stories are the life-blood of communities, their
unit of currency if you like. In swapping them people attempt to
discover commonality, a sense that someone else knows what it's like,
and, most importantly, what it all might mean. And in our pluralistic
society we shan't get close to understanding one another until we
have learnt to be attentive to the foundational stories at the heart of
our various faith traditions which resonate so powerfully with those
stories of day-by-day experiences which are of most immediate
concern to us.'

He continues: 'Our context is an avowedly inter-faith one. I thank
God for that. Our diversity should be a cause for great celebration.
Which is why hearing a story from so many different perspectives –
the South African apartheid story told to the Truth and Reconciliation Commission or the Stephen Lawrence tragedy recounted to the
Macpherson Inquiry – is so essential, because this models for us
patterns of listening and engagement to which we must all aspire.
And in a more mundane, but no less significant, way we are already
caught up in this process each day. You bump into a friend in Tesco's
and within minutes you are gossiping the gospel across the aisles
when you tell the tale of how your daughter's latest boyfriend has hit
her about and gone off with the rent, or of how your son has just won
a two-week holiday to Portugal. 'You are doing', he says, 'what the
first apostles were doing when they swapped stories of the ups and
downs of life in and around Galilee and Jerusalem. The preacher's
role is to focus this, to notice, for example, the small gesture which
might easily be missed, but which actually strikes at the heart of
things, and to bring it to the fore. What Vikram Seth does in a poem
about an airport departure lounge, I try to do week by week in the
pulpit, observing and interpreting some of what passes me by. The
context has changed a great deal in the last 2,000 years. But the*

method of approach is surely still the same? A widow dropping her mite into a collection box provides Jesus with a way-in to reflecting on how we may all best serve God. Finding the way-in is the key to good preaching. For in a market of wordsmiths the preacher is competing with many other forms of communication in an attempt to engage her congregation – though not necessarily to entertain them. Cheap gags rarely enhance discipleship. For the preacher – especially in suburbia – must be aware that this is perhaps the one chance in a given month to touch many of her hearers. Gone are the days of regular week-by-week church attendance. People's families are too widely dispersed for one thing. So they visit ageing relatives one week, the in-laws the next, take the children to a football tournament the week after, and only then are they able to come to church.'

Chris feels that this represents a huge shift and a major challenge for preachers. *'It's no use running an Advent or Lenten course of sermons these days. The chances are that almost no one will be able to make it through the whole series! Instead, what is required is an attentiveness to the issues and events of the present moment, an awareness that here, this morning, there is a chance to connect, to liberate, to affirm most especially those hearers who need to be – and should be – somewhere else next week. Too many people are made to feel guilty by the Church for fulfilling their legitimate and essential commitments to family and friends. For 2,000 years the Church has been telling its members to engage with the world, but when it finds that this means there is no one to do the coffee or to lead Junior Church, because the people who might fulfil these roles are busy doing the Lord's work elsewhere, the Church doesn't often cope too well.*

'It has been a bit of a change for me, coming from a stable, regular community like a school, where you see the same faces all the time, to a suburban church context in which there is a much more fluid pattern of involvement. I've had to adapt. Maybe there is less of a sense of the communal, more a sense of dispersed, journey. Perhaps church life is increasingly fragmented, as most commentators suggest. But certainly, as the preacher mounts the pulpit, there is still a great sense of waiting on the word of challenge, of hope and of affirmation – a palpable desire to be nourished and cherished.' He considers however that there is plenty of scope for complementing the set-piece sermon, the 'word for the week', with less formal, more interactive sermons which may perhaps better achieve in a church setting the mutuality he has so often found in a school context.

'Clergy must be prepared to take risks – to surrender their tendency to wish to control everything', he comments. *' "Father says" just won't do. No one's going to buy that line nowadays, thank*

goodness! Dialogue is the route to real spiritual maturity. Any preacher needs then to tap into the huge resource of experience and wisdom around him. Standing six feet above contradiction is no longer a realistic option, if, indeed, it ever was.' He also believes that the modern preacher must deploy his/her art in as many imaginative ways as possible. 'I love writing', he says, 'and over the last few years I've edited or written a number of short books – all taking the form of brief paragraph meditations – which are sermonic in style, I guess, and which, I hope, might fill the odd ten-minute slot for a parishioner stuck in the Tube on a Monday morning on the way to work. We must engage with people where they are. The Word can speak to them as much amidst a crowded carriage passing through Finsbury Park Station as through the relative calm of a Sunday morning in church.'

Text: Galatians 3:28

L ast Monday evening I was present in the Tricycle Theatre, Kilburn at a performance – if that is the right word – of *The Colour of Justice*: a dramatic representation of evidence submitted to the Stephen Lawrence Inquiry over many months during 1998. Taking 69 hours of material from the inquiry as a basis for his work, Richard Norton-Taylor, a journalist and writer from *The Guardian* has produced, in nearly three hours of script, what might be described as a tapestry of the inquiry's narrative. Over the next few months – and especially after the inquiry's report has been published in February – I have no doubt there will be many opportunities for us all to reflect on its findings. But for now I would like to give you some initial impressions based on what I saw and heard.

You will probably recall that Stephen Lawrence, a promising black 18-year-old and a prospective architectural student, was stabbed to death late at night on 22 April 1993 in Eltham, just south of the Thames. He had been waiting for a bus home after spending an evening with Duwayne Brooks, a friend of his, when they were both surrounded by a group of five or six white youths, one of whom was heard to say 'What ... what ... nigger'. At which point Stephen was set upon and stabbed several times in the chest before both he and Duwayne staggered off down the road away from the group. Within minutes Stephen had collapsed on the side of the road. And seeing this Duwayne dived into a phone box opposite to call for an ambulance. So began the train of events at the heart of the inquiry.

The first two people on the scene, arriving before any police car or ambulance, were Conor and Louise Taaffe – two local people walking home from a prayer meeting. It is on them that I wish to focus my impressions. For what emerges from their involvement in the Lawrence tragedy seems to me to lie at the very heart of the issues with which the inquiry was dealing. Seeing one man, Duwayne, standing in the road desperately trying to flag down passing cars, and another, Stephen, lying on the opposite side of the road, the Taaffes obviously became alerted to a very serious situation. After a few moments of thought, they went over to Stephen. They both bent down beside him and whilst Conor said prayers over him, Louise held his head. As Conor later recounted, they both had a sense he was in grave danger of losing his life; and knowing that hearing is the last sense to disappear before death, they said prayers to comfort him, Louise telling Stephen several times that he was very much loved – a gesture which of course meant much to the Lawrence family when they later heard about it. But as Conor revealed to the inquiry when they questioned him, his initial thoughts on arrival at the scene were not of the Good Samaritan variety, rather they were of the self-protective kind, for here potentially was a set-up. You had one semi-hysterical black man in the road and another black man lying down by the roadside. If I bend down to the man lying by the road, thought Conor, will I suddenly be attacked from behind by the other man? And I have to say that in revealing his thought processes with such amazing honesty and candour I think Conor Taaffe has done us all a great service. For what of course his reflections reveal is a train of sub-conscious thought-process which begins something like this: black youths spell danger: is it a set-up? – if so, this is a dangerous situation; will we be hurt? – this is really dangerous; and all of those thoughts well before one level of instinct is conquered by another: there's a man who's hurt – I must help him; there's another man distressed – I really must help him – so I give some help.

If you follow the logic of what can be uncovered from this opening scene of the Lawrence tragedy, you will perhaps have made the fundamental connection which needs to be made, namely, that racial prejudice – the instinctive, subconsciously conditioned response that the presence of young black youths late at night on the streets spells danger – has to be overcome at another level with sheer force of will, by an alternatively conditioned belief that I have a duty to help those in need whoever they are. And my reason for focusing on the motives and actions of Conor and Louise Taaffe is that they seem to me to represent exactly where most human beings are. They are basically good, decent, law-abiding people who endeavour to do the right thing. In the specific case of Stephen Lawrence they brought precious comfort and help to a dying man, which is a wonderful thing. But in order to do so they had to overcome other instincts, other forces deep within them. And it is those instincts which the whole Lawrence inquiry has sought to examine. For while in some cases – the case, for instance, of the five appallingly racist youths we saw on the television recently, threatening to 'skin niggers alive ... to chop off their arms and legs ... to throw them into the nearest river and see if they can still swim' – we see obvious and overt racism; whilst we have that blatant, despicable racism, we also have a racism much more subtle and all-pervasive; a racism which comes from the way in which we have all been conditioned to respond in our society.

Now is not the place – we do not have time – to recount the history of this racism in Britain. But now is the place to begin a process by which we acknowledge that we do make assumptions – whether conscious or unconscious – about people on the basis of their skin colour, because quite clearly we do, and to say that we don't, as a whole parade of police officers has so testified to the inquiry, is to live in the realms of fantasy.

Let me give you two examples. Let's take the black teenager who wins a competition of some kind at a predominantly white school, and is presented with a prize. We are sitting in the audience at Prize-giving. What do we often hear said, and in that faintly condescending tone, but 'Oh, hasn't he done awfully well?' – and what is actually meant by this is that he's done very well considering he's black. That's racism. Let's take another case: the way in which we hear people speak, as I have just spoken, of different colour groupings. 'Oh we've never thought of Indians as blacks' I was once told by someone here – and what of course is being said, even if it's not what is meant, is 'We really think of the Rector (an Anglo-Indian) as an honorary white'. That's racism too.

So there are two examples of this subtle, in-built racism – we all have it – which comes from the assumptions which we make – often very subconsciously for sure – but which manifest themselves all the time in our dealings with people – as we would see and describe them – of other races. And my reason for listing them, my reason for dwelling on such a small initial incident in the Lawrence tragedy, is that they all reveal something very deep-seated and ingrained within us, something which many people, the Metropolitan Police Commissioner Sir Paul Condon included, have failed to grasp, but which Conor and Louise Taaffe know only too well: namely, that all of us are stereotypers by trade – that is the nature of human beings – and that all of us thus bring to every human situation our baggage of prejudice. So, when one of the senior police officers heading up the initial Lawrence investigation folded into a ball – as Mrs Lawrence looked on – a piece of paper she had given him containing a list of suspects' names, he thought nothing of it. But she rightly experienced this gesture as a dismissive sort of racism. Because to her, by screwing up the paper he didn't appear to be taking seriously the clues she was presenting to him. And in the inquiry this police officer has not been able to understand how she experienced the gesture in the way in which she did. This is because he has not made – and seems unprepared to make – the connection which the Taaffes did make for themselves.

What am I saying we must do? Well firstly, I am saying that we must develop our self-awareness. We must think about our attitudes. We must examine the assumptions which we make and the things which we say. Secondly, I am saying that we must check out the motivation of our attitudes and actions. Let's please not say 'Oh, colour makes no difference to me – I just judge people as they are' because that isn't true, it's a lie. For we all judge people, consciously or subconsciously, on the basis of their skin colour, their education, their accent, their job, their appearance, whatever – that's the fallen nature of human beings. What's vitally important is that we all become aware that we do so, and aware of our fallenness. For then, as Conor and Louise Taaffe demonstrate for us, we will perhaps be able to redeem what is sinful within us, overcome our initial deep-seated prejudices, and conquer them by more worthy motives.

Today is the Feast of the Conversion of St Paul. And it seems to me that if conversion to Christ in whom, as Paul says, there is neither Jew nor Greek, slave nor free, but all as a new creation – if conversion to Christ means anything, if that new creation, the reality that all God's children are equal, if all that is ever going to be established in the depth of our hearts, it means our being schooled, our being trained, in that *scientia cordis*, that science of the heart as St Thomas Aquinas called it, by which we come to self-knowledge, so that in knowing ourselves we may have our baser instincts turned, converted, into the true love by which our neighbours will be nourished and served for what they are, as God's uniquely precious children, and through which God's kingdom will be realized.

We can do nothing, of course, to bring Stephen Lawrence back from the dead. We can probably do very little to alleviate the pain and suffering which his family have endured in their long search for justice. But we can face ourselves as we are; we can own up to the reality of what we see; and we can – as we must – work to transform all that into something worthy of his memory. Amen.

Comments

Ian Sweeney: '*From the horror of the brutal murder of Stephen Lawrence, he masterfully challenges us to reassess our prejudices in light of our Christian conversion.*'

Peter Graves: '*A good reflection on the Lawrence case, though more of an address than a sermon.*'

William Beaver: '*Totally precise and attractive exposition linking the conversion of St Paul with aspects of the Stephen Lawrence inquiry. Driving and challenging.*'

Jonathan Romain: '*He succeeds in taking a well-known theme and deriving profound lessons from it in a quietly directive way. The sermon gradually changes from being easy listening to very challenging.*'

The Sabbath

Sermon preached by Rabbi Shmuley Boteach in Oxford in February 1999

Rabbi Shmuley Boteach, aged 32, is an American-born Orthodox rabbi. Following rabbinical studies in Australia, Israel and the United States, at the age of 21 he was sent by the Lubavitcher Rebbe, the late head of the Lubavitch movement in America, to Oxford as the first residential rabbi serving university students for several decades. His aim was to stimulate students and share Judaism's timeless message of inclusion, tolerance and love as well as conveying its engagement in the modern world. The community he established has become known as the L'Chaim (Hebrew for 'life') Society and is now the second largest student organization in Oxford's history, with branches also in London and Cambridge.

In twelve years, the L'Chaim Society, inspired and driven by Rabbi Boteach, has become a central part of Jewish life in the United Kingdom, a hub of intellectual debate and religious celebration for Jews and non-Jews. Already regarded as a leading contemporary Jewish thinker, Rabbi Boteach believes wholeheartedly in the synthesis of heaven and earth, a message which challenges issues central to humanity.

The universal debates and lectures he organizes attract world figures from all fields. Visitors to the Society have included Binyamin Netanyahu, Shimon Peres, Mikhail Gorbachev, Bob Hawke, Elie Wiesel, Natan Sharansky, Simon Wiesenthal, Amos Oz, Diego Maradona, Jon Voight, Professor Stephen Hawking, Jerry Springer and Boy George. In debates held by the L'Chaim Society, Rabbi Boteach, runner-up in the 1998 Preacher of the Year Award, is involved in addressing subjects such as the existence of God, the role of women in society, the question of human evolution and the role of the media in representing the truth, to name but a few.

Rabbi Boteach appears regularly on radio and television. The BBC have produced a one-hour documentary about his work and the L'Chaim Society, entitled Moses of Oxford. *He has also appeared on* Many Questions, *a religious talk-back programme produced by ITN, along with many other programmes including* The Big Breakfast

(Channel 4), Thursday Night Live *(Carlton TV) and* The Moral Maze *(BBC)*. *Barbra Streisand's film company Barwood Studios, in New York, have been working on a script for a potential film on the life of Rabbi Boteach and a former President of the L'Chaim Society, Cory Booker.*

As the author of ten books including the international best-seller Kosher Sex, *Rabbi Boteach writes prolifically on all manner of contemporary issues: on relationships and sexuality, on broader social issues such as racism and gender equality, and on theological issues such as the existence of God and human suffering. Books published include* Dreams; The Wolf Shall Lie with the Lambs; Wrestling with the Divine; Moses of Oxford; Wisdom, Understanding and Knowledge; The Intelligent Person's Guide to Judaism; Kosher Sex *and its two sequels* The Jewish Guide to Adultery *and* Dating Secrets of the Ten Commandments, *this latest published in May 1999. He has built an international following as a spirited and lucid exponent of the role of Judaism in modern thought and life, through his weekly essays published in the* London Jewish News, The Forward *and the* Manchester Jewish Telegraph *as well as on the World Wide Web. He was also voted Newsmaker of the Year 1998 by the* Jewish Chronicle *in Britain.*

Rabbi Boteach, who lives in London and Oxford with his Australian wife Deborah and their six young children, believes without question that there is a place for preaching in the millennium. 'I think that the principle is we are a complex generation distinguished by our paradoxical desire to have more and more material possessions, but also to grow spiritually,' he says.

'On the one hand we are the most materialistic generation of all time. We are more financially successful, more professionally ambitious and more self-indulgent than ever before. On the other hand we are also reading more self-help books than ever before, trying to discover more spiritual and religious perspectives. This encourages people to climb the religious mountain and ascend to new spiritual heights. I believe that preaching is currently becoming more fashionable than ever before.'

But he believes preaching and religious worship must change if they are to survive, primarily by becoming more relevant. 'Religion has assumed a moral and pious manner and it is as if we are teaching people why they are doing bad things and why the world has so many flaws. Religion should be offering guidance. Preaching should show people how to be better parents and how to forgive their family for any wrongs that they may have done to them. Preaching can also teach us how to succeed in business but also how to remain ethical and moral at the same time. Religion should be the next self-help wave after the secular self-help wave which led to the sale of so many millions of books.'

He has seen some of these ideas reflected in the way his congregation at the L'Chaim Society has changed over the last twelve years. *'I have seen a great spiritual awakening of the students at Oxford and Cambridge Universities. When I first arrived in Oxford in 1988 the students all wanted to be investment bankers and make lots of money and their aim was to be professionally prosperous. Now we are seeing more and more students who want to pray during the day. They want more committed relationships, not just casual affairs, even in their early twenties. The 1990s have led to phenomenal financial prosperity. This is perhaps the most prosperous period of all time, and yet people are not happier. In previous generations when you heard that money did not make you happy or fame and celebrity status did not make you happy, people had to accept it as an article of faith. But now we are seeing it first hand. People are experiencing money and buying all the material possessions and they are still no happier. Hence they are looking for greater spirituality.'*

Text: Exodus 20:9–11

> Remember the Sabbath day to sanctify it. Six days shall you labour and accomplish all your work; but the seventh day is Sabbath to the Lord; you shall not do any work ... for in six days the Lord made heaven and earth, the sea, and all that is in them, and he rested on the seventh day. Therefore, the Lord blessed the Sabbath day and sanctified it.

T he Sabbath is a paradox. On the one hand, it celebrates *God's* activity. On the other, it is a celebration of *human* freedom. We subjugate ourselves to God's mastery and, simultaneously, rejoice in the mastery we have over ourselves. This is bizarre. Is the Sabbath about God, or is it about man? Is it about our dependence, or our independence?

In reality, the Sabbath encapsulates all these aspects. It is the day on which we release ourselves from the mindless slavery of materialism. It does not distinguish between master and servant, boss or employee. It is a sanctuary in time, an island of serenity from which the noise and distraction of life is excluded. And it is also the day on which, above all, we welcome God into our lives.

God made many wondrous things during the seven days of creation, but none so precious as the Sabbath. Of all the precious moments which dot the Jewish temporal landscape, none are as rich as the Sabbath. Indeed, the Sabbath is the crown jewel of the Jewish people. Of far greater significance than the duration of creation is the fact that it was crowned by the Sabbath (Genesis 2:1–3), bringing rest and refreshment to the toiling world. As one author so succinctly put it, 'The concept of the creative pause, sanctified by the divine example, is one of the greatest spiritual and social contributions to civilisation made by the religion of Israel'.

Freedom from slavery

Few people doubt that life today is busier than ever before. The labour-saving devices which are the gifts of modern technology do not relieve us of responsibility so much as spur us on to ever greater heights of ambition and achievement. This is the age of the entrepreneur, when the gates of wealth and success have been open to nearly everyone and there are millions of runners hell-bent on reaching the finish line. I have grown accustomed to having to wait three or four months to meet up with friends just for a simple dinner, such is the congestion of both our diaries. Most people today suffer from sleep deprivation as they fight to cram more and more into their frightfully hectic day. No doubt, social commentators could read much into the modern obsession with squeezing the most out of life and the endless lust for professional success. Some would call it capitalism gone mad. Others would see a value-less society in which money and material acquisition have supplanted family and the pursuit of knowledge. Others of greater morbidity might even speak of a subconscious death-wish on the part of young professionals who are pushing themselves over the abyss. The Jewish diagnosis, however, would be that this is the classic and misguided scenario, as old as the sun, of the earth's inhabitants sacrificing time in the acquisition of space, squandering their lives to make themselves the centre of an ever-expanding circle of possessions. Based on how people run their lives, it seems clear that they feel that their possessions and inflated bank accounts, are their most valued commodity. One of the principal objectives of Judaism, however, is to teach people to value time far more than space, to dedicate space toward the acquisition of time.

Creating sanctuaries of the spirit

In Judaism the empirical world is divided into three fundamental components: time, space, and man who acts upon time and space. The purpose of religion is the consecration of all three, through man using time and space in the service of the Creator. The man of faith seeks to make time and space holy by creating sanctuaries of the spirit, geographic areas as well as special moments of refuge and sanctity, in which God becomes manifest.

Man is meant to cordon off places and times in which God is experienced as a tangible and living reality. But whereas most world religions put the bulk of their emphasis on space, Judaism's emphasis is on time. Any traveller through Christian Europe will see the great monuments to space that the believers of old built for their Lord; wondrous cathedrals of unmatched splendour rise toward the heavens.

Judaism, by contrast, has never had such cathedrals. To be sure, there are some beautiful synagogues in existence and there was, of course, the great Temple in Jerusalem that was destroyed first by the Babylonians, and then by the Romans. Indeed, the land of Israel, a space consecrated by God as a holy Land, is central to the Jewish religion. But the fact remains that for the majority of Jewish history, including the past 2,000 years, the Jews have not been on their land and have not had a Temple. Rather, the Jewish religion thrives, as the great modern Jewish thinker Rabbi Abraham Joshua Heschel says, on cathedrals in *time* rather than cathedrals of space. The very first act of consecration recorded in the Bible is when God hallowed the Sabbath day. In fact, the very first time the word 'holy' is used in the Bible is in connection with the Sabbath day (Genesis 2:3): 'So God blessed the seventh day and made it holy, because on it God rested from all the work that he had done in creation.' Similarly, the first commandment, or *mitzvah,* given to the Jewish people upon their emergence from the crucible of Egypt was the sanctification of the new moon and new lunar month. They were to witness the monthly rebirth of the moon and consecrate the time as *Rosh Chodesh,* the first day of the new Jewish month.

Taking this idea further, in other religions space consecrates time. A geographic location is first chosen for a cathedral or shrine, and only then do actions, such as prayer or acts of confession undertaken within, become sacred. In Judaism, however, the reverse is true. It is special moments and supernatural events which have come to pass in a certain place that lend that location its solemnity and sanctity. In other words, time sanctifies space. A case in point: Mt Moriah, the domain where the Temple was built in Jerusalem, was sacred because, according to tradition, it was there that God took clay from the earth, fashioned it into the guise of a man, breathed life into it, and called that being Adam. On the same site, many centuries later, Abraham was commanded to bring his son Isaac as a sacrifice to God and ended up substituting a ram in the boy's stead. The site (space) became holy because of the great moments (time) which transpired there. Judaism is obsessed with holy and special moments, which then lend sanctity and become permanently ingrained within space. The Jewish year is like a spiral in which man continually comes back to the same periods of sanctity, each of which evokes a different season of the spirit and calls forth memories of an earlier period in the development of mankind and the Jewish nation. The bridge or field where a couple enjoyed their first kiss will always be special to them. So too, the places where God and the Jewish people consecrated their everlasting bond is likewise sacred.

Lost appreciation for time

Perhaps the greatest casualty of our modern, callous society is a lost appreciation for the sublimity of time. Modern man, with his computers and rockets, is permanently engaged in conquering and pushing back the frontiers of space. Indeed, the prototype for today's generation is the career-oriented man or woman who sacrifices all their time in the acquisition of material space. People spend their lives working themselves to the bone, and expending every waking effort to acquire money and possessions. Times for family and friends are regularly compromised in favour of business meetings and writing reports. Never in history have human relationships suffered as much as they do today. With the scarce amount of time which husbands and wives, and parents and children, have for each other, is it any wonder that divorce is at its highest ever rate, and that children are more acutely insecure?

Judaism conceives of life in a fundamentally different way. Man is meant to expend space in the acquisition of time. 'Remember the days of old, consider the years long past' (Deuteronomy 32:7). Man is conditioned by the Bible to embrace time as life's most precious gift. The Sabbath is designed around the idea that man should work six days, and get all his troubles out of the way, so that he can enjoy a totally tranquil and uninterrupted interval dedicated towards intimate, divine communion. The Sabbath is a day of relationships, prayer, and enlightenment. A similar idea pervades the festivals which punctuate the Jewish year, each of which represents time set aside for reflection on fundamental aspects of life. Similarly, on the many festivals which dot the Jewish calendar, the Jew works throughout the months in order to save up money and celebrate these sacred and precious moments with family, friends, and community. In Temple times, the Jew was obligated to make three pilgrimages each year in order to share these special moments with the Almighty Himself in His chosen home. Jewish life is about seizing the moment and living for glorious times as opposed to conquering vast tracts of land or owning glorious works of art. With the notable exception of King David, Jewish history has no famous conquerors. Our famous men are great sages throughout history who were celebrated for using their time wisely, devoting it to service of God and humanity, and the acquisition of knowledge and wisdom.

The lesson for each of us in our daily lives is to rededicate ourselves to an understanding of the preciousness of the moment. The time we parents have with our children when they are young and adorable is fleeting. If not captured now, it will soon be lost forever. We cannot work ourselves to the point of distraction, where all our time is dominated by the pursuit of success. Put people before property and relationships before riches. Carve out meaningful moments before, after, and even during work to read, think, love, and learn. The ancient rabbis warned that 'the more property one acquires, the more worry he acquires'. We must therefore use our prosperity as a *means* rather than an end. Spend generously if you have the money on plane and train tickets to visit parents, siblings, and children. Money should be used to buy time, to acquire sacred moments with all who hold us dear. A wealthy man once said to me that the only real blessing of wealth is the freedom it buys its holder. We undermine that blessing and turn it into a curse when we allow money to become a prison, when we become enslaved to our fortunes and our jobs. Money must be used to procure more and more quality and quantity time with loved ones. Only when wealth is used to release us from worry and liberate our time toward noble goals can it be construed as a blessing. Otherwise, it is nothing more than a gilded cage, devoid of both love and God.

And this is why God gave us the Sabbath. A day of rest, devoted to spiritual renewal and family, was utterly unknown in the ancient world. In fact, the Jews suffered ridicule on account of their day of rest from some of Rome's most prolific literary figures, including Seneca, Juvenal, and Tacitus. The seven-day cycle by which all humanity today reckons time and regulates its affairs has its origin only in the Hebrew Bible. All attempts at changing this pattern and moving the day of rest into a different time-frame or to change the seven-day week, have met with total failure. Such an attempt was made as recently as the French Revolution when all things were changed to a decimal system. The fathers of the Revolution tried to reconstruct the week into ten instead of seven days, but had to abandon the effort after it met with failure on all fronts.

The holy Sabbath is the goal of the week. Yet our business-oriented and money-making world today treats rest and relaxation as servicing the needs of further exertion of labour. It makes sense that workers will be more productive if they are given time to refresh and renew their energies. Many make the mistake of believing that the Sabbath was given by God to man to renew his energies so that he might be more productive in the coming six days. Leon Trotsky said that he would preserve the Sabbath, even in the atheistic culture of the Soviet Union, because all workers needed to rest. This misguided and shallow understanding of the Sabbath would have us believe that man's noblest goal is physical toil rather than moments of spiritual reflection. But the fact that the Sabbath is the holiest day of the week – by far transcending the six days of work – lays waste to this concept. On the contrary, in Judaism the six days of work are all a preparation for the one glorious day of rest. Echoing this point, the celebrated mediaeval Jewish sage Rabbi Judah He-Hasid said: 'One who goes to sleep on the Sabbath should not say "Let us sleep so that we can do our work when the Sabbath is over", but rather let him say "Let us rest for today is the Sabbath" ' (*Sefer Hasidim*). When man works hard to store some treasure, it affords him a meaningful day of relaxation in which, unencumbered by material concerns, he can focus on the purpose of his creation, the direction of his life, and commune intimately with God. He can strengthen his human relationships and bask in the glory of creation rather than dedicate more time to the domination of nature.

My son the Sabbath

But more than just teaching us to appreciate time over space, the Sabbath is actually a profound lesson in improving the quality of our relationships. Never before has life been so busy. The chaotic times in which we live are governed by constant emergencies in which everything is urgent and pressing. Never before has man been so harried. The ring of mobile phones drills a hole through our ears, as dozens of e-mails that must be answered clock up, and faxes and post stream through our in-trays. Just when we thought we could relax, we must travel hundreds of miles for an urgent business meeting. The greatest casualty of this harried lifestyle is that the urgent is always placed before the important. Modern-day man is no fool. Ours is arguably the most literate, educated, and informed generation of all time. We do indeed know the difference between right and wrong, the ephemeral and the eternal, the urgent and the important. So why are our lives and our relationships in such as mess? *Because although we know what is important, we never have any time for it. It is always superseded by the urgent.*

Sociologists point out that children today seem to be far worse behaved than at any other time in recorded history. Reports of young girls getting pregnant at age 11 no longer shock us. Soon the horror stories of children shooting each other with guns – a fact that has become almost commonplace in the daily news headlines in the

United States – will have the same deadening effect. Why is it indeed that children today seem to lack all guidance? Are today's children really such monsters? Of course not! Rather, the errant behaviour of today's youth is primarily a cry for attention. Our children are delinquent because we have no time for them, choosing instead to pacify them with television and toys rather than with attention and love. I once overheard a conversation between a young mother in her thirties and her elderly mother. The woman complained that it is so hard to raise children these days. Her mother responded 'In my day it was much harder. We had no television. We actually had to spend time with our children.' Children's misbehaviour and wrongdoing result from a lack of supervision and guidance on the part of neglectful parents, coupled with a deep-seated desire to get noticed. Children compensate for a lack of parental love with hurtful behaviour which is their appeal for affection.

Studies show that the average American parents give their children on average just three uninterrupted minutes of quality time per day. This is a shocking figure. Why is the time that parents spend with children today so pitiably minuscule? Why do we spend more time brewing coffee than playing with or reading to our children? Surely it is not due to the fact that parents today love their children less than in the past. When it comes to a moment of crisis, there is little that parents will not do for their children. The problem is because they always place the urgent before the important.

We all recognize that the time spent with children is important. So one sits down to play with one's children or to read them a story. But suddenly, the phone rings. And while one's children are much more important than the phone call, the call is *urgent*. If you don't run to pick it up just now, you will miss it. When you return from the call to continue the story you were reading, you notice that it is now seven o'clock, and there is a very important item on the evening news which again you just cannot miss. Later, when you return for the third time to resume your time with your children, you look at your watch and remember that the gym will only be open for another half-hour, and you once again run to accommodate the urgent and in the process compromise the important.

And so man continues, blindly trampling on everything which he knows to be dear to him. Later, when we retire in our old age, our deepest regrets will be that now that there is nothing urgent, we cannot pursue the important because the opportunity was squandered. The same parents who never had time for their children are confounded with far too much time because the relationships with children and grandchildren are non-existent. We wonder why our children don't visit us more in our retirement, and we remember that, like a neglected bank account that is empty through lack of deposits, it results from our not having built strong relationships with them when they were young. Furthermore, having devoted little or no time to study and the pursuit of knowledge, we have not developed a deep-seated craving for learning; so reading books is not sufficiently stimulating. Neither does religion engage us, since our lives were devoted to shopping and television. And since we have no relationship with God, we don't find His presence comforting. Having grown up in Miami Beach – America's largest retirement community – I can attest to the fact that so many of our dear elderly while away their retirement years playing cards and sitting idly in deck chairs in the sun. The Lubavitcher Rebbe once said that retirement should be about 're-tyreing', putting on 'new tyres', and going stronger than ever before, rededicating our lives to all that it is important, at the stage of our life when we finally have the time to pursue it without the distraction of the urgent. The problem is that by the time we arrive at this special stage, it is too late: we have largely forgotten what *is* important.

It is for this reason that God gave man the Sabbath, a 24-hour period in which nothing whatsoever is urgent. The Sabbath is not about learning a sense of priorities, the relative values of urgent and important. Rather, the beauty of the Sabbath is that on the Sabbath *there simply is nothing urgent.* On it we are elevated to a higher plane of reality. During the week, a father sits to read his daughter a bedtime story when suddenly he remembers that he must send an urgent fax. He wrestles with his conscience about what he should do. Should he leave his daughter and make the deal, or miss the deal and read to his daughter? But as he sits with his family at the Friday night Sabbath table, looking back in hindsight at the same scenario, he discovers that there never was any decision to be made. How could he even have thought of abandoning his child? On the Sabbath we discover that that which we think is urgent is actually non-existent. When a father discovers the true pleasures of playing with his children, he does not accept that doing so is better than making money. Rather, the two are utterly incomparable. One is real and everlasting, the other is ephemeral and illusory. Stated in other words, the key to becoming a good parent is to make one's child into the Sabbath. Treat your children like there is nothing urgent that can ever supersede them.

God wanted to *be* the Sabbath for the Jewish people at least one day a week, so He *gave* them the Sabbath. The Almighty understands how busy humans are throughout the week, and how they are almost totally consumed with providing for their basic human necessities. He understands, therefore, that man cannot devote all his time to overt

Godly activity. So the Almighty set aside one day a week and declared that for a 25-hour period, the Jew must put God first in all things. No sense of urgency should be attached to any matters on the Sabbath other than spiritual matters. Learning to make our loved ones into the Sabbath is the single greatest lesson for a successful relationship. A wife is forgiving and understanding of her husband's preoccupation with business. After all, that is what feeds the family. But if he is too busy for their anniversary, or her birthday, she feels unimportant and second-class. A woman wants to be her husband's Sabbath. On the Sabbath, therefore, man comes to know the sacred. And by indulging in an uncorrupted period lasting 25 hours, he learns to extrapolate beyond this once-a-week haven, and incorporate sanctity into other periods of his week by creating a daily Sabbath of a few hours at a time. Only the sacred can combat the urgent.

My dentist is an Orthodox Jew and a close friend. Although a consummate professional, on one occasion, he put a filling in my tooth which dissolved the next day. I could not eat on that side of my mouth and called him at home, telling his daughter that it was urgent. She returned to the phone saying that her father was preoccupied. 'Tell him it's an emergency', I said. 'My filling has fallen out.' She again returned to the phone. 'My Daddy said that he is celebrating his mother's 82nd birthday, and you will just have to call him in the morning at the office.' The Bible says that honouring one's parents is a sacred duty. My urgent tooth – not being as important as a mother's birthday – would have to wait.

When Moses first encounters the Almighty in the Wilderness, he sees a burning bush. He approaches the bush to investigate the wondrous sight. The Bible says that at that point the Lord spoke to him from the bush, and the first thing He commanded Moses was to remove his shoes 'for the ground which you now stand on is holy'. *Judaism is about teaching man to find the hallowed ground upon which no foot can trample.* Judaism sensitizes us to the moments of sanctity which must pervade our lives. And the Sabbath is the single greatest lesson in discovering that sanctity. We must establish time spent with parents, spouse, siblings, and children as hallowed ground upon which no commercial or recreational pursuit may trespass.

Now, imagine if we could each make just make two hours every day into a personal Sabbath. A mother sits to play with her children on a Wednesday evening. The phone rings, but she refuses to answer it, because the time she spends with her children is sacred, holy time. Her children are the Sabbath. A man talks to his wife when he returns from work. Rather than have his wife wait as he sends one last fax from home, he understands that the time he spends working on his marriage is sacred time upon which there can be no intrusion.

Suddenly, he has made room in life for the important. He is actually liberated from feeling that he is a slave born for toil.

And with this we can finally understand why God links the exodus from Egypt with the observance of the Sabbath. 'Six days shall you labour and accomplish all your work; but the seventh day is Sabbath to the Lord: you shall not do any work ... *And you shall remember that you were a slave in the land of Egypt, and the Lord, your God, has taken you out from there with a strong hand and an outstretched arm;* therefore the Lord, your God, has commanded you to keep the Sabbath day' (Deuteronomy 5:12-15). Without the Sabbath, we would still be slaves to Egypt, slaves to the Pharaohs of Wall Street and the whips of chains of bills, bosses, and clients. Only with the deliverance and emancipation afforded by the Sabbath can we really say with any real conviction: 'Free at last. Free at last. Thank God Almighty, I'm free at last.'

Comments

Jonathan Romain: '*A strong theme of distinguishing between the urgent and the important, and with good use of anecdotes. However, the central message is in danger of being engulfed by a welter of extraneous historical detail that makes the sermon over-long. It would be much more powerful if shorter.*'

William Beaver: '*Tackling the demon/friend, time, this rapid-fire, erudite sermon compels its auditors to re-evaluate how they use time and what it should be used for. Invigorating and compelling call to action.*'

Peter Graves: '*Clearly related an age-old theme to contemporary needs. Arresting and interesting.*'

Ian Sweeney: '*Rabbi Boteach reminds us of the importance of sacred time in this sermon which challenges us to make sacred moments available for God and our families.*'

Margaret Brearley: '*A passionate, thought-provoking eulogy on the Jewish Shabbat, theologically the meatiest sermon. Many profound insights distilled from earlier commentators and his own experience, beautifully expressed and well applied to social and familial crises of today.*'

Words on Love

SERMON PREACHED BY GRAHAM GILLMAN AT ST
FRANCIS CHURCH, NAILSEA, BRISTOL, ON 3 JANUARY
1999, THE SECOND SUNDAY OF CHRISTMAS

*Father Graham Gillman, a Roman Catholic priest in the diocese of
Clifton, has had many of his daily sermons published and is currently
working on a catechetical programme in what spare time he has as
parish priest of a thriving community near Bristol. Before becoming a
priest he served an engineering apprenticeship, finally becoming a
production engineer. Since ordination he has worked as a curate in a
number of parishes, a sixth form chaplain, chaplain to what was
Bristol Polytechnic (now the University of the West of England) and
has also been responsible for introducing a support programme for
the clergy of his diocese. He has four nieces and two great-nephews,
and so is no stranger to the joys and sorrows, pressures and privileges
of family life in today's world.*

*He was a founder member of the Bishop of Clifton's Committee
for Health and Healing, and has been actively involved with the
healing ministry for many years. He believes that healing is about the
whole person: body, mind and spirit. 'Jesus did not divide us into
body and soul – the soul to be healed and the body to be left to suffer
– He touched people's hearts with His love and in doing so brought
them to wholeness.'*

*He believes that it is the unconditional love of Jesus for every
single person that is at the core of the healing ministry, and this love
is a recurring theme in his preaching.*

*Father Graham was inspired to enter the Preacher of the Year
competition when he called into Southwark Cathedral for, as he
thought, a short time in prayer and reflection – only to discover that
the cathedral was hosting the final of the 1997 competition and the
building was full of people and television cameras, so he stayed to
listen and felt that he would like to give it a try.*

*He believes that preaching is a gift which carries a great
responsibility: the preacher is breaking and sharing the Word of
God for our world today. It must therefore be relevant to the lives of
those who are listening (Jesus Himself told topical stories to put His
point across) and must speak to their hearts if there is to be any*

conversion or transformation experience. Above all, for a sermon to be effective it must be sincere, it must come from the heart. You cannot share what you do not own yourself, and a congregation will always know if you don't believe, and live, what you are trying to say. This does not mean that you need to have all the answers (though it helps to have some!) but, like a good counsellor, you do need to be open to the Holy Spirit and know what questions need to be asked, leaving listeners with something to take away with them which will influence their faith and their lives in the days ahead.

He believes that there is a great spiritual hunger, albeit sometimes unrecognized, in the world today – you only have to see the number of people who are trying 'alternative' religions such as New Age spirituality, crystal healing and so on to realize that there is a longing for 'otherness' which is not being satisfactorily met. Preachers must address with understanding and compassion the challenges and problems that ordinary people are facing, whilst remaining true to the values that Christ upheld. They therefore have a responsibility to keep themselves informed about the political, social and moral influences that affect the lives of so many people in today's world, and strive to be inclusive, making the Church a place where all will find a welcome, not just the privileged few.

With the increase in car ownership and the advent of the seven-day week, congregations have become much more fluid in recent years, and worshippers much more flexible in their approach. Whereas once Sunday activities, such as they were, were arranged around attendance at church, nowadays worship, when it takes place at all, tends to be fitted in around the day's other activities. Where once people went to church every Sunday, the pressures of life today, regarding both work and social and leisure activities, mean that many will now only go to church once a fortnight or even once a month, at whichever service happens to be most convenient.

The importance of the preacher's task, in which Father Graham passionately believes, to share the Word of God becomes an even greater responsibility when that Word may be the only contact with the gospels that his listeners will encounter for a matter of weeks.

Text: The Gospel of the day – John 1:1-18

There are special moments in all our lives that mark change or difference; one of those moments is when we discover that our parents are not always right. As small children we see mum and dad as the source of all knowledge and wisdom – they teach us so much – but there comes that point when we find out that they can get things wrong. For me such a point came when my parents said to me 'Sticks and stones may break your bones but words will never hurt you'. Well, I knew they were wrong, because words do hurt; words can be life-giving or they can be destructive.

People's whole lives can be transformed, changed, by just a name and silly, childish behaviour like shouting, 'I hate you! Fatty! Specky Four-eyes! Shrimp!' To a young child such words can create an identity, and so often it is a negative identity, which stops them seeing themselves as they really are and can lead to disorders such as anorexia. Words have power – power to give life or to destroy.

Today's gospel is about God's word – a word which gives life. God so loved the world, in other words God so loved each one of us, that He utters a word of love and that Word is enfleshed, becomes real, becomes human. Through Mary's 'Yes' to God, Jesus is born; He is the utterance of God's love, uttered in love. And Christ goes on uttering the word of love when He heals, when He forgives, when He proclaims – and upon the cross, more than anywhere else, even wordlessly, He is uttering a word of love when He opens His arms to embrace the whole world in its suffering and in its pain: a word that says 'I am with you', for He identifies with every single one of us when we experience the pain of the cross which is part of life. He is there with us; the Word is real, the Word is enfleshed.

And you and I, because we are baptized into Christ and are given the life of Christ, have to continue that word of Jesus. We are the word for our world today and I would like to put before you three words, or phrases, that we might reflect upon.

The first is 'Thank you'. Whenever we share in the Eucharist, a word which itself means 'thanksgiving', we are, by our presence, thanking God. By sharing in Eucharist we are joining in that act of Christ in which He gives thanks for all that is good. So, during Mass, perhaps we could look back and thank God especially for that which has been good for us during the past year, for to give thanks is to recognize the blessings which we have and where they come from – that all is gift from God. Continuing the theme of thanks, we can go on to reflect upon whether or not we thank each other enough, within our family, within our community – for thanksgiving can be life-giving.

The second phrase is 'I love you'. God has uttered that Word in Jesus and the whole of Jesus' life is an utterance of love; we have to live it. How we use words can give life and build people, but it can also destroy them. Sometimes we are just longing to hear a word of encouragement or praise, a word that gives hope. One of the worst experiences of my childhood was waiting for my name to be called as the football captains selected their teams and as the other boys were all gradually being picked. I would be praying fervently 'Please,

please, don't let me be the last one!' I was never quite last, but almost: desperately waiting to hear my name called, desperately wanting to be chosen.

I wonder, in your homes, are there people waiting to hear a word? How many children have longed to hear, particularly from their fathers, the words 'I love you'. In counselling you quickly discover just how important that is for development, especially where fathers are concerned. Somehow, in our society it's perfectly acceptable for women to say 'I love you' and boys, no matter how big they are, can comfortably hug and kiss mum – but they also need that physical and emotional connection with dad. What is true for sons is, of course, just as true for daughters. Children need to experience being loved by both parents and so often, as fathers, we let our children down when we don't tell them how much we love them. It is so terribly sad when someone dies suddenly and we are swamped with regrets for the things we've never said: the 'thank you's' and the 'I love you's' – and now it's too late. Do it now; do it while you still can; do it every day.

And the third phrase, which is so necessary and so life-giving, is 'I'm sorry'. You see, you can't love without running the risk of hurting, and the more you love someone the more you open yourself to being hurt. So when we have hurt someone we love, the way forward is to make real the sorrow we feel for the pain we've caused. To love is to risk that pain; to love is to risk being hurt by the other and what restores us are those words, 'I am sorry', which is why every Mass begins with a greeting from Christ who tells us He loves us, followed by our repentance for any wrong or hurt we have caused. Well, I can only speak for myself, but I'm not perfect and I know that I hurt the people around me, the people who matter most, and I imagine that you are no different.

Do we really express our sorrow to others, or are we too proud to acknowledge it? Words can bring healing and give life – and so often we cannot be healed until we can forgive those who have hurt us, and we are liberated for that process when the other is prepared to say 'I'm sorry'. It can be a profound thought when we remember that on many occasions in the past few years the Pope has apologized in the name of the Church, particularly to the Jews for anti-Semitism over the centuries. We can't accept forgiveness until we say we're sorry, and healing cannot take place until forgiveness is given. Perhaps we need to ask God to help us in that today, and when we do, when we say I'm sorry, when we say, and live, 'I love you' and 'I thank you', then we are making God's word present in our life and in our world. We become the Word of God made flesh and He still dwells in our midst, just as He did as the babe in the manger.

Let us pray that we may truly be a life-giving community in our homes, in our places of work and in our world today.

Comments

Peter Graves: *'Clear, simple, to the point. Relevant.'*

Margaret Brearley: *'A beautifully straightforward presentation. Short, pared-down, challenging and encouraging – a model of a brief pastoral homily.'*

Kieran Conry: *'Quite brief and to-the-point, with a good lead into a central theme of "word". The illustrations are good and surely relevant to any listener, but a little more humour and anecdote would not come amiss.'*

Veiled in Chocolate

SERMON PREACHED BY GORDON GILES IN ST PAUL'S
CATHEDRAL ON 14 FEBRUARY 1999, ST VALENTINE'S
DAY

*Gordon Giles, 33, is the Succentor and Senior Cardinal of St Paul's
Cathedral in London. As one of the minor canons, he is involved in
singing and leading the regular worship there. As the century rolls
over into the second millennium, there are many big national events,
which must also be organized, planned and stage-managed. Gordon,
who has degrees in music, philosophy and theology, has a special
responsibility for music and liturgy at St Paul's. Before taking up his
post there in 1998, he worked in the diocese of Ely, at the church of
the Good Shepherd in North Cambridge.*

*'The contrast was remarkable, I was used to being closely in touch
with a lovely congregation of all ages, who attended regularly, some
of whom were responsible for actually building the church 40 years
earlier. I also had wonderful links with the local community, through
schools, and through the setting-up of the first Credit Union in
Cambridgeshire, which I chaired.'*

*He says: 'People and human relationships are just as important to
me at St Paul's, but there is less chance to form lasting relationships
with worshippers. In a parish, there is an underlying relationship,
built, not only through regular preaching to the same people, but also
through pastoral contact over weeks and months. In a cathedral like
St Paul's this is not so easy and there is only one chance to
communicate with those who are present.'*

*Tourism is a major part of the life of St Paul's, and the
congregations are often made up of many nationalities. 'Now I don't
get to preach so often; so when I do I am very aware that, for many,
English is not their first language, and that they may be with us for
only one day. In that context, it is our hope to send them away with
memories of sublime and beautiful worship, and of hearing a sermon
that is both clear and memorable. While the acoustic environment of
St Paul's lends itself to glorious music, it is not an easy building to
speak in; so clarity and pace are important too.'*

Mr Giles is also a founder member and Treasurer of Christians on the Internet (COIN) and advises various Christian media groups of the newest technologies as they become more widely available. 'It is important, in all aspects of Christian life, that we become familiar with new developments, so that we can assess them and use them, particularly in communicating the gospel in different contexts. As the world changes, we must adapt, but not necessarily go with the flow. We must observe where the flow is taking us, but constantly remind ourselves where we have come from, so that our pilgrimage of faith is authentic and coherent.'

He adds: 'It is unlikely that any form of virtual reality or inter-active technology will replace the spoken sermon. Not only is it still a very effective means of direct communication, it is also rooted in personality and relationship. Both are gifts of God, and are valued by almost everybody. For as long as praise and preaching involves people and communities they will be effective and will survive.'

Texts: Exodus 34:29–end; 2 Corinthians 4:3–6

'Heavenly Father, grant us wisdom to know your Word, generosity to share it, and love to receive it, in Jesus Christ our Lord, Amen.'

Today, St Valentine's Day, is a feast day of chocolate. And chocolate is very important to a lot of people. How many of us would want to live without it? Chocolate, that wonderful substance that can be drunk or eaten, without any physically or mentally destructive side-effects, and of which we consume thousands of tons a year. Chocolate is a daily ingredient in the lives of people of all ages, and those who market our major festivals are well aware of it.

For while chocolate is commonplace, it is also special, and therefore makes annual appearances as Christmas decorations and Yule logs, as Easter eggs and bunnies, and of course, today, as chocolate hearts with gooey soft centres. Wherever there is a Christian festival, the all-pervasive and delicious chocolate appears, and steals the show. Indeed, today, St Valentine's Day, is not so much a celebration of love, as of chocolate, and St Valentine's real place, in our pre-millennial hagiography, is as the patron saint of chocolate.

But this 'stealing of the show' is not a new thing, for it has happened wherever the Church and other traditions have competed for influence. It happened eighteen centuries ago, when the original Valentine gave his name to this day.

In the third century, in pre-Christian Rome, the Emperor Claudius II had terrible difficulty getting soldiers to go away to fight, because the men did not want to leave their wives and families. So, ever mindful of the root of the problem, Claudius abolished marriage, and prevented anyone from becoming engaged. But marriage, then as now, was held in high esteem in Christian circles, and Valentine, who was a priest in what was then a persecuted Church, continued to encourage couples to marry, and married them himself. The Roman authorities were not impressed, of course, and Valentine was beaten to death with clubs, and decapitated. His martyrdom is believed to have been on this day, in the year AD 270.

Today – 14 February – was itself significant because, ironically for Valentine, it was the eve of a pagan fertility festival called Lupercalia. And Lupercalia at the end of the third century was not dissimilar in form to Valentine's Day at our end of the twentieth century. On the eve of the festival, a grand lottery would take place, with the names of young women being drawn out of a jar by the young men. This Roman equivalent of the 'blind date' would lead to a meeting of two young people on the next day, 15 February, and they would spend time together during the festival, and sometimes the pairing would lead to love and marriage. The early Roman Church tried to clean up Lupercalia when, in the year 496, Pope Gelasius nominated 14 February as the feast day of the martyr Valentine. It remained as such until as recently as 1969, when it was officially dropped from the ecclesiastical calendar. But by then it had successfully over-written the pagan festival it had been intended to displace.

Or had it? In our age, we have seen the trend begin to reverse, and many have rightly wanted to resist it. Last Christmas, the local council authorities in a Midlands city seriously suggested renaming the Christmas period as 'Winterval'. And only a few weeks ago, the ghost of Lupercalia rose up in a new, high-tech media-centric form. For perhaps you remember that a 23-year-old model and a 28-year-old sales manager won a competition organized by a radio station in Birmingham. And their prize was each other. Two people, who had never met, were brought together by a game show, and were married and packed off on honeymoon to the Bahamas, barely knowing each other's names. A fly-on-the-wall documentary team have gone with them, and a brand new apartment and sports car await their return. I understand that they have just got back, and are, at this time of preaching at any rate, still talking to each other.

The assumption, on the part of the organizers, is that two people who hardly know each other have about as much chance of staying together as any other married couple do, and they have called it a 'scientific experiment in love', to test their theory. But, pseudo-science aside, it is not unlike what the Romans were doing at Lupercalia, in those days before the Roman Empire embraced the teachings of

Christ. A gamble, a game and a give-away spouse is a pre-Christian idea, revisited.

But the to-ing and fro-ing doesn't end here. While Lupercalia was superseded by the feast of St Valentine, which was itself superseded by the choco-centric, secular Valentine's Day, now we find that the Church has re-entered the fray with National Marriage Week. National Marriage Week has just ended, and, as you might expect, it seeks to promote and reaffirm the values of Christian marriage. Values of enduring love, of mutual support, of commitment through thick and thin, sickness and health, poverty and wealth.

So what we have, through time, is a continuing dialogue between Christian values that the Church wants to promote; and the practices and festivities of a contemporary culture. And this kind of engagement has always been a crucial part of Christian thought and practice. The Church has always been married to the world it inhabits, and is constantly having to adapt within that relationship, yet while always trying to maintain an integrity with the gospel, and with its own spiritual traditions. It is a marriage that is not always easy; but to which the Church is utterly committed. Some of the issues the Church has encountered and confronted are front page items, such as homosexuality and the ordination of women. Other issues are less famous, because rather than arousing controversy, many are indifferent to them. One such issue may well be that of the return of society to pagan values or behaviour.

Are we returning, then, to paganism? The spirit of modern Valentine's Day, while it does on one hand promote the friendly gesture of affirmation to friends, also seems to promote love-behaviour that can be damaging and confidence-destroying. The sending and receiving of Valentines can be fun, but it can also make people feel very vulnerable. The cards get bawdier each year, and we are now encouraged to give gifts to our pets, as in fact 3 per cent of pet owners do. And what was once a festival intended to commemorate what lengths a man went to in love of his Lord Jesus Christ has become a festival dominated by a love of chocolate.

The original purpose of a feast day – to help us focus on the love of God for humanity shown in the life, passion and resurrection of our Lord Jesus Christ, for the love and truth of which others suffered – has been obscured by a coating of candy. And that chocolate covering gets thicker and thicker, such that the kernel of truth at the centre becomes more and more insignificant. The truth and the joy of God's message of love in Jesus Christ is veiled behind a sentimentalized product that speaks often of sweet seduction and unreal relationships.

The escapism manifested in some of our modernized festivals is doubly ironic, not only because they used to be Christian, but because before that they were pagan. It is not a conscious move, nor a hateful one. The loss of the meaningful centre, as it were, is due to nothing more or less than indifference. And it is indifference, not hatred, that is the opposite of love.

Valentine's Day has become what it has become because of an indifference to love, not out of respect for it. If love can be seen as something that lasts barely longer than a box of chocolates, then it is no surprise that we devote only one day a year to it. But it is just as well that we only devote one day a year to whatever this kind of love is. And Valentine is still invoked as its patron saint. But Valentine is not, nor ever has been, the patron saint of love. He has become the patron of the trivialization of love; and of a form of emotional indifference to the gospel. The patron, perhaps, of the chocolatization of Christianity.

But we do not need a patron saint of love, because we have a God of Love. A God of the kind of love that leads to the altar and the kind of love that is found *on* the altar. It is a committed, enduring love, which we're not actually all that good at. It's a tough love, not soft-centred, and endures all things. It is patient, kind and forbearing, and it delights in the truth. Such love though we may only grasp it partially, is perfected in Christ. And by God's spirit, it is still present among us, in our hearts, in our faith, and in our relationships. And that is something worth celebrating, not just today, but every day.

Comments

Peter Graves: '*Very resourceful approach to Valentine's Day. Challenge to move beyond the superficial.*'

William Beaver: '*A powerful sermon with an unusual observation (Valentine's Day celebrates our indifference to love). Clearly given and well-wrapped from start to finish.*'

Kieran Conry: '*An interesting introduction featuring chocolate leads gently into central theme, well and carefully developed, that of the marriage of religious and "secular" values. The original icon of chocolate is woven well into the mix again and a clear enough message is drawn from what has been said.*'

Keep On Believing

SERMON PREACHED BY CHRISTINE SCOTT AT
RIDGACRE METHODIST CHURCH ON
7 FEBRUARY 1999

*Christine Scott, 58, who works as a training consultant, is a
Methodist Local Preacher. She attends Stockland Green Methodist
Church in Birmingham, which is part of the Sutton Park Circuit of
the Birmingham District. She preaches in her own circuit once a
month and also in the Birmingham (West) Circuit about once a
month. She would like to preach more often.*

*After attending a preaching course just over a year ago at Cliff
College, the Methodist college in Derbyshire, Christine came home
and tore up all the sermons she had written in the last ten years that
she had been a Local Preacher. She started again, trying to place more
emphasis on the love of God. She hopes that this is apparent in her
sermon.*

*She believes that a good sermon should inform, should encourage
and should always move the congregation to action – even if it's only
to throw something at the preacher! A good sermon should touch the
soul, so that the congregation goes out saying 'I'm a different person
because of what I've heard today'.*

*She firmly believes that there is a place for preaching in the new
millennium. 'If there wasn't, why would God still be calling men and
women to preach? It is certainly true that preaching is undervalued;
but isn't this the fault of the preachers? Most of us certainly don't
inspire our hearers. It seems to me that most preachers find true
preaching too difficult and so have given it up. It is much easier
simply to entertain.'*

*She thinks perhaps preaching does need to change to survive. 'Or
perhaps we should go back to the sort of preaching we should have
been doing all along. I believe that true preachers are there to deliver
God's message – warts and all. I believe that true preachers do not
bring their own thoughts and ideas into a sermon, they deliver what
has been given to them. Perhaps, as preachers, we should listen more
to what God is saying to the world and its problems today, and this
alone will be enough to change our preaching – and change our
congregations.'*

The congregations in her church in Birmingham have changed considerably over the last ten years, she reports. 'Ten years ago the church, which seats around 250, was always three-quarters full. Now a good Sunday morning congregation might fill half of it. A once-flourishing Sunday School went down almost to nothing, but now, with a change of name and a change of emphasis, the numbers are rising again and the work among children and young people is going forward. Changes in the family structure mean that children will often come with grandfather and grandmother to service, leaving the mother or father at home. Sunday opening hours mean that there are other things to do on Sundays.'

Text: Mark 9:26b–27

The boy looked like a corpse and everyone said, 'He is dead!' But Jesus took the boy by the hand and helped him to rise, and he stood up.

Bible: Good News Bible

He had always wanted a big family. A house full of noisy boys. But he had been married for over ten years, when, at last, he received the news that his dearest longings would come true.

When they put the small, warm body of his son into his arms, he thought his heart would burst – with happiness!

His friends rejoiced with him. 'He'll grow up just like you', they said. 'Tall and strong.'

But somehow the child didn't grow. When other babies grew plump and stout, he remained weak and thin. And, despite everything they did, the child never said a word.

Every cold in the village found its way to him. Hardly a week went by when he wasn't sick. His mother fretted.

'What's wrong with him?' she said to his father. 'Why isn't he like other boys?'

He made light of it, for her sake, but, deep down, he was as worried as she was.

The child was five years old, when he had his first serious illness. He had seemed so much better that week that they had let him go out to play with the other boys. His father had been so happy.

But his happiness was shattered by shouts and screams. 'Come! Come!' said the boys breathlessly, as they pulled him out of the house.

They had been playing by the stream when the child had fallen and hit his head. Suddenly, he was writhing uncontrollably. When he reached him, the child was foaming at the mouth. His arms flailing wildly, he rolled over and over, and then he stiffened and lay still. The boys were terrified.

He just couldn't believe it. Surely, this must all be a dream?

Three weeks later, as his wife came running to fetch him, he knew that it had happened again.

This time, it wasn't a dream.

That night, his wife burst into tears. 'He's never going to get better', she sobbed, 'He's never going to be like other boys.'

As he put his arms round her he felt something burst into life inside him. 'Oh yes he is', he said, 'Somewhere, there is someone who can cure him. *I know there is.*'

Over the next few years, he spent a fortune on doctors. He and his son travelled all over the country. Each time they came back with some new diet, or some new medicine. But nothing did any good. The fits might cease for a time, but they always came back. And still the boy didn't speak.

He began to neglect his business. He was reluctant to take on the big, well-paid jobs. For he never knew when his son would be ill, or when he would hear of a new doctor.

His family and friends thought he was mad. 'Don't the words "Give up" mean anything to you?'

But how could he 'give up' when there was still a chance that the boy could be cured?

Sir Douglas Bader lost both his legs in a flying accident. But he didn't lose his spirit. When he was getting better he was fitted with artificial legs; and he did more on two artificial legs than most people do on two sound ones. He always had time to spare for other people who had lost limbs.

A 14-year-old boy had lost a leg in a car crash. Sir Douglas visited him, and gave him some advice: 'Don't listen to anyone who tells you that you can't do this or that. Have a go at everything. Go anywhere you want to. And never, never, let anyone persuade you that things are too difficult, or impossible.'

'Give up' had never occurred to the boy's father.

At first, it was his hope that kept him going. Then, as disappointment followed disappointment, he kept going on sheer will-power alone. He was convinced that somewhere there was someone who could cure his son.

But the temptation to give up was strong.

He was running out of time. He was running out of money. And – even more important – he was running out of doctors!

Then he heard about the man from Nazareth. The man called

Jesus. They said he was travelling the country, preaching and healing. They even said that lepers had been healed.

It was with very mixed emotions that, once more, he and his son took the road together.

He only had to follow the crowds to find Jesus' disciples. But Jesus himself wasn't there.

He'd gone off somewhere in the hills, they said.

'Do you think he could possibly cure my son?' One of the teachers of the Law heard his question. 'You don't need Jesus', he said. 'These are his disciples. Ask them to cure him.'

He had to admit that they tried. They tried everything. But nothing happened.

Seeing their efforts, the teacher laughed.

'The world's full of these quack doctors', he said. 'Obviously, this man Jesus is the same. It's all talk. He can't really cure anyone.'

Almost before the man knew what was happening, arguments broke out. People took sides, harsh words were exchanged. He found himself at the centre of noise and confusion.

Frightened, his son clung to him. He put his arms around the boy, and held him tight.

So it was to be just another disappointment, after all. They had travelled all this way, only to see another man who could do nothing. Oh! Why had he bothered to come at all?

A man went to stay with his friend in Cornwall. Near his home, there were a large number of disused mine-shafts. These were deep holes in the ground, many with no rails round them.

One day, he went for a walk and got lost. Darkness came and he realized that he was near the holes and it was dangerous to walk in the dark. But it was too cold to sit down and wait till morning; so he walked on.

Suddenly, his feet slipped, and he started to slide down into one of the mine-shafts. He managed to grasp a rock, and held on, terrified, his feet dangling.

He hung on for about twenty minutes, but his arms were in such agony that he knew he would soon plunge to his death. He was about to let go, when he saw a light and knew that help was coming. With all the energy he had left, he shouted 'Help! Help!'

When the rescuers arrived and shone their torches on him, the first thing they saw was that his feet were dangling within a foot of solid earth. The mine-shaft had been filled in! All his agony and fears had been for nothing.

Had all *his* agony and fears been for nothing?

Deep in his misery, it took the man several minutes to realize that the noise had stopped. He turned, to see the crowd running to greet a tall young man.

'What's happening?' Jesus asked his disciples. 'What are you all arguing about?'

Depressed and despondent, the man came forward.

'It's my fault, Teacher. I brought my son to you because he has an evil spirit in him and cannot talk. I asked your disciples to drive the spirit out, but they couldn't.'

Jesus looked round at them all. At the teachers of the Law, trying so hard to trap him. At the disciples, trying so hard to understand him. At the crowd, trying so hard to keep up with him.

'How unbelieving you people are! How long must I stay with you? How long do I have to put up with you? Bring the boy to me!'

Slowly, the crowd parted, and someone brought the boy forward. But, even as they brought him, he began to shake uncontrollably. He fell to the ground, and rolled around, foaming at the mouth.

Helpless, he looked down at his son, lying in all the dust and dirt of the open road. Just a spectacle for the crowds to gape at! He sank to his knees by the boy's side, and gently put his hands on the shaking body.

'Oh, son, my dear son', he said silently. 'I love you so much. You are my life. I only wanted to help you. I only wanted to make you well and strong. And all I've done is brought you to this.'

He looked up to find that Jesus was standing by his side. Jesus' face was filled with tenderness, and his eyes were filled with understanding. 'How long has he been like this?' he said gently.

Inexplicably, the man felt his eyes fill with tears. 'Ever since he was a child. Many times the evil spirit has tried to kill him by throwing him in the fire and into water.' He felt the tears begin to run down his cheeks. 'Have pity on us, and help us, if you possibly can!'

The calm eyes of Jesus looked deep into his own. 'I can – if you can', he said. 'Everything is possible for the person who has faith.'

The man thought back over the years of disappointment. The long years when only his faith had kept him going. 'I do have faith, but not enough. Help me to have more!'

Again Jesus' eyes looked into his own. Then, confidently, his voice rang out. 'Deaf and dumb spirit, I order you to come out of the boy and never go into him again!'

The boy began to shake – this time, harder and harder. He gave one scream and then was still. His body lay, pale and lifeless, like a corpse. Someone in the crowd whispered loudly 'He's dead!'

The boy's father heard nothing, for he had his eyes fixed on Jesus. He had always known that there was someone who could cure his son. Now he was certain. For, if anyone could do it, then it was this man.

Again, the eyes of Jesus met his. Suddenly, he felt the tears dry on his cheeks. Suddenly, he felt safe and secure and loved. He felt his worries fall away, as he rested in the peace of those calm brown eyes.

He had come home.

Gently, Jesus leant forward and took the boy by the hand. The long eyelashes flickered, and the boy looked up, into Jesus's face. Smiling, Jesus raised him to his feet.

It's not easy to keep on believing when everyone says that it can't be done – that it's never been done – and that you're only wasting your time. It's not easy to hold on to your faith.

There are times in our lives when we are faced with problems so overwhelming that we struggle to believe that even God can overcome them. We read our Bibles, we recite Scripture verses, we ask our friends to pray for us. We want to believe, but, deep down, there are still those niggling doubts.

I believe that Jesus still asks us the questions he asked the boy's father: How much faith do you have? How far will you go?

When President John F. Kennedy's grandfather was a boy in Ireland, on his way home from school, he often passed stone walls that were ten feet high. He always wanted to climb them, but he was afraid.

One day, he took his cap off and threw it over the wall. The moment he did, he knew he had to climb over and get it back, because he didn't dare go home without it. He had to climb over.

So often, we are afraid of the unknown. But only because it's the untried.

We need to put our faith in Jesus, ask him for strength, and then start climbing. God has a plan for your life, but to find it, you've got to throw your cap over the wall. For, as the boy's father found, without faith, nothing is possible. With it, you can conquer the world.

The only one who can stop you believing – is you!

Comments

Peter Graves: '*Good example of a narrative sermon – a good story-teller!*'

God and Suffering

SERMON PREACHED BY CLARE HERBERT AT
ST ANNE'S CHURCH, SOHO

The Reverend Clare Herbert was one of the first women to be ordained priest in the Church of England in 1994. She attended St Hild's College, Durham, New College, Edinburgh, and Lincoln Theological College before being made deacon in 1987. Before becoming Rector of St Anne's Church in Soho, she was project manager of Websters, a resource and spirituality centre for women in central London, honorary curate at St Paul's church, Clapham and senior curate at St Martin-in-the-Fields. She contributed to a book, Crossing the Boundary *(Mowbray, 1994), which examines the impact of the ordination of women priests.*

'*My path to St Anne's was tortuous because I was unable to become a priest when I first sensed that that was my vocation – 27 years ago, when I was 18! Nevertheless the experiences of child-care social work, university chaplaincy and being a lay adviser in pastoral care all play their part in making my present role fruitful for me. It is certainly the toughest assignment I have ever had!*'

Clare was one of the 30 preachers shortlisted in 1994, the first year of the competition. Of the sermon below, she says: 'It seemed to mean a great deal to the congregation of St Anne's. The reference to "this weekend" is important. The sermon was preached in the middle of Lent after a week in which tourists in Africa had been brutally murdered, in which members of two families, including children, had died in a house fire in the east of London, and in which it began to become clear that the movement of refugees fleeing massacre in Kosovo would end in NATO air-strikes. There is always plenty of suffering on the streets of Soho, and within the congregation, but this week it seemed as if we had been swept into the suffering of the whole world.'

She says Soho is changing all the time. 'While threats to the strength of the local community arose twenty years ago from "the vice" or schemes for new roads, today we are threatened by the commercialization of Soho, by the noise surrounding the late-night clubs and bars, and by the drugs trade. The challenge for any church lies not so much in trying to meet the needs on the streets – many organizations are attempting to do that – as in remaining confident in our own relevance when confronted by so colourful and strong a secular culture.'

The original church of St Anne, Soho, was bombed in 1940. Ten years ago a new church was built, small by design, and set within a community centre. It is shaped around two basic human needs: to find peace and quiet, and to belong – both challenges in an area where all is bustle and the pavements throng with visitors. 'In such a church preaching can sometimes feel strange – a little like standing up in someone's front room', says Clare. 'The space looks more suited to sitting in a circle, playing or discussing. While I think the formal sermon will survive as an art, a poem which at its best enlivens a congregation again in faith, perhaps smaller spaces in which people share rather than perform will become more relevant, as people seek to make theology together rather than hearing it from one source.'

Text: 2 Corinthians 12:8–9

About this thing, I have pleaded with the Lord three times for it to leave me; but He has said 'My grace is enough for you: my power is at its best in weakness.'

I n the name of God, our Creator, our Redeemer and our Sustainer, Amen.

A friend of mine, enjoying her belonging to a church for the first time, said to me, 'Do you realize why we all get on so well, what makes us pull together?' And I said 'No?' expecting some profound answer about vision, or shared radicalism or life in Christ. 'It's because we're all nuts in some way', she said, '– crackers, barmy, all of us – you look round on a Sunday morning and you will see what I mean. We're all of us one-offs, but we don't feel so odd together.'

Behind the joke of someone who had at last come home there lay a deep understanding. Another way of putting it is to say that as Christians it is clear that our weaknesses are not taken from us.

'About this thing, I have pleaded with the Lord three times for it to leave me.' We, many of us, have our private sufferings:

- bereavements
- illnesses of body and mind knowing no easy cure
- lack of confidence
- or simply those haunting regrets that life has not turned out for us exactly as we would have wished.

And we share in common, this weekend, our flinching at the sufferings of society – a sensitivity heightened for us by our faith in

God's love and hope for this world.

How is our suffering linked with that of Christ? How may it be redemptive – that is, saving and healing?

I don't pretend to be able to unravel the problem of why there is suffering in the world at all. Anything I said would sound trite, measured at the level of pure reason – I have only some glimpses.

My first glimpse into suffering is that it has to be met at a level past reasoning, the level of love. The Eucharist moves us so profoundly by meeting us on that level: we are given bread and wine, the broken body and blood of our Lord, in whom we see our own brokenness and that of our world, and we no longer reason – we may only accept and yearn to love more completely each time we take it.

My second glimpse into suffering is that it is rendered yet more terrible by the loneliness which goes along with it. Those who suffer feel that real life is going on elsewhere and that they have no part in it.

'What's the point of going on living with this illness of mine, I've not done half the things I hoped to in life?'

'Why should I be sitting here alone this evening?'

'I've lost the one I love, so my reason for existence is gone.'

This sense of loneliness is understandable, and we often have to face it before we take the next step, which is realizing that in our suffering we may actually be entering, not losing, the full stream of life, that no part of our experience need be lost or purposeless. Certainly if our picture of true living is all of fun, social acceptance and success, then suffering will cut us off from some of that. But it cuts us off only to join us up with the true picture of what humanity is like, real humanity, not colour supplement living. From our experience of pain springs the chance to actually be a part of the human race, not let it pass by as if we never were.

My third glimpse is that those who suffer may feel they are forsaken by God. But anyone who cries out to God in her pain echoes the cry of the dying Christ. There, God is not just a hidden someone, to whom she cries, but in a profound sense the human God who cries with us where we are dumb.

Where is God? Where the hell is God watching all the suffering of this world?

And an answer comes deep within us: he is in the middle of that hell.

When we suffer we do not stand apart from the life of the world nor the stream of God – we enter them more fully and contribute to them.

How? How is it that those who feel so useless and so lonely may contribute to the life of the world and to the love of God? How are they able to heal, to save us?

They are able to heal when they have, to some extent at least, entered the depths of their own pain and found there hope again; when they have grasped the uselessness of basing our security on material possessions, on popularity or success, even on the closest of personal relationships. When all these have been mysteriously shattered by suffering, they have learned a little what it is to be the Son of man with nowhere to lay his head, the wounded Christ whose words were visible even in his resurrection, and from that position they are able to help us by their steadfast refusal to join in the game of avoiding our own suffering.

Many of us suffer because of the false suppositions on which we have based our lives – that there would be little fear or loneliness, little confusion or doubt. But these are wounds integral to our human condition, and the one who suffers confronts us with this. He or she does not allow us to live with illusions of wholeness or immortality. He keeps reminding us that we are broken and mortal, and that our healing cannot begin until we recognize our condition. The one who suffers offers us no palliative solutions, no easy answers, but performs the service of watching and waiting with us, allowing us to voice our deepest fears and anguish.

We may see in the one who knows pain that same mixture of suffering and strength, that same flame of love in the surrounding darkness, that we perceive in Christ on the cross.

But often the Christian Churches foster false suppositions: by putting on an appearance of power and success they deny, with their show of comfort and self-confidence, the bloody and despised body of their Lord. Where there is the pretence of invulnerability and the denial of the raw and painful realities of life the Churches are drained of compassion and can tolerate only those who conceal their wounds.

I want to end by reading you a poem by R. S. Thomas called 'The Musician', because it shows God bound up in human life and not only in its sunnier moments.

> A memory of Kreisler once:
> At some recital in this same city,
> The seats all taken, I found myself pushed
> On to the stage with a few others,
> So near that I could see the toil
> Of his face muscles, a pulse like a moth
> Fluttering under the fine skin,
> And the indelible veins of his smooth brow.

I could see, too, the twitching of the fingers,
Caught temporarily in art's neurosis,
As we sat there or warmly applauded
This player who so beautifully suffered
For each of us upon his instrument.

So it must have been on Calvary
In the fiercer light of the thorns' halo:
The men standing by and that one figure,
The hands bleeding, the mind bruised but calm,
Making such music as lives still.
And no one daring to interrupt
Because it was himself that he played
And closer than all of them the God listened.
                    (R. S. Thomas, 'The Musician' from *Tares* (1961))

Making such music as lives still – in all of us – if we can only bear
to listen.

Comments

Jonathan Romain: '*There were parts of the sermon in which I felt myself physically nodding in agreement, "Yes, she's got that right". Always a good sign.*'

William Beaver: '*A bold, reassuring sermon, valuable for seeing where God is in the pain and suffering. Critical and thought-provoking.*'

Peter Graves: '*Very sensitive and helpful meditation on suffering.*'

The Baptism of Christ

SERMON BY CANON BARBARA BAISLEY PREACHED AT
ST JOHN BAPTIST, BERKSWELL, ON 10 JANUARY, THE
FIRST SUNDAY OF EPIPHANY

Barbara Baisley, 52, always intended to become a teacher. She studied painting at Chelsea School of Art in the 1960s, thinking she would go on to teacher training college, but was waylaid by marriage, parenthood and later, God.

During her theological training for the Church of England ministry, Barbara was initially terrified at the thought of preaching. However, she quickly discovered that not only was she excited and energized, but she recognized the same impulse that had pushed her towards teaching and painting: 'The wish to make you see what I see, to show you what I've found.'

At its best, Barbara believes that preaching offers the opportunity for this very personal communication to take place, creating a space where ideas can ignite. 'The formal address offers one way for this encounter, but increasingly we do not need to be limited solely to a set piece delivered from a pulpit. The growing variety of styles of worship, alongside the traditional, allow for informal chats, "spots" illustrating a theme, and short "links" between periods of meditation or music, which can all do the work of a sermon. Of course this is a complex form of communication and may take more time, work and planning to organize. But some will find it easier to hear and respond to than a formal sermon. We have to take that seriously, and continue to preach traditionally as well. It's about being flexible, and using whatever works, whatever helps to create space for God.'

Much is being said and written about exploring new ways of doing and being church. Barbara feels there is some danger of the Church losing its nerve in this new situation, instead of making the most of new opportunities. In the parish where Barbara serves it is noticeable that 'belonging' no longer means being in church every Sunday. People come when they can, juggling work and family commitments, perhaps attending a mid-week or informal act of worship, or a house group. Barbara wants to affirm this looser membership as a way of helping people to recognize that Christianity is indeed a seven-day affair. A second change she has observed in her own church has been a growing hunger for Bible teaching, coupled with a growing confidence in discussing the Christian faith. This has clearly emerged from the Alpha courses that have taken place. Few if any newcomers have joined the church, but a good number of existing members have found their faith revitalized.

Since returning to the Church as a young mother some 25 years ago, Barbara has trained for ministry and become variously a deaconess, university chaplain, Diocesan Adviser for Women's Ministry, one of the first women to be ordained priest in the Church of England in 1994, and Head of Vocations and Training in Coventry Diocese. By 1997 she had also lived for ten years with breast cancer which had appeared in her skeleton, and she retired from full-time ministry at the age of 50. Barbara is still involved in some vocational work, leads retreats and has written a book about her experience of facing the questions that cancer brought her. She is still trying to find a publisher for her book, which was one of the motives behind her decision to enter the Preacher of the Year award.

'I have had cancer for thirteen years', she says. 'It has raised so many questions for me. Questions like: "What the hell are you playing at God? I thought you were on my side! What am I supposed to DO with all this?" Cancer rocked my faith completely. I wondered if it was my fault, and thought I should be able to cope, because I am a Christian. I wondered if the cancer recurred because I didn't have enough faith, or because I wasn't positive enough.'

She still receives treatment for the cancer. 'I have regular chemotherapy to stop my bones going soggy. I had a partial mastectomy initially, and I now have a piece of metal in my back because it was falling to pieces. But I am really quite well. I never understood that cancer can be an ongoing illness.'

She has found that one of the hardest things to deal with has been the attitude of others. 'There are those who glibly suggest that my faith will see me through, or that if it were adequate I would be completely healed. Remarks like that hurt. It is hard enough dealing with the disease, without having to defend oneself for being ill in the first place! I think it is people's own fears that make them talk such rubbish. It is not just Christians, of course. One person told me to drink green tea, another that having cancer meant part of my life was "out of control!" Probably, but I don't think that is why I have cancer.'

She now writes and speaks about suffering. 'One doctor, recently told me that my cancer was not aggressive – "That's good news", I said. She then went on to say that it will probably become aggressive in time! While it remains in the bones it is not life-threatening. If it moves into the liver, brains or lungs, that's a different story.'

She is currently licensed as non-stipendiary minister in the parish where her husband George is Rector, on the outskirts of Coventry.

She feels it is important to remember that ultimately the world, including the Church, is God's responsibility. 'It is even possible he can accomplish the redemption of the universe without our hindrance or our help. All that is required is that we do what we can with love. Preaching offers the chance to stir others with the same longings and hopes that fire us. It allows us the privilege of opening a door.'

Texts: Isaiah 42:1–9; Acts 10:34–43; Matthew 3:13–17

I don't know how you passed your geography lessons. But never having been further than St David's, I had little interest in the wheat belts of North America or 'SHEEP' written across the map of Australia. So I was mostly off on horseback, delivering a vital message to King Richard, disguised as a stable boy; or heroically saving the class from an outbreak of fire; or – later on – bringing up amazingly beautiful and talented children, two boys and two girls, who never answered back.

As I grew up, nothing changed. I had a strong idea of myself as 'doing good', saving the world. Many and varied are the motives for offering for ordination! I was intent on becoming the best possible university chaplain, and 'Women's Adviser', all by my own enthusiasm, drive and hard work. I loved it – and I needed it. I was desperate to earn approval, to be loved, by God and by other people.

It was a shock to discover that this is not always God's way of accomplishing things. When I studied theology I found that there is a shadow side to God's activity. That Christ is presented as passive as well as active. He began his ministry at his baptism, an event that happened *to* him. You cannot baptize yourself. Three years later, the salvation of humanity is accomplished on the cross, a supremely passive moment. Jesus was betrayed and taken into custody, tried and condemned, and his hands and feet were pinioned. It is in his loss of control and self-determination that Christ alters the direction of the universe. In his helplessness and dereliction, his glory is made known to the world.

I have found, too, reading the mystics, those great genius figures of prayer, that they speak of entering the darkness of *un*knowing. Not 'doing' or striving, not actively praying and interceding, but instead allowing God to mould and to shape. Learning to be passive under his gaze. It seems that this passive way, trusting God to be at work in us rather then feeling we must do it all ourselves, is the way we have to go in order to enter the depths of prayer. It is this that does most to move us on, to change and free us.

So where does that leave the frantically busy? Is it all a waste of time and effort? Are we doing it wrong, after all? Relax, it's all right, we need the activity too. If Christ had done nothing in his life, his death would mean nothing to us. We are given life and energy to use, to build, create, serve and enjoy. In Matthew's account of the baptism, John has been calling for repentance – for changed lives. 'Bear fruit worthy of repentance', he challenges. We are made to be active, to achieve and love and strive.

But here in today's gospel is a nudge to take note of the other side of the story. A reminder that we are not to look for our value in our actions and achievements. That was my mistake, and it is a common one. We work desperately to gain approval, only to discover that it is an endless and hopeless cycle. But the gospel tells us that contrary to all we expect, our value is not in what we do, but in the fact that we are created beings.

First of all we are objects, made by God. He is the subject of our life, we are the object. Our value is that we are beloved. 'My own, my beloved' says God of Christ at his baptism. But the words are for us too, we are, after all, the body of Christ. We hear it week by week at the Confession: 'God so loved the *world*, that he gave – he loves each of us, Jane and David, Stan, Gill, you and me. We are loved. Our value is that we are redeemed. Jesus goes down into the waters of baptism, and we have the first glimpse of his going down into the depths of hell to save us, to reach us and to bring us home. And we are in the process of 'being saved', by definition a passive role. Think of life-saving, or a cat up a tree. It helps if the victim, or moggy, will only do *nothing*!

It is the shadow side of all our activity and New Year's resolutions, our frantic efforts and good works. The picture of Jesus' baptism, coming at this time of year, reminds us that sometimes the most important thing is to do nothing. Just to be. To be 'baptized' with his presence. In other words, to be filled and swamped with God. It is then, when we are loved and comforted, touched by God, reminded of him dwelling always within us, that we want to offer all we have and are. It is when we are 'baptized' with his love that we respond with the love of our own hearts, and the service of our lives. And we might even manage the really heroic things like letting go of ancient resentments, or the grudge, the self-righteousness.

It is this passive side, the receiving, the being loved, that spurs our actions. It is at the heart of our struggle to live as Christians. It is the impulse, the initiative for it all. The idea that there is something to be gained by being passive can even change our perspective in the hard times.

So when you are stuck, frustrated with life, and there is nothing you can do to change the situation, remember Christ's passivity. When you have the flu, or have been passed over for promotion. If you are threatened with redundancy, or ill, or getting on in years and feeling it. If you are facing a crisis in self-confidence, or the house won't sell, or your partner won't budge. Maybe, contrary to all your mind tells you, you are at your most useful to God. Maybe something is being accomplished, far beyond our imaginings. Perhaps God is at work.

If we can let God use these experiences *in* us, not give way to bitterness or recrimination, but be available for God to work – see them as opportunities to learn to trust, if we can be open to him, and let him do things in our inactivity, it may be the most precious service we ever accomplish. We won't know it, or feel it necessarily, but he was baptized, he was crucified. These things were done to him, and save us. We can offer our failure, frustration and pain, as well as our efforts, and believe he will show his glory through them.

This is the season of Epiphany, the 'showing forth'. Christ's glory shines out to the world, and we see it in God's affirmation, as Jesus takes his place in the queue of sinners at the Jordan. When he puts himself on equal terms with us, the voice comes: 'My beloved, with whom I am pleased.'

We see his glory shining out of the New Testament story, the first non-Jewish converts at Cornelius' house: 'I truly understand', says Peter, 'God shows no partiality.' And the gospel message leaps across the gulf into the Gentile world.

We see God's glory in the Old Testament lesson. The promise that God will establish justice, will heal the world – through his servant, the one coming dripping up out of the water. And we are part of the fulfilment of that prophecy, if we can believe it.

If we can know we are beloved, both in our hectic activity, and our waiting for God to reveal himself, he will be at work in us and through us. Our achieving and our enduring are Christ's, and are in Christ. We are one with him and he is one with us and we offer our weakness as well as our strength as part of God's answer for the world.

Through it all, if we will see it, God is at work. Through us, Christ's glory is shown forth to the world.

Amen.

Comments

William Beaver: '*One hit after another of common sense, reassuringly applied, reinforcing and strong.*'

Jonathan Romain: 'A good opening that gets us on the preacher's side and then allows her to take us where she wants. A sermon should be a journey, and this certainly is. She has a warm style – not talking to the congregation, but with them.'

The Darkness Shall Not Overcome

SERMON PREACHED BY DAVID HATTON AT THE UNITED
REFORMED CHURCH, CLARE, SUFFOLK, ON
27 FEBRUARY 1999

*David Hatton describes himself as 'an exceptionally young 80-year-
old who has forgotten what it was like to go out to work'. He and his
wife Joan live at Clare, Suffolk: a lovely little town going back to pre-
Saxon days and proud of its Iron Age earthworks, Norman castle
remains, and priory with lovely ruins and continuing buildings, home
of the first Augustinian friars in the British Isles and of their
successors today. He was privileged recently to be invited to write and
present a pageant to mark their 750th anniversary. The couple's
garden is adjacent to cornfields where swallows and other birds
swoop, he says. 'A glorious country park with river and much natural
life just five minutes walk away completes our paradise. It is a town
and scene which inspires one to write poetry and books about it!'*

*The Hattons have a daughter and two grandsons whom they
describe as 'superb in every way. We must say that, because they are
both karate champions!' They also had a son, but sadly he died aged
46 in 1998 after working for 25 years amongst children who were
both physically and mentally handicapped. He also produced a
unique style of art work depicting the twentieth-century in a striking
way, which so far the world has only had a chance to see at a
posthumous exhibition at Wakefield Art Gallery.*

*Mr Hatton trained as a Methodist minister at Richmond College,
London, and spent nearly half his working life in that work, including
a spell with the late Donald Soper as organizing secretary of Order of
Christian Witness campaigns. In 1962 he became a secondary school
RE teacher, where a chance contact with a BBC producer led to his
becoming involved together with his pupils in a number of schools
broadcasts. This could have led to a career in broadcasting, but he
decided to stay in teaching. Various experiences made him dissatisfied
with much of contemporary RE, so he applied for a post in teacher
training, and finished his working years as Senior Lecturer in Religious
Studies at West Sussex Institute of Higher Education. 'I have always
believed that religious studies in state schools should not attempt
conversion but fulfil the essential educational function of helping*

students to grasp what religion is about – through their feelings by taking them to share worship with diverse groups, and through their minds by considering religion intellectually', he says. *'In explaining religion I believe thoughtful questioning ranks high, and this belief found expression when the Methodist Publishing House issued a series of booklets I wrote under the title* The Questioning Christian.

'*As a teacher I felt it better for the end result of my teaching to be a thoughtful atheist than a thoughtless Christian (though if a thoughtful Christian happened to emerge, that would be best!) I cherish the words of a mature college student who said "I remain an atheist but your lectures have made me realize the Bible is a book worth studying".'*

So – *what of preaching in the new millennium?* 'There will always be a need for it, whether in church or other appropriate public place, as long as there are any who have not grasped the message or reached full understanding of it and its relevance to an ever-changing world – which takes us on for a few years yet! But I believe it must be preaching which does not disregard the mind: after all, in giving the Two Great Commandments, Jesus said that his followers should serve God with their minds, thus making an addition to the original words as given in Deuteronomy 6:5.

'And as regards worship, I believe very firmly that the essential element every time should be a sense of "the magic of Holiness" which can be really felt by whoever is present. There is room for humour, and expression of joy, but these must never be at the cost of the congregation feeling God's presence. Religious entertainment or mere time-filling are no substitute. For some places this will mean just continuing as at present into the new millennium, but perhaps for others there can be pause for thought.

'The church I currently attend is small, and seems variously to flourish or look thin as young families move in and out, but I reckon that it, together with the other three churches here, has grown in liveliness and relevance over the past few years, and certainly gives wonderful support in efforts to help the world's many victims of all kinds. I am told that the computer age requires visual presentations and the shortest of sermons, but still believe that the carefully prepared sermon which says something which meets people's needs cannot be beaten!

'The following sermon was composed after a year which had started with the death of my son at the age of 46, and which ended with the discovery that my wife had cancer. I wanted to explore the theme both for myself and also because I knew there were others who face parallel problems.'

Text: Isaiah 45:7

> I create both light and darkness, I bring both blessing and disaster.
> I, the Lord, do all these things.

Bible: Good News Bible

'**I** create the darkness and bring disaster!' – surely these words in Isaiah are among the hardest passages in the Bible to understand.

Elsewhere Isaiah says (60:2) 'Darkness shall cover the earth, and gross darkness the peoples'. This century has seen plenty of darkness covering the earth: the unmitigated horror of trench warfare between 1914 and 1918; the Holocaust visited upon the Jews and others; the millions murdered by Stalin, and more recent 'ethnic cleansings'; many nations still under oppression; vast regions of hunger and disease. Widespread clouds throwing darkness over millions.

Even within favoured areas there are smaller clouds which are no less dark for the individuals under them: ordinary people taken hostage or children abducted, and those who await news of them; old people attacked in the street or at home; people suddenly hit by some disease which is not easily treated; and the grim possibility of AIDS which faces children born HIV-positive today.

I am not thinking of people who *choose* to place themselves in a hazardous situation, but of ordinary people going about ordinary life, the situation in which they have been placed.

Perhaps the time my own eyes were first really opened to such darkness in people's everyday life was when I went as a young untrained minister to a Welsh mining valley more than 50 years ago: a church organist facing a lingering death by silicosis, a girl dying from tuberculosis, a family hit by a pit accident. Details change over the years; those hazards have faded, but other kinds of darkness come. Even Mary, so willing to become the mother of Jesus, found things 'went dark' for her. When she took the baby Jesus to the Temple, the aged Simeon told her 'A sword will pierce through your own soul'. It did. Thirty years later she stood at the foot of a cross, watching her son die. As someone said of Francis Gay's lovely *Friendship Books*, 'The daily readings always have a nice ending – but life ain't like that'.

The psalmist declared (Psalm 37:25): 'I have been young and now have grown old; but never have I seen the righteous forsaken', to which Edmund Blunden, the poet, responded:

> I have been young, and now am not too old;
> And I have seen the righteous forsaken,

His health, his honour and his quality taken.
This is not what we were formerly told.

I have seen a green country, useful to the race,
Knocked silly with guns and mines, its villages
 vanished,
Even the last rat and the last kestrel banished –
God bless us all, this was a peculiar grace.

(Edmund Blunden, first two verses of 'Report
on Experience' from *Poems 1914–1930*,
Carcanet Press Ltd.)

Jeremiah came to curse the day he was born. Job's name is synonymous with suffering. Isaiah felt compelled to say 'You have rolled up my life like a weaver when he cuts his work from the loom'. Even Jesus came to the point where he said 'My God, why hast Thou forsaken me?'

Darkness can become a reality for any one of us without bringing it upon ourselves – not only through great world-scale events, but also at any moment in common everyday life.

My first encounter with the darkness of death in that Welsh valley came within a few days of my arrival: a miner finally conquered by dust in his lungs. He had a deep faith, and, with his family around, I asked him 'Have you anything to say to us?' His reply was 'Have *you* anything to say to *me*?' I had no answer, and people the world over have often searched for a suitable explanation for the darkness which can hit ordinary people undeservedly.

Ancient Chinese philosophy used the idea of *yin* and *yang* – *yin* associated with darkness, *yang* with light – pictured by a diagram in which black and white halves are joined by an S-line so they flow continuously into each other. We may see this as the universal pattern of life: darkness and light inseparably bound together. Day and night flow into each other, neither conquering the other. The desert – for the hermit a place for contemplation, so of light; for the traveller, a pace of hardship and disaster. The continuous flowing of light and darkness into each other is an underlying fact of existence, working out in every facet of life. We can never escape the darkness – it will return, inexorably.

So, one answer to the problem of darkness is that we can't have light without it. But this is not true: there are many people who have darkness with no relief, and there are others who have sunshine all the way. I know somebody who even feels guilty because nothing ever goes wrong for her!

A second explanation for the claim that 'God sends darkness' lies in a prayer of St Augustine which I recently saw on a sheet from our local Augustinian Priory: 'May God in his mercy grant that we are shaken every day, tempted, tested, in order that we may make progress.' St Augustine was echoing a thought in Hebrews (chapter 12) and Paul' s epistles – we are disciplined for our own welfare, the shaking is to strengthen us. A diamond needs polishing to make it perfect. So we should ask for troubles because they can make us better people.

No doubt encountering trouble *does* sometimes make people stronger. A recruit in the army may be put in a tough spot to make him more fit for combat, a father may want to help a son stand on his own feet. But can we really put the kind of darkness I am describing into this category? The masses who live under oppression, the millions who never have a square meal, the children born with some terrible affliction – can we say that such darkness is the action of a loving God, intended to strengthen the people concerned? As Victor Meldrew would say, 'I don't believe it!' I don't pretend to know all of God's will; perhaps I lack faith. But I still want to know 'Why should this person or group be put to such testing, while that one escapes it?' I'm happier with the prayer taught us by Jesus, 'Lead us not into temptation', which is more accurately translated as a plea, 'Don't bring us to the testing point!'

So, why does 'Isaiah' have God saying 'I create both light and darkness, I bring both blessing and disaster'?

The passage occurs in what is often described as the Second Isaiah, which is set in Persia, the modern Iran. The religion there, Zoroastrianism, held that there are two powers behind the universe, one good and one evil, and that these are in conflict. The prophet wants to fight that dualism, so asserts as emphatically as he can that there is only one God, and He is supreme. He expresses this by going on 'I am the Lord, and there is none other: apart from me there is no god. There is none besides me.' Our God is the only God, and holds all power in his hands, therefore He *is* ultimately responsible for everything, and 'Isaiah', determined to demolish any thought that another power exists, has God going on to declare starkly 'I create darkness and disaster'. As a Hebrew, he wouldn't be concerned with the problems this would raise for those with philosophical minds, but we are.

Zoroastrians appear in the Bible again, centuries later, this time in Israel, for the 'Wise Men' in Matthew's nativity story were magi, Zoroastrian priests. These believers in supreme powers of both darkness and light have chosen to follow the light of a star. The Isaiah who said 'Thick darkness shall cover the earth' went on to speak of 'a light to which nations would come from afar'. The opening passage of St John's Gospel, one of the greatest passages in the Bible, includes the words 'The light shines in the darkness, and the darkness cannot overcome it' . Thick darkness covers the earth, but it is defeated by that Light which ultimately appeared in a manger.

Return for a moment to the *yin* and *yang* symbol, half light and half dark. I didn't mention previously that each half has a dot of the other within it – there is a dot of light in the dark half. Throughout history there have been 'dots of light' in the midst of 'gross darkness'. The Light of God is not overcome by darkness.

Sometimes that light has shone forth where gross darkness had been. The French composer Messiaen's deep Christian faith finds expression in his music. He was a prisoner during the last war. On one occasion he was to be allowed to give a concert. The German camp commandant provided him with a clapped-out piano, a cello with only three strings, and a couple of other scratch instruments. There, in the prison, Messiaen wrote a new composition, *Quartet for the End of Time,* based on words in Revelation: 'I saw an angel coming down out of heaven, and his face was as the sun … And he swore by Him who created the heavens and the earth and the sea, that there shall be time no longer.' The final movement of this piece expresses, through the composer's strange but haunting music, the resurrected Christ and his ultimate victory over time. Despite the awful circumstances and bitter cold, the music is said to have enthralled his 5,000 fellow prisoners. Light appearing in the darkness of a prisoner-of-war camp.

Light can appear in the most gross darkness. Jesus, dying on the cross, was offered a drink via a sponge on a stick. Always, God's light shines in the darkness – through the quiet word or kindly act of a sympathizer, the hand stretched to reach someone who is stumbling, a worthy contribution to a life-giving charity – and through actions such as those of a person I know in sheltered accommodation who 'accidentally' cooks too much dinner for herself and pops the extra along the corridor for some other 'old lady'.

I still remember a scene from 65 years ago at a Scout camp. We were on a night manoeuvre. It was pitch black, yet within the field was a host of tiny lights – glow-worms. There are many such lights within a world which sometimes seems very dark.

And on an international scale, ultimately darkness does not overcome the light. Augustine writing of the enduring City of God while the Roman world was in turmoil: the discovery, when a chink came in the Bamboo Curtain, of little groups of Christians who had held their faith through dark decades in China. Sometimes widespread darkness is scattered suddenly – remember how the Spanish dictatorship collapsed like a bubble directly Franco died, how suddenly the Iron Curtain across Europe ultimately fell and millions found freedom to live as they chose – whether they choose wisely or not.

It is a fact that darkness, to a greater or lesser degree, can come over any of us at any time. Various religions and philosophies have tried to account for it, but I don't believe it is explained by *yin* and *yang*'s darkness and light flowing into each other eternally, nor by Zoroastrianism's struggle between two great powers. But neither can I see the kind of afflictions of which I have spoken being deliberately sent by God to test or build up those 'chosen' to receive them.

I can't offer any better answer – but believe it is just part of the in-built structure of life in this kind of world. Today I still couldn't give a *rational* explanation to that dying miner – but I *do* believe that such darkness is not the whole story. The 'Second Isaiah' said (65:20) 'I am creating a new heaven and earth ... No child there will ever die in infancy, no old man fail to live out his span of life.' How, when, where this could ever apply, I can't guess, but it says something, even if we can only see it as a poetic image offering some kind of hope. The fourth-century bishop Ambrose said: 'Here the sun is succeeded by the darkness of night, but there is a Light which knows no setting.' No glib 'Don't worry, it may never happen' – which deserves the reply it frequently gets: 'It *has* happened!' – but an assertion of an ultimate faith, whether in or beyond this world, which is perhaps what Mother Julian of Norwich meant when she repeatedly said, through her *Revelations of Divine Love*, 'All shall be well and all manner of things shall be well'.

Meanwhile, we are not left without light. A family was being shown around Chartwell, Winston Churchill's house. In the study the guide said 'and this room is just as Sir Winston left it all those years ago'. A child's voice piped up 'He left the light on'. God has left his light on in this world, in a myriad places, no matter how dark the night may seem.

And the darkness can never overcome it.

Comments

Jonathan Romain: '*What is distinctive about this sermon is that the preacher is prepared to say "I don't know" and share his doubts and puzzlement. We respect his honesty and willingly join his search for answers. Even if some of us come to a different conclusion, we have been forced to think about the issue and to confront the question marks he raises. That is one of the prime tasks of any sermon.*'

Peter Graves: '*Thoughtful, wrestling with dark experiences of life.*'

Margaret Brearley: '*A rich, multi-faceted exploration of darkness and light, with an unusually wide range of cultural reference (Blunden, St Augustine, Messiaen, St Ambrose).*'

Coping with Stress

TALK GIVEN BY CAROLINE LAWRENCE AT ST PAUL'S
ANGLICAN FELLOWSHIP, ONSLOW SQUARE, LONDON
SW7, ON 14 FEBRUARY 1999

Caroline Lawrence, 45, a Californian who first came to England over twenty years ago to read classics at Cambridge, became a Christian during the pudding course of a dinner party. 'I was doing my usual, asking one of the other couples at the dinner table what star signs they were, when they said "We don't believe in that, we are committed Christians" The man was a doctor and he told me of some experiences of healings he had seen which he couldn't explain. Our hostess was at this time holding the trifle in mid-air, while the doctor wrote down a prayer for me. I knelt down and said it that night, and I felt different when I stood up. I haven't looked back since then.'

She began attending St Paul's, Onslow Square, a church plant of Holy Trinity, Brompton, the Knightsbridge church which was the originator of the Alpha course. Her conversion awakened an interest in her Jewish ancestry and she later studied Semitic languages in London, writing her MA thesis on a tenth-century Syriac manuscript of the book of Esther. Today she lives in Battersea, where she teaches art, Latin and French at a Christian primary school.

Having attended St Paul's for more than ten years, Caroline was recently invited to give a talk on the Jewish roots of Christianity. Since then she has been asked to speak several times as a lay preacher. She has subsequently taught courses in Hebrew and the Old Testament at St Paul's and also helps run a Lone Parenting Course at Holy Trinity, Brompton.

A single mother for several years, Caroline now lives with her 18-year-old son, Simon, and her second husband, Richard, a graphic designer. Her other interests include psychology, writing, memory techniques, and the cinema.

Commenting on the view in some circles that the turn of the millennium marks the end of this era, she says: 'End of the Age? People in every century have thought they were living in the "end times". The Syriac-speaking Christians of the seventh-century, for example, suffered devastating floods, earthquakes, fires and finally the Arab invasions. They were convinced they were experiencing the end of the world. And for most of them, it was. When you think about it, we are all living in the last days, because when we die – as far as we are concerned – this world comes to an end. Still, any specific sense that time is running out causes us to search for the things that really matter. I believe the Holy Spirit is often behind that sense of urgency. It is at such moments of transition – like the onset of the new millennium – that preaching can have the greatest impact.'

Caroline, a film lover, is inspired by the cinematic aspects of the Old Testament and the parables of Jesus. *'Jesus spoke so that we can easily visualize the scenes he described. Instead of using abstract verbal concepts, he used vivid images, symbols, and stories. I believe that is one of the best ways to reach people in the next year, decade, century, millennium: we need to appeal to all their senses, especially the visual, just as Jesus did. I'd also love to see worship and even the space in which we worship appeal more to all five senses'*, she adds. *'Of course, none of that means a thing unless we have the Word and the Spirit. True worship and teaching will survive with or without our efforts; if he wanted to, God could make the stones preach. But I believe he takes pleasure when we get enthusiastic about making the gospel exciting and accessible.'*

The congregation at St Paul's, in common with most HTB plants, has been growing over the past years. *'Many young, single professionals have become believers as a result of the Alpha courses that we and other churches hold. It is strange to be one of the oldest members of the congregation at 45.'*

She loves living in London. *'It's an international cultural centre and home to many people involved in the media and the arts. In our congregation these past few years there has been a growing interest in using the creative arts as a vehicle to express the gospel; not just traditionally "churchy" arts like music, drama and painting, but dance, film, creative writing and multi-media. Our pastor, John Peters, believes that each one of us in the church has gifts to contribute. I'm just a school teacher and would never have thought of myself as a preacher, but John has been brave enough to let ordinary people like me make our first fumbling attempts at discovering what gifts we might have.'*

Text: Luke 10:38–42
Bible: New International Version

Today's reading is the well-known story of Jesus at the home of Martha and Mary. As I read this passage, in preparation for this talk on 'Coping with stress', I had an exciting revelation about the way we have been created and how that can help us reduce stress in our lives.

There was a fascinating article in *The Sunday Times* (9 November 1997). It was about an American company called Heart Math that went into high-powered firms and businesses to help the executives lower their blood pressure and stress levels. At one company in Florida, for example, 25 per cent of the workers had high blood pressure. Six months later, after using the Heart Math technique and nothing else, they all had normal blood pressure.

What was this amazing technique? It was actually very simple. They got the executives to do some deep breathing and relax (something not many people are taught how to do these days), and then they got them to imagine something pleasant like holding a baby or walking through the park on a sunny day.

I got very excited when I read this article last year, because it confirms my discoveries about the different functions of right and left brain. Studies done in the 1960s by a man named Roger Sperry demonstrated that the two hemispheres of the cerebral cortex – the bit that controls higher brain functions – control different modes of thought. (Betty Edwards, *Drawing on the Right Sight of the Brain*, HarperCollins.) Sperry won a Nobel prize for his research, which demonstrated the two different functions of left and right brain.

The left side of the brain – which controls the right side of the body - is the academic side of the brain, governing processes like speech, vocabulary, numeracy, logic, linear thinking and abstract concepts. The right side of the brain, by contrast, is the non-verbal side of the brain. It governs the imagination, daydreaming, colours, visual-spatial perception, the intuitive, the holistic, the concrete.

Although both sides work together, one hemisphere is always 'in control'. Most of us work out of the left side of the brain because that's what our particular culture encourages. Think about what we emphasize in school. When kids are little, they get a balance of reading, writing and maths (left brain functions) with art, dance, and music (right brain functions). Pretty soon the artistic subjects are dropped and the academic subjects are emphasized. Children are told to stop daydreaming and get down to work.

As a primary school art teacher, I get my pupils to do the opposite. Using various exercises and techniques, I encourage them to put the right brain in control, because when they do *that*, their drawing improves dramatically. Because the right side of the brain is non-verbal, I can tell when I've got them working from the right brain: the room goes totally silent.

The more I saw the benefits of understanding the principle of left and right brain functions in the classroom, the more I started to think about its implications for our spiritual lives. I realized that when I prayed not in words (from the left side of my brain), but with my sanctified imagination (from the right side), it had a powerful emotional effect. For me, using my imagination became a powerful way of getting my knowledge of Jesus from my head to my heart.

That was when I started to wonder if the right brain isn't synonymous with heart. In the Bible, 'mind' and 'heart' are often placed next to each other in a verse, the way the two hemispheres of the brain lie next to each other. Perhaps the left brain was the rational, thinking *mind*, and the right brain the non-verbal, intuitive, feeling *heart*.

So you can imagine how excited I was when I read in this article that electrical impulses from the imagining part of the brain go directly from the vagus nerve to the heart. The stressed-out executives discovered that when they imagined being in a beautiful place or holding a naked baby (in other words when they went into the right brain mode), that immediately their heartbeat grew steadier and stronger, pushing blood to parts it otherwise couldn't reach, and that as a result, stress levels fell dramatically.

I have been convinced for a long time that God meant us to pray like this – that is, to use our sanctified imagination to put ourselves in his presence. I often do this as an exercise at women's groups I speak to. We invite the Holy Spirit to help us imagine we are in a beautiful garden with Jesus. Not saying anything. Just being with him. Afterwards, women have come up to me with tears in their eyes, often having met with the Lord in a amazingly powerful way, and they say 'I didn't know I was allowed to use my imagination'. Others say 'I used to do something like that but I kind of forgot about it'.

'Be still and know that I am God ...' says the Psalmist in Psalm 46:10. I think we often need to read this as 'Be silent and know that I am God'.

The left brain – the rational, verbalizing, 'in-control' part of the brain – doesn't like stillness or silence, and will offer a running commentary which anyone who has ever tried to pray will be familiar with: 'This is stupid. You're wasting your time. Why are you just sitting here? That's not God's voice, it's just your imagination. You're making all this up.'

Even if we succeed in stilling the criticism, then we get the distractions. Suddenly you remember all the things you have to do. Did I ring so-and-so? Did I buy the whatsit? Oh, I have to do that thing!

Once we know this is just our rational side, complaining because it's not in control, becoming distracted because it is the organizer, we can let those thoughts go. If they come to us when we are trying to pray or meditate on his word, we just acknowledge them and let them go. After a while our left brain, our rational side, will grudgingly allow our right brain some free rein.

Let's look at today's reading again, Luke 10:38–42.

As Jesus and his disciples were on their way, he came to a village where a woman named Martha opened her home to him. She had a sister called Mary, who sat at the Lord's feet and listened to what he said. But Martha was distracted by all the preparations that had to be made. She came to him and asked, 'Lord, don't you care that my sister has left me to do the work by myself? Tell her to help me!'

'Martha, Martha', the Lord answered, 'you are worried and upset about many things, but only one thing is needed. Mary has chosen what is better and it will not be taken away from her.'

There is a painting in the National Gallery which some of you might be familiar with. It is by Velazquez, and it depicts Christ in the house of Martha and Mary. In it we see Martha working hard preparing the meal. At first it seems she is staring resentfully out at us, the viewers, but then we notice the mirror on the wall. Mary sits at Jesus' feet, listening to him while her sister works. Martha's resentment is directed at Mary, perhaps even at Jesus, who allows this selfish conduct.

Now I know quite a few people, especially women, have a deep empathy for Martha. She, after all, is expressing her love for the Lord in the most wonderful way, through the preparation of food.

My husband Richard and I have a favourite joke from the *New Yorker* magazine. A man wearing suit and tie – you feel he is very strait-laced – is sitting at a table while his prim and proper wife presents him with an enormous decorated birthday cake. This is his plaintive appeal: 'Food as a metaphor for love, again?'

Food *is* a metaphor for love. One of the greatest practical expressions of love you could find. Richard is a wonderful cook, whereas I find it pretty boring. But I do like to eat. And when I come home after a long day teaching, and he presents me with a delicious hot meal ... Well, it's a very powerful way of saying 'I love you'. Martha was preparing the meal because she wanted to express her love for the Lord.

I have a close friend whom I don't see very often. She is Greek and very hospitable. It used to be that whenever I was invited to dinner, she would spend hours cleaning her house and preparing an elaborate three-course meal and getting herself all made up. But by the time I arrived she would be so exhausted and keyed-up that the evening would invariably be a disaster. She would quarrel with her husband, who didn't really notice how clean the house was or how much work had gone into the meal and so she would resent him. I always used to say 'It's *you* I've come to see, not the house. Just bread and cheese will be fine.'

Well, for some people their house *is* them. The food they prepare *is* them. My friend was very much like that, but she taught herself to clean strategically and prepare a simpler meal. And now she is much more relaxed and fun to visit, though she is still and always will be a wonderful hostess.

I think Christians all through history have been a bit aggrieved on behalf of Martha. Here's a story told by the desert fathers as long ago as the fourth century AD:

> A certain brother came to Abbot Silvanus on Mount Sinai, and seeing the hermits at work he exclaimed: 'Why do you work for the bread that perishes? Mary has chosen the best part, namely to sit at the feet of the Lord without working.' Then the abbot said to his disciple Zachary: 'Give the brother a book and let him read, and put him in an empty cell.' At the ninth hour the brother who was reading began to look to see if the abbot was not going to call him to dinner, and some time after the ninth hour he went himself to the abbot and said 'Did the brethren not eat today, Father?' 'Oh yes, certainly' said the abbot, 'they have just had dinner.' 'Well', said the brother, 'why did you not call me?' 'You are a spiritual man', said the elder, 'you don't need this food that perishes. We have to work, but you have chosen the best part. You read all day and can get along without food.' Hearing this the brother said 'Forgive me, Father'. And the elder said 'Martha is necessary to Mary, for it was because Martha worked that Mary was able to be praised'.

So we need to find a balance between Martha's example and that of Mary. Look again at verse 38: 'As Jesus and his disciples were on their way, he came to a village where a woman named Martha opened her home to him.' As I read that, it occurred to me that we have all opened our home to him. Those of us who have invited Jesus to come and live in us by his Holy Spirit. Then I realized that we all have Mary and Martha in us.

Then, as if a light bulb had appeared over my head, I saw it so clearly! Martha is the rational verbal part of us and Mary is the watching listening silent part. Martha is Left Brain and Mary is Right Brain. Martha the Mind, and Mary the Heart.

Martha is necessary because she is the one who invited him in. We invite him in with our words, by an act of our will. Martha is also the part of us that works hard to please the Lord, but which is often too busy to spend time with him. Look at verse 40: Martha was distracted by all the preparations that had to be made ... and in verse 41, Jesus says to her 'you are worried and upset about many things ...'.

And notice that throughout this passage, Martha does all the talking. She is like the rational worrying part of us that carries on little monologues and finds it terrifying to sit in silence.

Mary, on the other hand, is silent, non-verbal. She just listens. Elsewhere, in John 12:3, Mary breaks the seal of fabulously expensive nard and pours it on Jesus' head, again, in silence.

We need both our Martha and our Mary. They are the two sides of us that need to be in balance if we are to live the victorious Christian life. We need the rational part of ourselves to let Jesus into our lives initially and to do the many practical things he asks of us. And we need the silent intuitive part that can sit at his feet and silently be in his presence.

In verse 41, Jesus says 'only one thing is needed'. He doesn't say what that one thing is, but any good Jew who knew his Bible would immediately think of Psalm 27:

> One thing I ask of the Lord,
>   this is what I seek:
> That I may dwell in the house of the Lord
>   all the days of my life,
> to gaze upon the beauty of the Lord
>   and to seek him in his temple.

Seventeen years ago, when I first became a Christian, David Watson was a hugely influential figure on the Christian scene. Later he got cancer and died, but in his last book he wrote something which I have never forgotten.

He had been through chemotherapy and was weak and for the moment unable to carry on his duties as a vicar and in his ministry. He was praying one day, apologizing that he couldn't do God's work. As he lay there he felt God's loving presence and heard God say: 'David, I don't want your ministry. I only want you. This is when you are most precious to me. When you come before me with nothing to give me except yourself.'

Many of us find it hard to sit before our Lord with nothing to offer. Probably because, growing up, we got the impression – rightly or wrongly – that our parents' love was dependent upon what we *did*, not who we were. We often make that mistake with God. He doesn't love us any more or any less because of ministry we do or do not have. All he wants is us.

One of my favourite psalms, Psalm 131 says

> I have stilled and quietened my soul;
> like a weaned child with its mother,
> like a weaned child is my soul within me.

A weaned child, an active toddler, comes to its mother not for milk, not because it wants anything from her, but merely to sit in her lap and be cuddled. Those of you with active toddlers know how precious, and sadly how rare, it is for that little bundle of energy to come and snuggle quietly in your lap. You can cuddle their solid warm little bodies and feel the silky touch of their hair on your lips and smell their fragrance.

That's all Father God wants from us. Just to hold us in his arms of love and let us be. He doesn't demand anything from us except that we be still for a few moments so that he can delight in us.

In his wonderful book *Following Jesus Without Embarrassing God,* Tony Campolo tells the story of a reporter who was interviewing Mother Teresa. Upon hearing that she prayed for several hours a day, he asked 'When you pray, what do you say to God?' She answered, 'I don't say anything; I listen'. 'Well, what does God say to you then?' he asked. 'He doesn't say anything. He listens!'

Campolo goes on to say: 'It is in such listening that we hear the soft still voice that, paradoxically, says nothing. But the stillness in such times of prayer moves more powerfully than an earthquake, a hurricane or a raging forest fire. It has been said that the soul is like an atom but more powerful than an atom bomb. If the soul can root itself in stillness for just a little while, the laser power of God's spirit will penetrate the electrons that keep warding it off, split the nucleus, and release the kind of power that can stagger our imaginations. For this to happen, in mind and heart, we must retire to "a secret place" where in quietude He can penetrate our personhood' (p. 69).

I was talking to two Christian women the other day. They had been asked to do an exercise: to sit in the Lord's presence silently for fifteen minutes. They found it almost impossible. One of them emptied her mind but found all sorts of distractions flooded in. The other could only endure it for five minutes. But after being encouraged to use the sanctified imagination, they sat in silence easily in God's presence. And as they just sat being quiet with him, he unexpectedly spoke to them both.

We don't need Heart Math, or drugs, or anything else, to lower our stress levels. We only need to spend time in the Lord's presence.

At his feet. Just listening. Letting him love us. If we do that for twenty minutes a day, not only will our stress levels drop, but our relationship with Jesus will deepen into something much more wonderful. We'll begin to soak up his love like a sponge, and as we soak up his love, that love will displace the pain, the anger, the bitterness, the regret.

One thing I always emphasize is that we never empty our minds; rather, we focus on him. And we always invite the Holy Spirit to sanctify and protect our imaginations. Without the Holy Spirit we can do nothing.

Let's put some of this into practice right now. God loves to speak to us and he will use any means he can. One of the most powerful ways he speaks to us is to use our sanctified imagination.

We will have to take certain steps of faith in our imagination, but then he meets us there. Any words or verbal commentary from the left brain, just acknowledge them and let them slip away.

Holy Spirit, please come and fill our minds with your holiness and purity. Please wash us clean and protect us from all outside distractions or thoughts as we focus on Jesus. Help us to let go of those things that distract us for just a few minutes. In Jesus' name. Amen.

Let's just still ourselves for a moment.

Put down any Bibles or handbags and get as comfortable as you can on the church seats. Close your eyes; it's almost impossible to do this with your eyes open. Remember that God by his Spirit permeates every cell of your body, and he is in every breath you take. Focus on your scalp and forehead, imagining God's gentle touch.

Focus on your jaw and tongue, where we often store tension. Relax them, imagining God's light and warmth flowing through them.

Let the rational part of yourself, the talkative Martha, be silent for a moment. She'll be saying things like 'This is stupid.' or 'How long am I going to have to sit with my eyes closed?' or 'This is a bit New Age-y' or, in true Martha fashion, 'I hope the roast doesn't overcook.'

Just encourage your Martha to be silent and wait, so that the Mary in you can receive.

Now focus on the tension in your neck and shoulders and again imagine God's warmth and love flowing through them to relax them.

Think about your hands and fingers. Be aware of how they feel.

Relax your chest and stomach. Feel God's warmth flowing through.

Relax your legs and feet and the soles of your feet. Feel the tingling of God's presence even down to the soles of your feet.

Now imagine that you are in the most beautiful place you have ever been. A garden perhaps. Or the seashore. Or a mountain.

Let your imagination create the time of day.

What is the temperature?

What can you feel? Cool grass on your bare feet? The warm sand? A breeze on your face? The warm sun on the top of your head and shoulders?

What are you wearing? What is its colour? Weight? Texture?

What can you smell?

What can you hear?

Now imagine that you are sitting at Jesus' feet.

What do those feet look like? Are they bare or sandalled? Clean or dusty? Pierced or whole?

Is Jesus speaking or is he silent?

Let your sanctified imagination lead you.

Perhaps he is resting his hand lightly on your head or shoulder. Feel his touch.

If your imagination allows you to, look up into his face and see the immense love there for you.

For the next few minutes, just rest silently in his presence, not speaking, just listening.

Amen.

Comments

Ian Sweeney: *'A practical and relevant sermon that not only talks about stress, but can lower your stress levels too.'*

Kieran Conry: *'Good introduction, a bit of science, a story or two and a personal invitation to look at our own experience. Then the text turns solidly to the Scriptures and a specific text, and illustrates that well in a number of different ways. It might benefit from being a little shorter – some might find it difficult, especially when it moves into the "experiential" time at the end.'*

What Are You Looking For?

SERMON PREACHED BY RAY SCHROEDER AT FAITH PRESBYTERIAN CHURCH, SUN CITY, ARIZONA, USA, ON 17 JANUARY 1999

The Reverend Dr Ray Schroeder, 47, and his wife Kathi have three children, aged 24, 20 and 13, and have lived in the desert community of Peoria – just northwest of Phoenix, Arizona – for the past five years. Dr Schroeder serves as an associate pastor of pastoral care at Faith Presbyterian Church, a church composed of 1,400 retirement-aged parishioners (average age 79).

Realizing the value of personal visitation in ministry, Dr Schroeder has had articles published in The Christian Science Monitor *('Making Religion Relevant', 29 December 1998) and* The Presbyterian Outlook *('Caring for our Elderly', 3 May 1999) on the importance of listening and the skills it requires. He is currently in the process of publishing a book,* To Love Is to Listen.

Ray, who was baptized as an infant in the Presbyterian Church, attended worship regularly with his family while growing up, and was confirmed at the age of 12. 'When I was 14 or 15, my minister invited me to read the Scriptures from the pulpit during the worship service on several occasions. Saying that I had special talents for public speaking and reading, he encouraged me to consider a call to the ministry. He gave me and my parents information on church schools and vocations, and urged us to pray about it.'

However, Ray did not feel called to the ministry. 'After high school I went on to get married and earn a degree in business administration. My wife Kathi, and I continued to be actively involved in church life working as part-time paid youth workers for a Presbyterian church while we lived in Texas.

'It was while we were serving at that church as youth directors that I came to realize God was calling me into the ordained ministry. The youth group was responsible for planning and directing the worship service for what was called Youth Sunday in April, and the young people agreed to do all of the service except the sermon. Finally, giving in to their entreaties, I agreed to do the preaching.

'After the service, my parents took Kathi and me and our two

children out for lunch. While we were eating my father asked me 'Have you thought about entering the ministry?'

' "Not since high school", I said "but it really felt 'right' up there in the pulpit this morning. Sometimes I do feel like I'm not fully using my talents and abilities working as an accountant. Why do you ask?"

'My father said: "After the service a couple of church elders asked if you had ever felt led to enter the ministry. I told them you had considered it when you were younger, but I didn't know what your thoughts were now. They said that they believed you would make a good preacher and that the church would be willing to support you through seminary." '

Although he was experiencing disappointment in his secular career, he had not talked to anyone at the church about entering the ministry. 'I felt that this was God's way of guiding me into a new and correct path for my life – a path which I had been offered before but had not taken. Now I was being given a new opportunity. After several days of prayer and discussion with Kathi and the children, we agreed to step out in faith. So at the age of 30, married and with two children, I enrolled in the Austin Presbyterian Theological Seminary in Austin, Texas.'

He has now been ordained for over thirteen years, and has earned a Doctor of Ministry degree as well as a Master of Divinity. 'I am grateful for having the opportunity to serve the church as a minister and preacher, and can't imagine my doing anything else.'

Dr Schroeder is the first preacher based in America, although not the first American-born preacher, to make the final 30.

In an age of increasing technologically advanced methods of communication, he believes the sermon continues to serve an important function. 'Preaching remains a powerful means of conveying one's deepest values and beliefs to a group of people, face-to-face and in person. We are losing sight of the importance of face-to-face communication as we spend more time faxing and e-mailing one another in what we call virtual reality. Preaching will continue to play an important role in the church and in society in the new millennium. It is an active symbol of God's desire for us to speak personally to one another–in the sense of "I-and-thou".'

He believes preaching needs to be the result of honest and active listening: 'Listening both to God – through Scripture and prayer – and to one another. Preaching that does not proceed from listening is hypocritical and false. It is of no value. But preaching that is the product of focused and intent listening is a sharing of one's search for meaning and truth, and is a means of connecting and caring. Such preaching will become more important in a time when meaning is increasingly seen as something unobtainable and unknowable.'

He says that amusing oneself in isolation from others is seen as the one 'honest' reaction to living in a world of increasing mobility and information-turnover. 'In the creation account in the Bible, God says it is not good for "man" to be alone. Community is God's call to men and women to love and care for each other, including the stranger. Although modern electronics have increased the networking of people, that does not create community. Preaching that is personal and honest helps create real community.'

He believes worship in the new millennium should not try to copy the ways of the world in an effort to retain people's attention and interest. 'Giant television screens and web-pages will not replace the preacher speaking from the heart to a gathered group of people. God will continue to use preaching that is honest and personal to speak to people's hearts and souls and minds in a powerful way.'

His congregation has felt the impact of today's attitude of social isolation and the desire to be left alone. 'Membership in all voluntary groups and societies, including the Church, seems to be down over the past 30 years. The Church must meet this challenge through preaching that shows that it cares for people. Like someone once said, "People don't care how much you know, until they know how much you care". I think that applies to the Church, as well.'

Text: John 1:35–49

'What are you looking for?' Jesus asked. I'm not sure the two disciples really knew, because they responded with a question, 'Where are you staying?' Jesus invited them to come and see, and they stayed with him all day.

They were seeking something, even if they weren't quite sure what it was. In this man, Jesus. they found it. They found the answer to their own ill-defined questions. They found the Messiah.

What happened that day they stayed with him? I'm sure Jesus taught them many things – new and exciting ways of looking at the world; a new understanding, perhaps, of parts of the Old Testament; and renewed hope. Jesus also listened to them. In the course of an entire day with these two, I'm sure Jesus did a lot of genuine listening. He made them feel as if someone had understood them for the first time – with all their ill-defined longings and questions. He listened to them like no one else had ever listened them, and he made them feel understood and valued.

Most people long for that kind of personal listening and understanding. 'For what are you seeking?' can be answered with the statement 'I'm seeking someone who will really listen to me, who won't cut me off, someone who will hear me without judging, someone who will make me feel that I'm genuinely understood and valued for who I am'.

Jesus did all these things. He is the great listener, who understands our hearts and offers us love and acceptance. When we pray, we pour out our hearts to him, knowing that he hears us. As the old hymn says,

> Can we find a friend so faithful
> who will all our sorrows share?
> Jesus knows our every weakness.
> Take it to the Lord in prayer.

We can take anything to him in prayer, for he understands and listens.

This is what the two disciples found that day. Andrew was so excited that he went and told his brother, Simon Peter, to come and meet him – the Messiah – Jesus; Jesus, the man who listened and understood, a person who made you feel valued and took the time to spend all day with you.

In Taylor Caldwell's novel, *The Listener* (Doubleday, 1960), she tells the story of an architect who retires to a small town. He decides to leave a memorial to the town and erects a new building. Over the door, etched in gold, are the words 'The Man Who Listens'. When the architect dies, the building is finally opened. People from all walks of life go there to talk to a mysterious man who quietly listens to them from behind a curtain. They wait in a small anteroom, or waiting area, for a light to come on signalling their turn to go in to another room by themselves and talk to the man. Each person goes into the room with the curtained wall at a time to share their innermost burdens with the 'Man Who Listens'. No one knows who it is who sits behind the curtain. After each visitor is done talking, they press a button and the curtain is drawn, revealing a painting of Jesus. Their need was for someone to listen to them.

Caldwell argues that our basic needs are few. We don't need to go to the moon or stars. We don't need all the things advertisers try to sell us. We certainly don't need more missiles or better bombs. We do need bread, shelter, and lots of listening. The most desperate need of people today, she states, 'is not ... a new religion, or a new way of life'. People's real need, their most terrible need, 'is for someone to listen to them, not as a patient, but as a human soul. They need to tell someone of what they think, of the bewilderment they encounter when they try to discover why they were born, how they must live, and where their destiny lies.'

There are few who truly listen. One of the most frustrating

experiences is to have an illness or ailment of some kind, and to go to a doctor who doesn't really listen to us. Perhaps we're hospitalized, and we long for the doctor to spend some time listening to our concerns and questions. Too often, however, we feel like a 'case' to be treated instead of a person to be listened to.

In the film *Patch Adams*, Robin Williams plays a young man who commits himself to a mental hospital after a long period of depression. In one scene he is shown talking to a psychiatrist, one-on-one, in the privacy of the doctor's office. However, the doctor is busy reading the medical file, putting cream and then sugar in his coffee, generally being preoccupied. Never once does he look at his patient eye-to-eye. Finally, in frustration Patch leaves the office, vowing to become a better listener himself.

We long for doctors and other professionals to treat us as human beings, and to listen to us with patience and understanding. As the essayist Anatole Brovard wrote shortly before his death from prostate cancer: 'I wouldn't demand a lot of my doctor's time. I just wish he would brood on my situation for perhaps five minutes, that he would give me his whole mind just once, be bonded with me for a brief space, survey my soul as well as my flesh to get at my illness. Just as he orders blood tests and bone scans of my body, I'd like my doctor to scan me, to grope for my spirit as well as my prostate. Without such recognition, I am nothing but my illness.'

We have put so many demands on doctors to be proficient in the latest technology, while also demanding then to be cost-efficient, that, sadly, they have little time left to listen. Ministers, too. seem to be too busy to listen. Again, Taylor Caldwell put it this way:

Our pastors would listen – if we gave them the time to listen to us. But we have burdened them with tasks that should be our own. We have demanded not only that they be our shepherds, but that they take our trivialities, our social aspirations, the 'fun' of our children, on their weary backs. We have demanded that they be expert businessmen, politicians, accountants, playmates, community directors, 'good fellows', judges, lawyers, and settlers of local quarrels. We have given them little time for listening and we do not listen to them, either.

To love someone means to listen to them. If we don't listen to a person, how can we say we love them? Jesus demonstrated the power of love by his listening and understanding. He took time to be with people and to listen to them. He calls us all to listen to each other – not just doctors, ministers, and other professionals. 'Love one another as I have loved you', he told us. Listen to one another, as I listen to you. The one sign by which the world would know we are his disciples, Jesus said, was how we loved one another, nothing else but that.

Where do we start? We begin by learning to become comfortable with our own silence. Until we learn that, we can't listen to others. The gospels tell us that on many occasions Jesus would go out by himself and pray all night to his Father in heaven. Although he was amongst great crowds of people during the day, and was always present with the Apostles, Jesus sought time alone – to pray in total silence.

We live in a noisy world. It's hard to find that silence today. My family and I live in Peoria, and our backyard borders on Olive Avenue. Day and night we hear the rush of traffic and the scream of sirens along that busy thoroughfare right behind our house. I have always liked to go outside in the early morning, to enjoy the stillness of that time, but now there is the constant interruption of the noise of rushing cars and trucks.

It's not just the noise of the city that interrupts our silence, however. The media today is a noisy and ever-present stimulus. It surrounds us. From radio and TV talk shows to news interview programmes, no one on them is silent long enough to allow the other person time to finish their remarks. Talk shows are aptly named, for no one listens to anyone else in that format. Listening, for those on such shows, is to just bide your time until you can say what you're thinking. No one seems to really hear what the other person has said, nor do they seem to care.

Even the Church has become uncomfortable with silence. In many congregations it seems that every minute of the worship service must be packed with talking, preaching, or teaching. The frantic pressure to get everything in offerings, announcements, music, sermon, readings, prayers, almost would make one think that silence is a sin and the need for solitude a sickness. How different from when the Church intentionally sought to offer a sanctuary of silence for its people.

'Christianity no longer listens', one young mother said recently. 'All the Church wants to do is talk – lecture, reprimand, and command – never really listen.' Unfortunately, she is right. Christ calls us to be listeners, and to be comfortable with our own silence.

The Church could take a lesson from the world of business on the importance of listening. One of the latest and most publicized business management skills is called MBWA: Management by Walking Around. Basically, it says that unless people are listened to, they will not feel valued as human beings, and the workplace will suffer. People are more than cogs in a production machine, and the best way to ensure they are treated as human beings is to listen to them. In his book *A Passion for Excellence,* Tom Peters stresses the importance of 'naive listening', staying in touch with workers and customers by going and listening to them, regularly, with no agenda except what's on *their* minds.

Who's got time to do such listening? We've got things to do, meetings to attend, projects to complete. In my own visits with people in their homes I have listened as some people told me they are fine, and that the church should be visiting those who really need it. I agree that we should be visiting those with special and acute needs. However, we all need someone who will listen to us, whether it be a neighbour, a relative, or a fellow church member.

There is a cost to not listening. Small difficulties not shared develop into large ones. As any professional counsellor can tell you, little hurts and needs grow to unmanageable proportions if not addressed. In an article entitled 'Deep listening', Harry Farra puts it this way: 'Few now have time to listen to the average person's slight skirmishes of soul. Ironically, neglect often causes those overlooked folk to become themselves people in crisis. Untended little problems easily become big. If people can get their share of attention only by being in crisis, they will learn to have major disturbances rather than small ones.'

'What are you looking for?' Jesus asked. We respond today that we're looking for someone who will listen to us, really hear us, and make us feel valued and understood. In Jesus Christ we have the one who does all those things. He hears our prayers and understands our needs. And he invites us to be what Martin Luther called 'little Christs' to one another, and to learn to silence ourselves and listen to others. May we grow in the grace of Christ that enables us to listen and to be obedient to the one commandment of Christ, loving one another, as he has loved us. To the glory and honour and praise of the living God, in Christ Jesus our Lord. Amen.

Comments

Ian Sweeney: *'Dr Schroeder challenges our presuppositions that religion is about telling people what they ought to be doing, by stating that religion is more about listening. Listening to God and to the hearts of our fellow men.'*

Peter Graves: *'Good on importance of listening.'*

Kieran Conry: *'Although it goes straight into the heart of the topic – not always a good tactic, perhaps – this is a lively and engaging text. It is well illustrated with useful references and has a good personal feel to it. It is Christ-centred and ends in a very positive and encouraging way.'*

Making Sense of Images

SERMON PREACHED BY MARK HART IN ST BARNABAS
CHURCH, BROMBOROUGH, AT AN ALL SOULS SERVICE
ON SUNDAY 8 NOVEMBER 1998

*The Reverend Mark Hart is married to Karen and they have three
small children. He entered the ordained ministry of the Church of
England in 1998 and is serving a curacy in the parish of St Barnabas,
Bromborough, on the Wirral. He was educated at Cambridge
University, reading mathematics and taking a doctorate in engineering, and was employed in industry for eleven years as a research
engineer, working on the aerodynamics of steam turbines. He trained
for ordination at Trinity College, Bristol.*

*It was at Trinity where his tutor annotated his first sermon draft
with 'ZZZZZZZ'. 'At last someone was giving me some honest
appraisal', he says. 'He was absolutely right. There were long
paragraphs which were sound but soporific. Who cares whether it's
heretical or not if nobody is listening? I learnt the need for a sermon
to be thoroughly down to earth – to build a bridge between an
ancient text and a modern world, between an almighty God and
human creatures.*

*'For me one of the most wonderful and inspiring aspects of the
Christian gospel is the mystery of the incarnation, that God is such
that he could be born and live and die as a fully human being in Jesus
Christ. The fullest manifestation of divinity is in one like us.*

*'So we encounter God best, not in rarefied preaching, but in
preaching which reveals the power of the gospel in the nitty-gritty of
life. We enter a new millennium in a culture increasingly impersonal
and escapist. Preaching at its best is neither. It is a word addressed to
a specific community concerning their particular needs. It is delivered
live by a human being who is one of the people. It is in the nature of
God that he can thus become personally present and heard.'*

*He believes the same principle applies to worship generally. 'In it,
heaven and earth are united. It should not be an attempt to escape
earth (as if God were merely alien). Nor should it be an earth-bound
parading of the talents of the worshippers (as if God were merely
human). It will always be necessary to strive to make worship
contemporary and relevant, yet such that we are drawn to apprehend*

the transcendent through the immanent, to sense the mysterious in the mundane. Through a human preacher we hear the word of God. Receiving bread and wine we share the risen life of Christ.'

When he looks at St Barnabas church as a whole, he asks himself to what extent it looks indigenous to Bromborough, and to what extent it is a community which points to something more. 'For as the body of Christ it should be both. It has been (and still is) gradually changing from a traditional institution from a bygone era to a community which is bound together by a common spiritual life centred on Christ. The anti-institutional trend in society is thus reflected in the life of the Church – and in its diminished role in the community over decades. However, the widespread hunger for "spirituality" is also evident in signs of renewal in the Church. The challenge is for the Church's perceived distinctiveness to shift from being simply a custodian of ancient tradition to being a witness to the life of an age to come – the kingdom of God.'

Text: Revelation 5

I wonder if you have ever studied a 'Magic Eye' picture? Here's one from yesterday's *Daily Mail*. At first glance they appear to be just a detailed, random pattern of colour. But the trick is to look at the picture in a special way. You need to hold it a certain distance from you and focus not on the picture, but some way beyond it. Then out of that randomness and chaos appears a clear, 3-D image, in this case of three interlocking circles.

Sometimes we might look at our lives, or at the world around us, and wish there were such a technique. A way of seeing things which allowed everything to make sense. A new vantage point which could give some ultimate purpose to the seemingly random pain and grief and suffering. There is certainly no shortage of methods these days. Just note the widespread interest in astrology, mediums, drugs, the paranormal, the extra-terrestrial. All these in one way or another are a search for a new dimension on life, a trick which changes how things look, a trip which suspends the present reality.

We're born. We live. We die. But we're made, it seems, with a very strong sense that there is more than this. There's a verse in the book of Ecclesiastes, in the Bible, which says that God has set eternity in our hearts. Different experiences evoke this awareness in different people. I find that watching cricket gives me a real perception of eternity. Some are stimulated by the majesty of the natural world, as in our last hymn: 'O Lord my God, when I in awesome wonder consider all the works thy hand hath made.' But perhaps these words of a well-known Christian writer strike a chord with many of us today. He said: 'Eternity is born in time, and every time someone dies whom we have loved dearly, eternity can break into our mortal existence a little more' (Henri Nouwen, *A Letter of Consolation*, Harper & Row, 1982).

I know that in my limited experience, to lose someone close, to be faced with our mortality, can greatly sharpen our perception of life. What really matters in life becomes so much easier to see. It's as if we're given the opportunity to step back and view the bigger picture, to consider where we have come from and where we are going.

There is no book in the Bible quite like the Revelation to John, where our second reading was from, for giving the big picture. This is the Stephen Spielberg or James Cameron production of the Bible. Full of special effects and epic scenes. A sequence of panoramic views of earth and heaven, of all of time, of all of life. A resource for seeing God's ultimate purpose in creation. A book of encouragement given originally to a church experiencing pain and suffering and martyrdom.

The beginnings of the book were quite mundane. John was a prisoner, and had the good fortune, we might think, to be sent at taxpayers' expense to a Greek island. But on arrival he didn't just find that his hotel was next to a building site, as we might fear. He was, very probably, put to hard labour in a quarry. This really was material for the TV programme *Holidays from Hell*. On the Sunday, not surprisingly, John was found praying. And at that point he is transported and begins to experience the visions which now form the book of Revelation. His holiday had become quite literally a holiday from heaven.

But where we pick up the story, John is in tears. A week or two ago a very sad news item also gave me a little amusement. I tried to picture the editors of certain of our national newspapers weeping bitterly in their offices. They had a tantalizing half-story surrounding the resignation of the Welsh Secretary. But they just could not get the full picture they craved. John, however, is here on the verge of something monumentally bigger. There in God's hand is a scroll, promising to reveal the divine purpose in all the events of history. Yet no one is able to open the seals. Or so it seems.

At this point John's guide tells him that the Lion of Judah's tribe has won the victory and can open the scroll. Now this is all symbolic imagery, of course. But John must have taken heart from the picture of a lion, a beast of strength and majesty. The nations of this world like to use such symbols: the British choose the lion, the Russians the bear, the French the tiger, the Americans the eagle – all powerful, ravenous beasts. But when John looks, it's not a lion he sees but a lamb. Which nation ever chose a lamb as its symbol? And more, the lamb looks as if it has been killed! And yet it's standing and alive. It doesn't make easy sense, but in the world of symbols and special effects you can do this kind of thing.

Of course, the lamb represents Jesus, who died and came to life again. But it seems there is something about his death which is always present. It reminds me of how when Jesus was raised he made himself known to his disciples by his wounds. Those nail marks in his hands and feet hadn't gone. They didn't disappear like wounds in the body of the android in the Arnold Schwarzenegger film *Terminator 2* which re-forms perfectly, whatever weaponry is unleashed against it. The resurrection has not left the cross behind, but revealed its victory. God has not left us behind in our still broken world of pain and death. God himself in his son Jesus has identified with all of that. The revelation of God's purpose to John lies not so much in the scroll but in the one who could open the seals.

For me the most moving part of the film *Titanic* was not where the heroine Rose finds the hero Jack has died, and lets him go to an ocean grave. It was at the point when the lone violinist began playing 'Nearer My God to Thee'. It was the point where the illusion of calm could be no longer maintained by the orchestra. It was the point where the reality of the scale of the tragedy and the loss of human life had to be faced. And where was God? Well, he couldn't be nearer, for God is forever the God of the cross.

Someone has said these words of the crucified Jesus: 'this is God and God is like this. God is not greater than he is in this humiliation. God is not more glorious than he is in this self-surrender. God is not more powerful than he is in this helplessness. God is not more divine than he is in this humanity' (Jürgen Moltmann, *The Crucified God*, SCM, 1974).

I believe that it is only as we look to the cross that we can begin to make sense of our lives and of this world. No tricks or trips will stand the test of time like the story of Christ. The cross is where God's eternity has broken into our time, our humanity, our pain, our grief. We may only see it at one point, but it gives us hope and reason for faith.

Suppose I were to go on holiday to Blackpool and bring you back a stick of rock. You might break it and look at the cross-section and read the words 'With love from Blackpool'. Now you would only be able to see that at one point. Yet you would believe that it said 'with love' all the way along the stick.

God has demonstrated his love for us at the cross. He has shown us that the cross leads to resurrection. We still can't see the whole picture. A lot is simply tough and does not make sense. But because we've seen that one point. he wants us to believe that through all our lives it says 'with love'. Throughout all the earth and all of history it can be said: 'God so loved the world.'

Now if God's eternity has broken into our time and our mortality, maybe we should think there is a way for us to reach beyond this existence to a new dimension? Perhaps we can from here have a part in heaven. Perhaps we can even at this distance be united with angels and the Christians who have gone before us.

And sure enough, as John watches, that is what becomes apparent. First, he notices the four living creatures and the 24 elders worshipping God and the Lamb. When he looks more closely, he realizes that thousands and millions of angels are also singing in loud voices. And finally he sees that every creature in heaven and on earth is singing praise and honour and glory and might to God.

Throughout the whole book of Revelation, worship is the real battleground. And it is such an encouragement to suffering Christians because it shows that when we meet to worship, we are simply joining in with the worship of heaven which goes on endlessly. We are anticipating, tasting now, a future when God is worshipped by all and everything is made new.

You must have seen all the advertising for digital TV. It expands your mind. It broadens your horizons. You are no longer a passive observer, removed from the action, you get in there, you can interact and make a difference. And then there's the Internet, a vast network which can link you up instantly with millions of people.

But worship has always been digital. And the fellowship of all believers, living and departed, has been linked together on the heavenly Internet since time began. Our worship is in unison with that of heaven. Our praises echo the praises of saints and angels. Our prayers are received in heaven. John pictures them as bowls of incense brought by the elders before the Lamb, before Christ.

It really does seem to be possible to experience this whole new dimension to life. I look at this picture which is just a mess, flat and two-dimensional. Then suddenly there appears in 3-D an image of three interlocking circles – rather like a symbol of the Trinity, God the Father, Son and Holy Spirit. I wish you could all see it. Where is God in this mess? Well, he's there right in the middle of it.

When looking at our lives and this world there's no simple trick, but the first step is to place ourselves at the cross. Then things may begin to become clearer. Then God's love may be felt. Then we see a new dimension open up. God is there. We can bring our prayers to be heard. We can worship together and be a part of a vast multitude of living and departed who exist to bring glory to God. To him be praise and honour for ever and ever.

Amen.

Comments

Jonathan Romain: *'What a lively style. The preacher takes Revelation as his text but manages to pack in the* Daily Mail, *Arnold Schwarzenegger,* Titanic, *Blackpool rock and digital TV!'*

Peter Graves: *'Good insights into Revelation. Clearly presented with a winsome style.'*

Problems, Problems

SERMON PREACHED BY CANON IAN KNOX AT
LWAKHAKA, BUNGOMA DIOCESE, KENYA, ON 2
DECEMBER 1998 (NOW SLIGHTLY ADAPTED FOR A
BRITISH CONGREGATION)

This is the third time Ian Knox has been part of The Times *Preacher of the Year award. As Director of the 40:3 Trust, he is widely used in evangelism and teaching throughout the British Isles and beyond. 'There was never a time when we needed preaching more than now, as we enter the new millennium', he asserts. 'A world full of bad news needs Good News more than ever.'*

Married to Ruth for 26 years, with four sons, he lives in Coventry, where his work is based. Psalm 40:3 is the key to his ministry, speaking of the Lord putting a new song in our mouths, so that many will 'put their trust in the Lord'. In the last year, his work has taken him back to the diocese of Bungoma in western Kenya to help train clergy and laity in the Anglican Church, where the Bishop installed him as a lay canon of Webuye Cathedral.

Canon Knox is currently researching the relationship between the Church and older people, and is concerned about the dilemma facing preachers. 'We have to be continually relevant to a new, modern and largely unchurched generation, whilst not pushing out those who have come faithfully over many years. I believe the secret is to be simple but not simplistic, caring but not patronizing, and showing that God is for now, as well as then. A friend of mine said that we preachers should stay close to God, close to people, and bring God and people together.'

The great change in churches over recent years has been the impact of so many coming in who have no spiritual or biblical background. This has meant that churches have to modernize their methods. Sadly, many churches fear that this will lead to compromise – which is not the case. The message of the gospel is the same, but must be presented to make it real for twenty-first-century people. As long as the baby is not thrown out with the bath-water, and the best of the old preserved, then both older and newer churchgoers will feel part of a renewed vision.

'In many ways it is the original message of Jesus which speaks

most clearly', says Canon Knox. 'When I speak of God's love, the forgiveness Jesus purchased on the cross, the power through the resurrection and the presence of the Holy Spirit, people respond with joy. If we are to change our preaching, it must be to stop being so cerebral and speak to the heart-needs of our people. So many are over-worked, or bereaved, or lost, or lonely, whilst others need to be helped to see the relevance of God in a secular world. We have so much to offer from God. We must be faithful sowers of the seed which is the word of God, which is why I preached this sermon.'

Text: Mark 4:1–20

What scares you most? A national radio station recently asked its listeners to answer that question – I wonder if you'd agree with what they said? In Miss World style, the third most scary thing was: the car behind yours putting on its blue light. I think we'd go with that one! Number two was: coming home and finding your front door open. Yes again. But the thing people feared most was really amazing. It was: being asked to speak in front of three or more people in public. Even if it wasn't our number one, we'd have voted for that somewhere in our top ten, wouldn't we? When the church is looking for volunteers to get up and do something, especially sharing our faith verbally, we take a few quick paces backwards. Is that why we sit at the back – so we can hide when this danger lurks?

'I wouldn't know what to say.'

'I haven't the time to do it.'

'I'd be a complete failure.'

That's what we think. At least, I do, very often. What, me? Tell others about God? It's panic-button time. Which is why I get so much encouragement from one of Jesus' most famous parables, the one about the sower and the seed, because it faces my problems head on.

Problem number one is not knowing what to say, or how to say it. How can I speak to others when the Bible is so hard to understand, and my knowledge seems so poor? What a relief it is to find that the disciples had the same difficulty! You can almost see Jesus raising his eyebrows and lifting his shoulders as they confess their ignorance about the parable: 'Don't you understand this parable? How then will you understand any parable?' He asks them (verse 13). In other words, this is the easy stuff – wait till we get on to the A-level section!

So does Jesus throw them out, as a hopeless class? Of course not. He sits down with them and explains the meaning. It's not how clever we are, it's how brilliant our Teacher is that matters. 'Don't be wise in your own eyes, fear the Lord', says Proverbs (3:7). One of the very disciples who was there that day, James, later wrote 'If any of you lacks wisdom, he should ask God' (James 1:5). When we don't understand, and don't know what to say, Jesus will teach us – through his Word, the Bible, through other teachers, and because, as Paul says, 'We have the mind of Christ' (1 Corinthians 2:16).

You don't have to be a know-it-all: we all have invisible L-plates. Get into the car with your expert beside you and learn, before you drive. The world is not wildly interested in our doubts, which the Church seems brilliant at expressing. The disciples saw Jesus privately – why don't we do the same, and then share the certainties we discover?

If wisdom is a problem, so is work. 'I've no time.' 'I'm too busy.' 'It's hard work.' And, of course, that's all true. 'A sower went out to sow' is how Jesus begins his story in verse 3. Spreading the Word – the seed – is no easy job. 'We have all got to work, and we have got to work until we drop. And then we have got to pick ourselves up and go on working.' Was it a religious leader who said that? No. It was Chris Patten, Chairman of the Tory party, addressing his workers before the 1992 election. Are we saying we care less about God's Kingdom than politicians do about their kingdom? Shame on us!

Who sees the farmer as he sows the seed? He is out in all weathers, working so hard for a good crop. Where is our commitment to God's work? Let me throw you a wobbly by changing the scene from a sower to show you what I mean. I hope you can cope! The other summer, we went as a family to St Ives, at the far end of Cornwall, for our holidays. The day we arrived, they were opening a new lifeboat house. It was all very grand, with a brass band, the mayor, and the lifeboat crew in dress uniform. It reminded me of a great open-air church service. That week, on a lovely calm day, there was a fine display of how people were rescued. You had to imagine the rough sea, but the show was great, volunteers were plucked from a delightful bay, and a collection was taken up. It was like the 'church on parade' – a March for Jesus for all to see.

But the third time I saw the lifeboat was at two o'clock one morning. I looked out of our holiday home window, and there was the boat, with its crew on board, slipping into the sea. Four hours later I watched again as the lifeboat returned, a burnt yacht in tow. The lifeboat was pulled up the beach, the crew wearily getting out of their oilskins. No one saw them. No one applauded. When the world got up, the boat was back in its house, and the men were going to their day jobs. But lives had been saved, and the real work done. I realized again, that morning, that sharing God with others is like that – hard work, often unappreciated, but so important. That's how a sower feels when he's sowing, too.

Which brings me to the last problem, which is a very real one – the fear of failure. 'I'd be no good at this "sharing my faith" ', we say. 'I'd be hopeless.' We live in a success-driven world, and the Church too often gets caught up in its craving. The parable of the sower is a great antidote, because the poor farmer has so much failure. The path rejects the seed, the rocks have too little soil, the weeds choke the growth, and only the good soil is of any use. Even then, some seed is 30 per cent successful, some 60 per cent, and only some 100 per cent. I accept that there may have been lots more good soil than bad, but there is no great sense of 'triumphalism' here. The farmer is more faithful than anything.

It was Robert Schuller who said 'I would rather attempt something great for God and fail, than attempt nothing for God and succeed'. One of the saddest questions Jesus asks is in Luke 18:8: 'When the Son of Man comes, will he find faith on the earth?' That's what Jesus wants – our faithfulness as messengers, as sowers, not a healthy balance in the profit and loss account. Is sharing the Good News of God with others full of problems, problems? Yes, it is! Will that be our excuse, or will we get on with it, like the lifeboat crew, and the sower?

Let's be faithful, and dare to be God's sowers with our lives, and with what he gives us to share with others.

Amen.

Comments

Jonathan Romain: *'Ian Knox's direct and deceptively simple style is very effective. Unlike with some sermons, we do not have to struggle to pay attention, and he gets his message across.'*

The Trial of the Pyx

SERMON DELIVERED BY JULIA FRANCIS TO SEVERAL
NONCONFORMIST CONGREGATIONS AND SHORTENED A
LITTLE FOR A SERVICE OF ANGLICAN MORNING
WORSHIP AT ST LUKE'S CHURCH, SNAILBEACH,
SHROPSHIRE ON 23 OCTOBER 1998

*Julia's family consists of herself, her husband, who is their chapel
warden, and their two teenage daughters. 'They have always given
me an incredible amount of support and encouragement and thus
continue to play a significant part in all that I do in my ministry as a
Reader', she says.*

*She was admitted to the office of Reader at Michaelmas 1986.
'Throughout the period 1988 to the present day I have attended
regularly the Summer Conferences for Readers as a delegate from my
diocese. I am currently the chairperson for Hereford Diocesan
Readers Association. In 1999, I was nominated for and established on
the Central Readers Council Executive Committee. I consider my
vocation to Reader ministry to be an integral part of my discipleship,
and I am daily humbled by the challenges that God places before me.
Apart from the attending of PCC, Deanery Synod and Diocesan
Synod I am a member of our local Bible Society Action Group. I am
also involved with the Ministry Among Deaf People, as lay co-
chaplain for Hereford.'*

*Her parish is in south Shropshire, in the diocese of Hereford: Holy
Trinity, Minsterley, with its daughter church of St Luke, Snailbeach.
'We have regular joint services with our friends from the Methodist
and Congregational chapels. Our typical congregations number 18 to
60 according to which building, festival time it is, and so on, and
whether it is an ecumenical event. Our incumbency group also
includes the village of Habberley. The congregation at St Mary's in
that village is generally about ten persons. I regularly preach in all
three churches.'*

She has always been interested in the image of God.

*'My entry is entitled "The Trial of the Pyx". I don't use titles on
all my sermons but it can make it easier for finding them amongst the
filing!'*

She has also been on the amateur stage since she was six years old under various guises: singing, dancing and acting. Now she also writes scripts and produces. The year 1999 saw the staging of her third pantomime in their local village hall. 'It is always a feat to get it to the final stages, but I love every minute. It has been wonderful to share the fun with so many of our locals since the venture began as a fund-raising activity. I love literature of all kinds and as well as reading I write copious amounts whenever time allows.

'As a child in the 1950s and 1960s I was aware that a majority of the children in my school attended some kind of Sunday School; we were from the many Christian denominations that typified England at that time. By the early 1970s this had begun to change. Thirty years on, it is a very small percentage of any community school which also attends any form of Christian nurturing activity aligned to the local churches and chapels. I ascribe much of the change to the impact of leisure and work patterns and the relative affluence of people. A generation who have been encouraged to put self first have not felt the need to form into cohesive spiritual groups for regular worship. Very often there is a sense that people are happy enough to leave others to do the praying whilst still very often relying on the Church in times of real distress. My own small congregation in a village of less than 150 households has remained fairly constant for sixteen years at an average figure of twenty persons per service, whilst the festivals are well attended. The building holds only 60 and is frequently full. The majority attendance, however, comes about when there is a funeral; we transmit the service into the churchyard for the bulk of the supporters to the bereaved.'

She believes preaching must be based in experience. 'We have to bring into our preaching the realities and experience of our lives so that our listeners can relate to the ideas we are asking them to grapple with. When Jesus was preaching on the hillsides, towns and lakes, he used stories and events that his listeners recognized. He made God a reality for them. We must in turn make Jesus himself a reality for our listeners today. If we are serious about tackling crime, addictions and behavioural problems, we must not neglect to make known the alternative reality that the peace of Christ brings. Perhaps, therefore, preaching in the new millennium may become more testimonial. By that I mean more laity sharing their own experiences of faith as well as the traditional pulpit role. We are generally a race of shy people, especially about our spirituality. We must create opportunities to take part in community activities and to shift witness and worship to those places where people are already spending their time. Christianity is growing world-wide as people value themselves as the children of God.'

Text: Mark 12:13–17

I tend to wander in and out of second-hand bookshops quite regularly, and recently I came across a little gem, which I bought for the princely sum of ten pence. It was printed in 1867. It was not the age, or binding that attracted me, but the title! *The Trial of the Pyx*.

Now to me that word 'pyx', which comes incidentally from the Greek word *pyxus* meaning 'box', is in regular use in our churches and cathedrals today and refers to a small metal container, silver or gold, in which are kept the Holy Sacraments.

I have one here in my pocket. I use it when I take Holy Communion to someone who is housebound for some reason and cannot attend our service of Communion. Inside the pyx the priest who administered communion at an earlier service that day will have placed a piece of bread, infused with wine, at the altar. I then take the pyx containing the sacraments to the house and we have a short ceremony in which the elements are given to the person who is ill. In this way the sacrament which has been prepared amongst the whole congregation is shared with this other member of the church.

Well, it was because I knew of this use of the word and receptacle that my attention was drawn to the booklet. To my surprise, I found that this was not the use of the pyx referred to in the title. The pyx in question was in fact the Treasury Pyx. Reading the introductory paragraph soon put me in the picture.

Briefly, I feel I should outline some of the salient bits of information.

It so happens that in Westminster, close to the Chapter House of the Abbey, there is a room known as the Pyx Chapel. There is a room in the Tower of London known as the Pyx Chamber. Both these rooms have been at one time in the charge of the Treasury.

Before the Bank of England was centralized it was necessary to check the standard of coinage minted at regular intervals from the early mints situated around the kingdom. It is recorded that in 1248, the reign of Henry III, the first public trial of the Pyx took place in London. Now this took place before the Barons of the Exchequer, twelve discreet, lawful citizens of London, and twelve goldsmiths, also of London. The Pyx was opened in the presence of the monarch. Inside were coins which would then be assayed for weight, standard and face value. This was the trial.

So what actually happened to the coins in the Pyx and how had they come to be in there? More details are made clear in descriptions from 1279, Edward I's reign, because it was at that time that the mints were consolidated under one mint-master, who too had the responsibility for the standardization of the coinage. Now are recorded quarterly standardization procedures.

Over the years, coins in circulation were the gold sovereign and half-sovereign and a variety of silver coins. Some of you may still remember the silver threepenny bit. There were no copper ones in those days.

During production an agreed figure was set. As the coins were counted out, each one at the certain number chosen, such as the thirtieth coin, would then be put aside. All the coins were then collected from each of the aside piles and put into the Pyx. It was then sealed. The Pyx could only be opened at the public trial. There was a ceremony of keys for the six locks. The keys were held in the hands of two of the main characters previously mentioned.

Remember there was no paper money until the days of Victoria, and the coins were only minted according to the amounts of gold and silver in the possession of the Mint. They were restricted to 22 carats for purity.

As each coin was taken from the Pyx, it was first weighed. Then, to test for purity, a small amount of metal was cut off, melted down and assayed. This was therefore a costly process. A small percentage error was allowed.

A sergeant-at-arms was also present and if it should happen that the coins were found to be less than face value the master of the mint from whence they had come would have been held in custody. Poor man, what a responsibility! You will be relieved to hear that the book recorded no such an arrest.

For more than 600 years the Trial of the Pyx was the standardization trial for all coins of the realm. The coins were tested for weight, purity, uniformity of design. Each coin was produced as an image of its fellow, each bearing, as we know too, the head of the monarch.

Hence the echo of our reading of St Mark: 'Pay to Caesar that which is due to Caesar.' That which bears the imprint of the emperor, or monarch, belongs ultimately to him.

Even though I have discovered a second use of the term pyx, I find that both are in essence very much the same.

The Treasury Pyx bears coins for comparison, whereas the church pyx bears the elements of the body and blood of the Lord, for the believer. However, just as the contents of the first are used as a measure of the worth of all the others, so too the contents of the church pyx are the reminder to us of the standard by which those others of the children of God measure themselves.

Uniformity of design. Weight of worth. Purity.

These three things we would hope to live up to and be able to measure ourselves against before our judge at the day of our trial.

To quote our Lord once again: 'Give to Caesar what is due to Caesar; give to God what is due to God.'

When our Lord took up the coin and saw upon it the head of Caesar, he turned to the crowd and saw reflected there the image of God, in those all around him, and so he spoke those words.

In Genesis we read: 'In his own image he created them. Male and female he created them.' That which bears the imprint of his image belongs to him.

The measure we have is that Christ was upon the cross paying full dues.

In 2 Corinthians 5, St Paul writes: 'For the Love of Christ leaves us no choice. With us therefore worldly standards have ceased to count in our estimate of any man.' Note that 'wordly standards have ceased'.

He continues: 'Even if once they counted in our understanding of Christ, they do so no longer. When anyone is in Christ, behold he is a new creation. Old things have passed away. Behold all things are new.'

Christ is the new standard. Christ shows us that which was obvious to us in Genesis, but forgotten, and even today not fully understood. We are all worthy of the Lord, because we have his image, and if we allow his dwelling within us, we are re-created to that standard of purity, value and uniformity with the Lord which is desired of us.

Do we use this standard as we judge one another and ourselves?

In an ideal situation we would apply God's standards, made known to us through, and made possible for us by, Christ Himself.

Paul says in 1 Corinthians 'God has made the wisdom of this world look foolish'. We can expect at times to be ridiculed for the opinions we have and the turnings we take in our lives because of our beliefs and faith.

'These have come so that your faith – of greater worth than gold, which passes through the assayer's fire – may be proved genuine and may result in praise, glory and honour when Jesus Christ is revealed' (1 Peter 1:7).

Many of you, here in Shropshire, will be familiar with Ellis Peters' Brother Cadfael novels. In those books many of her theological utterances show her own deep faith. Under her own name of Edith Pargeter she wrote a three-volume historical novel, one volume of which is *The Scarlet Seed*. In that book she makes an observation through one of her characters. Listening with a Christian ear, you know she fully intends the *double entendre* when she writes these lines:

'Harry picked up a carved stone portrait, a prophetic portrait of himself, carved by his father. He did not know himself even now, the head still daunted, bewildered, excited him with its promise and its clarity, but still he believed. There was some way yet to go but he had set his feet upon the road to that identity, and he would reach it all in good time.'

When asked about what he carries, Harry replies: 'It is a design of my father's. I thought someday I may manage to copy it.'

So meaningful, isn't it?

How easy it is to forget that we are the design of Our Father, a design which in all its promise and clarity is daunting for us to grasp.

So often we fall short of his intentions, so often we fail to use all that is within us of himself, in order to make our becoming like him so much easier.

Yes. There is some way to go, for each of us. And collectively certainly there is much to do. But what a goal!

How daunting to be told that we are made in his image.

How terrifying a responsibility for any child, but what a promise to us is that revelation.

When we learn to love in ourselves that which is God dwelling in us, and use it to overthrow our darker nature, then we learn to reach for that within others which is part of God. And so we gradually widen the circle, loving globally, not just parochially. Perfecting our love in near things. Expanding our love in far things, until we meet him face to face, and know that we are like him.

'Now are we the sons of God. And it doth not yet appear, what we shall be. But we know that we shall be like him, for we shall see him as he is' (1 John 3:2).

Comments

Peter Graves: *'Interesting development of the concept of the Pyx.'*

Ian Sweeney: *'A well thought-through sermon, which would have us measure our lives by the God we proclaim to serve.'*

A Pattern of Patience

SERMON PREACHED BY MICHAEL TOPLISS AT ST JOHN'S METHODIST CHURCH, BLOXWICH, IN THE MORNING AND AT THE NEW INVENTION METHODIST CHURCH IN THE EVENING, ON 13 DECEMBER 1998, THE THIRD SUNDAY IN ADVENT

Michael Topliss is a Methodist layman who has been a local preacher for 40 years. His wife is Hilary, and they have two children and three grandchildren.

Mr Topliss retired early from teaching, having been Head of Religious Education in a comprehensive school. He served on Walsall's SACRE, and helped with the framing of that borough's Agreed Syllabus.

In 1998 he was appointed County Ecumenical Officer for the Staffordshire Plus Ecumenical Council, whose area covers that county and the local authorities which were formerly part of it. The job entails the encouraging of all aspects of ecumenical activity involving Churches Together groups and the like, befriending and advising Local Ecumenical Partnerships, and acting as secretary for the SPEC Church Leaders' Meeting.

Being lifted off the shelf of retirement to take on this fascinating (in theory part-time) job has had a rejuvenating effect. The family has acquired a computer, and if you are reading these paragraphs, it is because he has achieved an e-mail to The Times.

He looks for a resurgence of preaching. 'Though I am beginning to understand the fascination of the Internet and the ready information it makes available, I think people will ultimately prefer the personal contact. The sermon may need to be more dramatic than the traditional homily, and the preacher should eschew sprinkling abstract nouns around and seek instead to excite the imagination by picture-language (as Jesus did). When the preacher is already known to the congregation, the essential rapport is already on the way to being established.

'One of the changes during the years I've been preaching has been that although Christians are just as committed as they ever were, they actually attend worship less frequently. This may be partly due to greater mobility, with families living away and week-ends being

required for visits. There is also in some places a reluctance to tread the streets at night or leave a car outside church and vulnerable to vandalism. In preparing to preach in a particular chapel, the preacher may (and this one would seek to) visualize the members of the congregation each in his or her customary pew. Where the attendance is unpredictable, the rapport might be less readily achieved.

'However, I am now preaching in a greater variety of situations, and that has its challenges. Whereas a nonconformist preacher is usually responsible for the conduct of the entire service (and can frame it as a whole), the "guest preacher" at a service where the local priest presides, may climb to the pulpit "cold" (and be expected to be through in twelve minutes!).'

Text: James 5:10

As a pattern of patience ... take the prophets ...

Bible: Revised English Bible

Today's sermon is worth £40. Each.
But you can have it free.

It comes with the usual problems that a sermon has: that it's dead easy to assent to its basic idea with the top of your head and it's very difficult to let it make any difference to the way you live. And that goes for the preacher quite as much as for the congregation.

On the night of 4 November, at twenty minutes past 10 o'clock, I was travelling back through Huntington when there was a bright flash just by the side of the road.

'These stupid idiots with their premature fireworks', I thought. 'They ought to be reported to the police.'

But the police know all about what was going on in Huntington at 10.22 p.m. on Wednesday, 4 November. And a couple of days later, a red letter arrived, saying that I had been caught on camera travelling at 42mph. And the £40 fine followed.

It has been an expensive way to learn patience. And irritating for someone who reckons to take the Bible seriously, who already knows perfectly well with the top of the head that if you want to know how properly to behave you don't seek to emulate the kings. (You thought road rage was something new: you've not heard of King Jehu!) Instead, you do well to pay attention to the prophets.

So I paid £40 to be taught that I must act more responsibly, but for you the lesson is freely available in today's epistle.

As a pattern of patience, says St James, take the prophets. We'll do that. How much time have we got?

You'd prefer me to be selective? Right, well, I've chosen four.

As a pattern of patience, take the prophets.

Take Amos.

He was a shepherd who might lead his flock by day, but at night he would be out on the hillside under the stars, wary but thoughtful.

I remember only one night up on Cannock Chase doing fire picket duty in the RAF, stomping round the coke compound on a frosty night cursing my luck. It was many years later that a star-struck old friend stood with me in Langdale pointing out Ursa Major and Orion's belt. But 28 centuries ago, there was Amos studying Orion and the Pleiades and the rest of the night sky and noting the disciplined movement of the heavenly bodies: and he was impressed also with the reliability of day and night and the regularity of the tides and the seasons.

And in his patient meditation Amos came to admire the God of nature and to understand something of the nature of God.

As a pattern of patience, take the prophets.

Take Hosea.

You've heard about his Mrs?

'That Gomer? Gone off again, hasn't she?'

'Moind yo, her wor a wayward wench when her wor a tainager.'

'And she's been trouble for him ever since she came to live in Market Street.'

'Ar! Her moight be the baker's woife, but hey doe [doesn't] know where her am!'

'Last time she ended up in the slave market.'

'Up? Down, I reckon: what did he pay for her?'

'15 quid, a sack of barley and a bottle of wine, the slag.'

'I don't know how he can have the patience with her.'

But he *has* got patience: haven't you seen him teaching that little kid of his to walk?

As a pattern of patience, take the prophets.

Take Jeremiah.

When he was gated from the Temple and forbidden to speak, he hired a professional writer, Baruch Neriahson, and dictated all the messages that he had been preaching for years, a considerable collection, but God's word for Jerusalem then. And then he got Baruch to take the scroll, all 30 feet of it, and read it aloud in public.

Well, the court officials knew they would have to report this to the King. But they were decent enough to confiscate the scroll but let Baruch go with strong advice that he and Jeremiah should disappear. And the scroll was taken to King Jehoiakim sitting in his winter-house with a brazier burning in front of him. And Jehudi, one of the courtiers, was instructed to read out Jeremiah's words. And as he did so, every time he'd completed three or four columns of the writing, Jehoiakim would take a pen-knife and slash the scroll into shreds, and he threw the entire book strip by strip on to the fire.

The arrest of Jeremiah and Baruch was ordered, but although these friendly courtiers told *them* what had happened to the scroll they informed the king that Jeremiah and Baruch 'could not be found'.

Now I won't tell you what I said last Sunday afternoon when I switched on my wordprocessor to put the finishing touches to this morning's sermon and found that somehow the night before I had wiped it all out. But do you know what Jeremiah said to Baruch when the only copy of his life's work, his record of what God wanted said, had been deliberately cut up and fired?

We'd have called down fire and brimstone on Jehoiakim – yes? I'll tell you what Jeremiah said ... to Baruch: 'Have you got your pen and ink? There's another scroll here.'

As a pattern of patience, take the prophets.

And on this day of course we must take John the Baptizer. To think of *him* as a pattern of patience, maybe we need to exercise our imagination. But I recall seeing a production of *Salome* (now, why was I watching that? Oh, I know!). The actor playing John was somehow below stage: you could hear him, but see only his fingers grasping the grating covering his prison.

Now if the reality was anything like that, think of this rough character, one of the wildest outdoor types there ever was. Tanned to dark leather by the sun, unkempt and exultant in the storm, in the heat leaping naked into his Jordan to wash off the desert sand, familiar with the feral sights and sounds and smells of the countryside, delighted to stone-bake fresh-netted locusts, guzzling his cannily-collected wild honey. This free agent has been incarcerated in a disused well, dropped down into a stale-stinking black hole. Fed by the occasional crust when a friend has dared to visit, and yet, there keeping his integrity, uncompromising in his condemnation of the adulterous Herod Antipas, and politely hoping that his living has not been in vain:

'You are the One we're waiting for, aren't you?' is the patient question he sent to Jesus.

As a pattern of patience, take the prophets.

Learn from Amos to use times of inactivity, sleeplessness, or traffic jams for meditation and prayer.

Exercise understanding and forgiveness like Hosea when people whom you have trusted let you down.

Seek like Jeremiah to cope gently when your creativity or your constructiveness is aborted either by accident or by someone's deliberate viciousness.

And if your way of life suddenly is disorientated, like the Baptist's was, and you are in the control of others, then seek to remain calm and collected and attain what has been called the 'stature of waiting'.

Now just very rarely I come home from a meeting at which I have learned before Hilary has that somebody we know has had a baby and *I'm* able to tell *her* that mother and child are both all right. Then I get quizzed:

When did it happen?

Did she get to hospital all right?

What was the baby's weight?

What are they going to call ... ?

She even expects me to remember whether it was a boy or a girl! And I get told that I've 'come with half a tale'.

But you are too polite. You should really have been jumping up and down by now, accusing me, in this message, of having 'come with half a tale'. But don't worry, you've only had £20's worth so far.

In thinking of the prophets as a pattern of patience we need to raise the question: Hey! What about when ... ?

So, what about when ... ?

Amos came in from God's country to man's 'civilization'?

He saw nagging women lolling in decadence on couches inlaid with ivory, swigging wine by the bucketful: 'Cows!' he called them. 'You're for the refuse tip!'

He lambasted the traders for cheating with weights and measures and demanding Sabbath-opening and wanting to work on Christmas Day!

He damned a father for leading his son into a brothel. And 'Hey, you: you've come into town from your holiday cottage: that was a human being you've just tripped over lying on the pavement!'

He spoke out publicly from the steps of Bethel's shrine:

'Why are you ruining the farmers?'

'How come you're selling your fellow-Israelites as slaves?'

'See those surveyors testing to determine if that wall is perpendicular? The Lord will set a plumbline against your lives to test if you are going *straight*, to see if you are *upright*; 'cos to me you look *bent*; you're *crooks*!'

'And with all this you *pretend* to be religious with your "Songs of Praise"and your ostentatious donations.'

'See that? There's a message there! That man with a basket of summer-fruit? God will bring you to a *summary* end! All your psalms and your charity stink *if* the orderliness ordained by God does not permeate this disorderly society!'

As a pattern of patience, take the prophets.

What about when . . . ?

Hosea wants the nation to understand how monstrous is their unfaithfulness to the God to whom they are covenanted. He has the terrible idea of naming his children with his message, so that every time he calls them his point is driven home.

He saddles Gomer's elder son with the place-name of a massacre. 'Come on!' he shouts at cock-crow, 'It's time to go to school. Get up, Dunblane!'

To the girl he gives a name which means 'Unloved'. 'Come along in, Anathema: your tea's ready!'

And the little toddler, who may well not be Hosea's son, gets utterly disowned: 'Get to bed now, you Bastard!'

Providentially, Hosea learns from this distressing marriage of his that if he, a mere man, can find it within himself still to love and care about this faithless slut, then God, being God, must for ever be seeking to restore his relationship with his wanton nation.

So his word has to be as good as he is.

He changes the messages broadcast each time the children are named.

The eldest is called by a name that means 'God provides': instead of Dunblane, something like Eden (Edinburgh, perhaps!). Unloved becomes Loved: Anathema becomes, say, Desirée. And the one-time Bastard is now properly acknowledged: Sonny.

Of course by our reckoning his method is appalling. But the urgent need to stir the national conscience, to disturb complacent people and to challenge evil-doers is highly commendable.

As a pattern of patience, take the prophets. What about when . . . ?

Jeremiah expressed his exasperation at the gates of the Temple?

'It's no good pouring in and out of these gates declaiming your words and spending your energies on this building!' he says. 'It's how you *behave* that matters.

'Are you treating people fairly, acknowledging each individual's worth? How in your society do you treat the immigrant or the incomer, or the person who is of a different orientation? Are you caring for the children of single parents? Are you looking after those whose partners have died? What have you really made your god . . . on what do you mainly spend your time and your energy and your money? You ignore half the commandments and you think you're OK because you spend half your time in church!'

Jeremiah presents God as telling him that these people are so mixed-up about matters of religion that really he needn't bother even to pray for them any more.

As a pattern of patience, take the prophets.

And what about when . . . ?

John the Baptizer excoriates the religious prigs at the back of the crowds who have come to Jordan to confess their sin. 'What are you doing here, you snakes? Who *do* you think you are? You imagine you're something special because of your Hebrew pedigree; you think you're *it* because Abraham was your progenitor?'

I see coarse John picking up two small round pebbles, to chuck on the floor.

'You fools, God can produce children for Abraham from *these* stones! Put yourselves right with God before the Day of Judgement comes!'

As a pattern of patience, take the prophets.

That pattern demonstrates that there is a time for righteous impatience.

Whenever like Amos, in society, in the world, we see things happening that cannot be part of God's intention for humanity; when like Hosea we really know that it is our responsibility to speak out and have to overcome our reluctance to make a scene; if, like Jeremiah, we see the church we belong to somehow getting wrong its priorities; and every time, like those targeted by John, we assume that the preacher's message is appropriate for somebody else but cannot possibly apply to us: then it's time as a pattern of patience to take the prophets, to take them to heart, and to give voice.

Whatever form 'standing up and being counted' takes, whether considered speech-making at church council, protesting in the union meeting, taking an unpopular stance at work, putting the alternative view over a pint in the pub, ringing up the local radio station to make a point, framing a letter to the *Express & Star*, taking ourselves to task, there are times when *we* need to assert a *prophetic impatience*.

One of our four urged that the qualities of the Divinity should pervade human society.

A few years back, I tried in verse to 'anglicize' Amos's message. I needed the name of a river, and I required a rhyme for 'love': on the Staffordshire/Derbyshire border I found the two in one.

> Let Justice roll down like High Force,
> And Righteousness flow like the Dove,
> Till humankind finds its true course –
> The arterial route for God's love.

But God's love is a strong and can be an impatient love, 'fit to burst'.

Amos knew the Nile. It was only a few days ago, however, that I learned of the power of the Dove. Driving (slowly and observantly) through Tutbury, we saw the sodden sand-bags in the street.

Great! Yes, let God's love flow like that!

Comment

Margaret Brearley: *'Brilliant. An arresting opening and interest sustained to the end. Highly original, witty, gripping, memorable. A biblical, fresh and individual approach to four Hebrew prophets. Outstanding use of language, with styles ranging from rhetorical to colloquial and dialect. At times earthy, well-earthed in ethics.'*

Finishing the Course with Joy

SERMON PREACHED BY THE REVEREND HARRY YOUNG
ON 11 JANUARY 1998, AT KINGSTON BAPTIST CHURCH,
SURREY, ON THE OCCASION OF A SPECIAL SERVICE TO
MARK HIS RETIREMENT AND FAREWELL AFTER MORE
THAN 50 YEARS IN THE BAPTIST MINISTRY

*The Reverend Harry Young, 79, and his wife Joyce have three sons
and six grandchildren. Brought up in Cumbria in the Open Brethren,
a grouping similar to modern Baptists, he left school at 18 to train as
a schoolmaster, teaching English and history. He became a
conscientious objector during the war and entered the Non-
combatant Corps, and by the time the war ended was qualified as
a lay pastor and a teacher. His first church as pastor was in Sipson, a
village close to Heathrow, and he continued working as a teacher in
Hayes, Middlesex when in 1955 he went to minister at Surbiton
Baptist Church in Surrey. The church was destroyed during the war,
and his induction took place the day it re-opened. In the meantime, by
1963 he had become head of department in a comprehensive school.
His next step was to read for a degree in English, history and
theology, studying part-time at Birkbeck College, London. When he
graduated in 1966 he had moved to become associate minister at
Duke Street Baptist Church, Richmond, Surrey.*

*In 1970 he was ordained and appointed part-time minister of
Kingston Baptist Church, while also working as a part-time lecturer.
Ten years later he retired from education and became full-time
minister at Kingston. Even though he retired in 1987, he remained
active in the Baptist Church, working still as a minister at Richmond,
Surbiton and Kingston.*

*Early last year, however, he and his wife moved to Westward Ho!
in Devon, and are now members of Bideford Baptist Church. The
publicity locally surrounding his being shortlisted has led to several
invitations to preach in churches near his new home. 'I was sitting
here moaning that I hadn't got any preaching to do when two friends
persuaded me to enter', he says. 'I was amazed to be shortlisted, not
just once but twice.'*

He believes preaching is a valuable educative tool. 'People love to

be challenged and taught, and we need to do more and more of that',
he says. 'We need to get to grips with the nitty-gritty of the Christian
tradition. But people don't just need educating, they must also be
inspired and uplifted. A sermon should also have aesthetic qualities.
Many preachers fail because they are too colloquial, too spontaneous
and impromptu.'

He believes the millennium is the best opportunity in a thousand
years of proclaiming Jesus Christ as 'God in human form; the
Messiah, Saviour of the world. This eminent fact must not be lost
amidst all the celebrations. We celebrate the birth of Christ.'

But he adds 'In evangelism where we are seeking to reach the
"outsider", preaching and worship must be attractive, relevant and
contemporary. An element of entertainment – music, drama,
audience participation, and especially with young people may be
acceptable. Worship, however, is not for our entertainment but for
the glory of God. The atmosphere is one of reverence, the music must
be as beautiful as can be provided, the dress appropriate to the
occasion, and importantly, the preaching – brief, challenging and
instructive in the manner and obligation of a Christian life.'

He says 'I am now retired, but visit congregations which vary
greatly: from where "two or three are gathered in His name", to
congregations in hundreds (rarely). People are less formal, organ
music yielding to groups of musicians, overhead projectors updated
with computer technology available. But one admires the enthusiasm
and sense of joy which prevails. It is contemporary and the effort is
made to meet the issues alive in society and – what is admirable – an
emphasis on human needs, at home and abroad.

'There is room for compromise in church life, providing where
possible, alternative styles. The impact of secular society is not
infrequently a "dumbing down" to coincide with what is fashionable.
I miss the richness and beauty of the English language, for example.
The Church risks too much conformity with the world.'

He has recently published a book, Understanding the Holy Spirit
(Autumn House), with a foreword by John Cole, formerly of the
BBC. His earlier book Major Themes from the Minor Prophets (also
Autumn House) is still available.

Text: Acts 20:17–38 (St Paul's farewell to the Ephesian elders)

Bible: Revised Standard Version

I am grateful to the apostle Paul for words which have become my
motto as we say 'Goodbye and God bless'. 'Finishing the course
with joy', however, has a double meaning for me. It refers to my

ministry, but since Joy is the name of my loving wife of 54 years, it also applies to my marriage!

Retirement is an open-ended word, a pause for breath, perhaps, before continuing the marathon of ministry in all its challenging diversity.

'Retirement isn't a good idea', said Lord King. 'What would I do?', he added, 'Sit on the QE II somewhere?'

'Live as though you are immortal', said Lord Weinstock.

'At my age', said Sir Ian McGregor, 'some men do gardening, some play golf, some chase girls, some just become cabbages. I do business!'

Those last words remind me of a certain boy of twelve who, when found by his anxious parents in the Temple in Jerusalem, replied 'Don't you know that I must be about my Father's business?'

'You are not finished yet', said a kind friend, and quoted encouragingly the Psalmist's words: 'The righteous flourish in the courts of our God ... they still bring forth fruit in old age; they are ever full of sap and green.'

Paul's farewell address to the Ephesian elders is surely one of his most emotional utterances. He speaks so fearlessly, living so independently, facing the future so gallantly. The address is threaded through with deep affection, though touched with apprehension about the future. Paul is on his way to Jerusalem. He looks back over his years of service with all humility, and in spite of tears and trials, he has, without shrinking, fulfilled his ministry. He has heard the Spirit's testimony of what may await him and he knows he may never see these dear friends again. It all adds poignancy to this wonderful farewell message. The ship will soon carry him beyond the horizon, the limit of our sights.

As I read St Paul's words, I discovered priceless jewels of truth which seemed so appropriate to this occasion also.

The first is *an unchanging message.*

To both Jews and Greeks, in public and in private, the gospel is a call to repentance towards God and faith in the Lord Jesus Christ. This is still the message for today: repentance, made without compromise, but with compassion, a call to make room for God, to make room for Jesus. A garish banner outside a public house in Surbiton bore the message 'No room in the inn – try the off-licence!' It was torn down – scarcely an act of vandalism, more of righteous indignation. The world prefers the off-licence instead of receiving Him who left His throne and kingly crown to come to earth – for me.

The second truth is the *unknown future.*

'I am going, not knowing what shall befall me', says St Paul. What someone called 'the ignorance of perfect rest', that is, not knowing what the future holds, but knowing Who holds the future! 'God holds the key of all unknown, and I am glad!' – words I have sung so often.

The third truth is an *unqualified ambition*. That is, to finish the course with joy. Using this familiar athletic metaphor, what matters most to the apostle is that he should complete the race, looking to Jesus, the author and finisher of faith. His Master endured the cross, despising the shame for the joy set before Him. Paul might well have sung the words 'It is the way the Master went, Shall not the servant tread it still?'

Bells of encouragement ring out when the winner reaches the last lap of the race, soon to cross the finishing line with leaps of joy. At the time when his departure from this world was imminent, Paul could confidently say 'I have finished the course' – words of joyful triumph and quiet anticipation.

Paul's apostolic heart is revealed as he expresses *an unceasing care* for the church at Ephesus. He has never shrunk from declaring the whole counsel of God, nor has he ever faltered in his care and concern for the flock. He warns these elders of the fierce wolves, that is, the false leaders, who, by speaking perverse things, draw other believers after them. Such a grave warning is by no means irrelevant even now. He recalls his own experience when over a period of three years he exercised a self-supporting ministry, and then recovers words of the Lord Jesus, not previously recorded, *an unforgettable rule* that it is more blessed to give than to receive, retranslated helpfully as 'Happiness lies more in giving than in receiving'. Paul had given them his time and his talents without seeking any reward, save that of doing God's will. In our acquisitive, selfish world where so many are self-contained and undivided in their pursuit of personal happiness with little sense of community and social holiness, his message and example are very relevant now.

As Paul regards an emotional end to his 'tender, last farewell', he faces *an unavoidable reality* as, through his tears, he realizes that they will see his face no more. It will not be a tragic anti-climax, but a triumphant end. He will surely face martyrdom when eventually he reaches Rome, but his future is bright with immortality and a crown of righteousness awaits him. Death holds no terrors for Paul, nor for all who believe. As someone recently put it quite beautifully, 'Death is not the extinguishing of the light, but a putting out of a lamp because the dawn has come'.

'Let us treasure the time we have and resolve to use it well', wrote Viscount Samuel in his book, *An Everyday Philosophy*, and continued: 'Let us count each moment precious, – a chance to apprehend some truth, to experience some beauty, to conquer some evil, to relieve some suffering, to love and be loved, to achieve something of lasting worth.'

As we continue to run the race set before us, with Paul's moving words to inspire, caution and encourage us, may we also aspire, at whatever cost, to finish the course with joy.

Comment

William Beaver: *'Sprightly yet totally directional, this sermon is packed with "go thou and do likewise" common sense.'*

The Word is God

SERMON PREACHED BY IRENE AHRENS
ON 3 JANUARY 1999

Irene, 59, and her husband Gustav live in a second marriage, and between them have three children and one grand-daughter. Irene is honorary curate in Kew, Surrey, for two churches: St Philip's, also called 'the Barn Church' because it is a sixteenth-century barn, and St Luke's. Gustav, who worked for Agfa UK, retired early and works now for Relate as a counsellor.

Irene was born in Berlin, did a PhD in art history and then changed to the practical side of art and studied graphic design in Warsaw with Henry Tomaszewski. Coming to London, she first worked as a freelance designer, mainly for the design group Pentagram and for the Royal Opera House. Then she had a happy year as art director with Saatchi's. She still works from time to time as a free-lance illustrator. She achieved something near celebrity status with the angels she designed for the 1998 Christmas stamps, a commission from the Royal Mail.

'The death of my son, Jan, in 1980 brought me back to God, whom I had practically forgotten since my teenage years', she says. 'After some years it came as a surprise that God seemed to call me to the ministry. To test this vocation I studied theology and finished with a MTh in systematic theology from King's College, London.'

She was ordained deacon in 1995, and priested in 1996. 'My time with the two churches in Kew were some of my happiest times in my life. In January 2000 Gustav and I shall move to Berlin, though, because we want to see our grand-daughter a bit more before she is a teenager. I shall work as honorary curate again, this time with the Anglican church in Berlin, St George's, and Gustav will continue his work as a counsellor.

'I see what is traditionally called "spiritual direction" as part of my work as a priest. A better word for this is to be a "soul friend". I was trained to be a spiritual director and to give retreats in the Jesuit tradition by a three-year ecumenical course in Ignatian spirituality in Margaret Street, London.

'One of the great longings practically in every human heart is to be able to talk with someone about things spiritual in the widest

sense. A friend of mine once said: "One thing I long for is that every member of my congregation could speak with someone else on a regular basis about their faith and their doubts, their prayer life, or lack of it."

'In our society we talk about almost any topic. But imagine yourself at a dinner party saying to your neighbour at table: "Yesterday, as I prayed, I had an amazing experience of God." Or imagine yourself chatting to someone at an office party and complaining about your difficulties in prayer. It is simply not the done thing. And at the same time the spiritual hunger of almost everyone I meet is enormous, whether people overtly say so or imply it. People would find a lot of help being able to talk about the spiritual side of their lives. As an old lady of 81 said to me the other day: "Speaking of God gives you confidence that He exists."

'An important focus of parish life is for me the work with small groups. We use an adaptation of the so-called Alpha course in our parishes, a course in Christian basics. These groups consist of ten to twelve people who all take it in turns to prepare the presentation of a chapter of the Alpha course book by Nicky Gumbel, Questions of Life. This encourages people to look at the text very thoroughly and to come to grips with the questions raised there in a personal way. This makes the ensuing discussion in the group more interesting. These groups have developed into a number of small groups who continue to meet and have become friends.'

She believes that people cannot be expected to come to church as something taken for granted. 'The Church still plays a role on special occasions like baptisms, weddings and funerals, or as something like a family outing on Easter and Christmas. But church as an integral part of day-to-day or week-to-week life is only relevant for a minority. Therefore, I think that preaching is not the primary tool for spreading the Good News. Listening to sermons usually only comes when someone already had some kind of a conversion experience. But good preaching will always have an important role in the Church because we are never converted once and for all. We need conversion daily – so we need the work of God proclaimed and explained to help us in our on-going change of heart.

'But because the spiritual hunger of the so-called unchurched majority is so immense, there must be a wide-ranging activity of the Church: on personal and friendship basis like spiritual direction and small group work, as well as on a larger scale like Christian rock groups, or Christian music generally, evangelism in various forms and simple outreach in parishes to help people feel less lonely. The loneliness of the busy middle classes as well as the loneliness of the "unsuccessful" in whatever form you can think of is crying out for *community. And that is something the Church can provide in a natural way, across age and status borders.*

'*So there is an important place for preaching in the new millennium for people who are already on their way to God and need a weekly or monthly uplift and food for thought, even something that they may discuss with others. To help such discussion along, I started a monthly sermon-cum-discussion slot. I ask people to read the Gospel text used for the sermon in advance and to think of questions or experiences and feelings they would like to share.*

'*Another important aspect of preaching in the new millennium is, I think, to use the times when people who do not regularly come to church do come. Sermons for weddings, baptisms and funerals as well as Easter and Christmas sermons are so important because they are perhaps a rare opportunity to speak to the heart of someone who never hears the word of God otherwise. Such a sermon can be an invitation to look for something deeper, something more meaningful than everyday life on the whole can offer.*'

*But, she says, good preaching is not just done with words. '*Not even mainly. What the Church as a whole and individually does and is – that is the best sermon. I can think of dozens of people in St Luke's and St Philip's who preach the gospel beautifully, simply by being who they are. The centre of their lives is God and that speaks louder than words. But at some time the word has been preached to them in some form. And I know that these "walking sermons" do like a good sermon on a Sunday to lift them up and to act as something like a spiritual take-away for the week.*'

Text: John 1:1–18 (The Word)

Today I would like to speak about just one single word in our Gospel reading, about The Word. And with 'The Word' I would like to take you into the ancient world, to see what St John was doing when he called Jesus 'The Word'.

Christianity began as a form of Judaism, and all its first members were Jews. So the idea that with Jesus the long-awaited Jewish Messiah had finally arrived was indeed good and great news. But St John, who lived in Ephesus in what is today Turkey, wrote for a Greek as well as for a Jewish audience, and Jewish thinking was completely foreign to Greek thinking.

If St John had used St Matthew's approach and tried to prove that the Messiah had indeed arrived in Jesus by quoting widely from the Jewish Bible, the Old Testament, no Greek would have understood what he meant. Most people in Ephesus were not interested in any Messiah. Archbishop William Temple said that 'it would have been like trying to excite an English audience by proclaiming the arrival of the Mahdi, so fervently awaited by the Arabs'. (*Readings in St John's Gospel*, London, 1955, p. 4).

What was St John going to do in this dilemma? How was he to proclaim to Greeks and Jews alike that with Jesus something incredibly wonderful and great had happened? His inspired choice was the concept of 'The Word': the word he was looking for as – 'The Word'! Without naming Jesus in the Prologue, St John conveys that 'The Word' is what everybody was waiting for.

'The Word', *dawar* in Hebrew and *logos* in Greek, was a widely used concept, well known both in Palestine and in Greece. It had acquired a special status throughout the centuries, both for Jewish prophets and theologians, and for Greek philosophers and wisdom teachers.

Let me first look at the Jewish background of 'The Word'. The whole of the Old Testament shows that the Hebrew language saw in words much more than mere sounds. Words had something like an independent existence. A word was not just a soundwave, it did something.

The veneration Hebrew had for the spoken word becomes clear already from the first verses of the Bible: 'God said "Let there be light", and there was light.' The word of God does something. It creates. God creates by simply saying a word. God says 'Light', and light there is.

St John deliberately evokes associations with the creation story, when he starts his gospel echoing Genesis: 'In the beginning God created heaven and earth . . .' St John writes: 'In the beginning was the Word, and the Word was with God and God was the Word . . .'

St John speaks of 'The Word' as an independent agent, who was there before creation even began. 'The Word' was there as the creative power of God. By mentioning 'The Word' or 'The Word of God' he will have captured the attention of his Jewish listeners immediately. And as he goes on speaking about 'The Word' it becomes clear that this 'word' is a person. The question St John deliberately evokes is: 'Who is this word?' instead of 'What is this word doing?' So St John takes an astonishing step from 'The Word' as God's creative power to 'The Word' as God become man.

But for St John's Jewish audience there was still another association when the idea of 'The Word' was used. Already 100 years before Jesus, nobody spoke Hebrew any more. The spoken word among Jews was Aramaic. Aramaic compares to Hebrew like modern English does to Anglo-Saxon English. Hebrew was still used and read in the Synagogue, but for the people on a Sabbath it was always translated into Aramaic.

In these translations a significant change had taken place. While the Hebrew Bible quite daringly attributed human feelings to God, people of the time round about Jesus' birth who translated these texts into Aramaic were greatly concerned about God's holiness and that He therefore must be utterly and completely different from anything human.

Aramaic never spoke directly of God.

So wherever the Hebrew Bible says 'God', the Aramaic translation substitutes 'The Word of God'. For instance, Deuteronomy states that 'God is a consuming fire ...'. Already this is too irreverent for the Aramaic translators, so they say 'The Word of God is a consuming fire'. Or in Isaiah, God says 'My hand laid the foundation of the earth and my right hand spread out the heavens' (Isaiah 48:13). The Aramaic changes this to 'The hand of the Word of God laid the foundation of the earth ...'.

The great advantage for St John's task to express that 'Jesus is God become man' was that whenever St John used the expression 'The Word' or 'The Word of God' every pious Jew would have made the following connection: 'The Word of God ... well that means God, doesn't it?'

Let us look next at the Greek background. The concept of 'The Word' was already 600 years old when St John used it to reach his Greek audience. The Greek philosopher Heraklitos, who like St John lived in Ephesus, only 600 years earlier, was famous for his statement 'Everything flows'. With it he gave us a memorable picture. He said 'You can never step into the same river twice'. What he meant was that the water will have flowed on. So next time you put your toe in, it's already a different river.

But that was not the end of the story. Because if the only thing you could say about the universe was that nothing stays the same and everything flows, you would have chaos. But there is order in the universe. Heraklitos claimed that the reason for this order is an underlying Rational Principle that gives unity and significance to all that exists. Heraklitos called his Principle 'The Word' or 'The Logos'. The Greek word *logos* means two things: it means 'word' and it means 'reason'. And Heraklitos uses it to describe his idea of a divine principle that underlies the whole universe. This concept of 'The Word' had never lost its popularity during the 600 years preceding John's Gospel.

So when St John spoke about 'The Word' or 'The Word of God', he had captured his Greek audience too, because, following the evangelist's argument, they would have realized that he was announcing something amazing when he said: 'The word became flesh and dwelled among us.' A Greek listener of the time would have made the connection: 'The Logos, the mind of God, that orders everything, has become a person.' St John was claiming that all a Greek had to do was to look at Jesus and know the mind of God, the Rational Principle.

Imagine St John's Jewish and Greek audience. The Jews of the time held that you could not really say anything human about God. God was far too far away and much too holy. You had to paraphrase in order to speak at all about God. You had to say 'The Word of God' instead of God. Everybody knew what you were talking about, but you didn't really do it directly.

The Greeks of the time held a similar view. God or the 'divine principle' was far removed from the imperfect and changeable physical world, though it gave this imperfect world an underlying order and direction. 'The divine principle' or 'the word' was truth and goodness, everything else wasn't.

To use these Jewish and Greek concepts that describe both the far-removed and the unattainable, and to apply them to a human being, to Jesus, and say 'He is the Word, and the Word became flesh and dwelled among us', must have been simply amazing. And it must have been exhilarating and refreshing, inspiring and freeing.

The Jews had started to doubt. Did God really care for his people? Hundreds of years of foreign rule in Palestine seemed to speak against God's care. But if he, 'The Word of God', really became flesh and dwelled among them ... then he really cared, didn't He?

And the Greeks with their mythology of wild and immoral gods, who just masqueraded as humans from time to time to have a bit of fun, but never really cared ... or the Greek philosophers with their 'Divine Reason' that dwelled in unattainable spheres ... If this *logos*, this divine reason that ruled the world, really became flesh and dwelled among them, then 'The Word', the Logos, cared, didn't he?

Greeks and Jews longed for a God who cared and who was not far away. And so do we, don't we? We long for God to be close. One way of feeling God's closeness is to use language reverently, because God gave us brains to invent language. But as with all good gifts of God we can make good and bad use of it. If St John used the Greek and the Hebrew concept of 'The Word' in order to speak meaningfully about Jesus, perhaps we can imagine 'This Word' standing close by when we speak, encouraging us to speak gently and thoughtfully.

Let me end with the words God says to the prophet Isaiah: 'My word that goes forth from my mouth will not return to me empty, but it will accomplish what I desire, says the Lord, and it will achieve the purpose for which I sent it.'

Let us pray: Lord, please bless the words we shall speak in this coming year so that we, too, will achieve what You desire, a world that is more loving and peaceful. Let our words contribute to 'Your Word'. Amen.

Comments

Peter Graves: *'Good, clear, scholarly exegesis. Relevant to under-standing.'*

Margaret Brearley: *'Scholarly, highly informative – yet so transparently written that even a relatively uneducated congregation could enjoy this sermon.'*

An Angel on the Window Ledge

SERMON PREACHED BY NEIL BOOTH AT BOLTON ST
JAMES CHURCH, BRADFORD, WEST YORKSHIRE, AT
HOLY COMMUNION ON EASTER SUNDAY, 4 APRIL 1999

Neil Booth, 57, is a Reader in the Church of England and this is the second successive year in which he has been shortlisted for The Times Preacher of the Year Award. *Last year his entry was a Christmas sermon, this year it is an Easter sermon. 'I find that quite ironic', he says, 'because, as someone who used to belong to the Plymouth Brethren, I don't really believe in Festivals at all! I was taught to regard every day as Christmas Day, Easter Day, and so on. But, who knows, after this I'll probably submit a Pentecost sermon next year!'*

Neil has two children from a previous marriage and has just become a grandfather for the third time. He is married to Yvonne, who has had multiple sclerosis for the 21 years of their life together. Yvonne is sufficiently stable both to teach music at home and to share fully with Neil in ministry at St James, their local parish church. She plays keyboards in the church band and is generally involved there in all things musical while, at home, she helps Neil run a Thursday fellowship meeting. Such fellowships are, Neil believes, vital to the health of the Church and the only context in which serious spiritual growth can occur. 'That is where real Bible teaching takes place', he says. 'The sermon slot is no longer the place for it. It cannot be, with a time constraint of ten to fifteen minutes and a congregation which often includes baptismal parties etc., for whom references even to Paul, Calvary, grace, salvation and the like are utterly meaningless.'

Neil is a chartered accountant and was a partner with KPMG until, in 1994, he retired following a heart attack and a quadruple heart by-pass operation. For many years he was regarded as the country's leading expert on National Insurance and wrote a number of standard works on that subject as well as on other aspects of taxation. 'Lecturing professionally to many and varied audiences up and down the country helped me greatly in my Christian ministry', he explains. 'You cannot keep folk interested and entertained for hours on end with yawn-inducing subjects such as "Contribution Planning for Employers" without developing a colourful style of speaking that carries over into your preaching.'

Despite his belief that little serious teaching can take place in the sermon slot, Neil is convinced that there will always be a place for such a slot, provided it is used for preaching the gospel: 'The ending of one millennium and the start of another does not change that. The good news of Jesus does not become less good with the passage of time nor is there any less need for it to be proclaimed and heard.' But he insists that while the message remains the same, the way in which it is delivered must change so that the content of the message becomes as accessible as it can possibly be to each new audience. He quotes C. S. Lewis: 'You must translate every bit of your theology into the vernacular', and says that, for him, the 'vernacular' means not just the language of the group to be addressed but also its learning patterns and thought forms. He believes that this has always been true, but thinks that preachers probably need to take it to heart today more than ever before. Why? 'Because the first post-modernist generation is all around us – intuitive, informal, experience-orientated young people – and we, with our reasoned, structured, intellectual approach to the faith, are, by and large, failing to make any impact upon it.' As proof of this, he points to the established Churches. 'In the vast majority, the old and elderly predominate, the teens and twenties are conspicuous by their absence.' He suggests that there can be no greater challenge to any preacher standing on the threshold of the new millennium than this: How can I reach the members of 'Generation X' and communicate to them the good news of Jesus Christ? 'Unless by the Spirit of God we meet that challenge', he says, 'we shall not be far into the new millennium before all our churches are either heritage centres or carpet warehouses or worse.'

Neil himself is persuaded that one of the major communication tools that Christians ought to be mastering and using is the Internet. As well as his existing website (www.bbb.ndo.co.uk), which has been up and running for two years now and which includes all manner of Christian content, Neil is presently building a new and innovative site aimed particularly at Generation-Xers (members.spree.com/lifestyles/areopagus).

Text: Matthew 28:1–10

Bible: Revised Standard Version

I wonder if you will believe me when I tell you that there is an angel in church this morning? Back there … sitting on the ledge under the east window. Look carefully and you might just detect a shimmering in the air, a shifting of the light – though angels *are* difficult to see, unless they want you to see them.

This one is none other than the angel who featured in our Gospel reading a moment or two ago. Then (you will recall) he was sitting not on a window ledge but on a stone: the great circular stone that, in New Testament times, was rolled down a sloping track to come to rest across the entrance of a tomb. A stone that was designed to keep the body within the tomb safe from both man and beast, and that, once in place, could be moved only with the greatest difficulty. A stone that he, the angel, being an angel, had moved without any difficulty at all.

We are told that there are all kinds of angels, angels of mercy, guardian angels, recording angels, angels of light – but this one, the one watching us from the east window, is what I suppose we might call a 'waiting angel'. Two thousand years ago, in that garden near Jerusalem, his task was to await the arrival of four women, possibly more, and to give them a message: a message from God. That is what angels do, of course. It is what their name means. An 'angel' is a messenger.

Two of the four women were mentioned in that part of the Gospel according to Matthew that I read to you this morning. They were Mary of Magdala – a woman whose life had been dramatically changed by Jesus – and someone described as 'the other Mary'. In the Gospels of Mark and Luke, this 'other Mary' is identified as Mary, the wife of Clopas and the mother of two, possibly three, of Jesus' disciples: James the Younger and Judas, not Iscariot, and possibly also Simon Zelotes. Mark also tells us that Salome was there. Salome was a sister of Jesus' own mother, Mary, and the mother of James and John, two of Jesus' closest disciples. And Luke also tells us that Joanna was in the company. Joanna had been healed by Jesus and was the wife of Chuza, a steward in the royal household of Herod Antipas.

Of the four, the first three were certainly at Calvary and witnessed the crucifixion of Jesus, and Joanna may well have been there also. And Mark records that, of the four, the two Marys went with Joseph of Arimathea when he took the body of Jesus to the garden tomb, and saw where the body was laid. It is clear that they saw, too, the massive stone being released from its moorings so that it rolled into its place over the entrance to the tomb. According to Mark, as the four women made their way through the darkness before the dawn of that first Easter morning, that stone was the one thing on their minds. 'Who will roll away the stone for us?' they kept asking each other.

'Knowing the stone was there, why go at all?' we might ask. After all, Jesus was dead. He had been dead since mid-afternoon on Friday and it was now Sunday morning – almost 40 hours later. The third day. If they had wanted to anoint his body with spices, why had they not done so before the tomb was sealed? If they had wanted to pay a last visit, why had they not gone the morning after Jesus' death, on the Saturday?

The two questions have a single answer: the Law. The Law had prevented them from doing so. Jewish days began at six in the evening and ended at six the following evening. The Sabbath began at six in the evening on Good Friday, just a few hours after Jesus breathed his last; and during the Sabbath nothing whatsoever could be done.

Hence the rush to get his body into a decent place of burial before the Sabbath began. Hence the unseemly manner of that burial: the apparent failure to anoint the body with sweet-smelling spices that lessened the stench of decay in that hot climate. Hence, too, the lack of opportunity for these four heartbroken women to say their last, long farewell to the one they loved, in the quietness of the garden tomb away from all the noise and horror of Calvary.

And hence the visit now, despite the problem of the stone. The Sabbath had ended nearly twelve hours ago, at six on the Saturday evening, but by then night had already begun to fall. So now they were making their way to the tomb through the last of that darkness, timing their arrival for the breaking of the dawn.

The angel no doubt heard them coming as the first flush of pink lit the eastern sky. He heard Mary Magdalene, the youngest of the four women by many years, calling behind her in a loud whisper: 'Come on, this way. It's down here past that big olive tree.' And the other Mary saying 'Just hang on a minute. Some of us aren't as young as we used to be.' And then the angel did what I imagine all angels are able to do; as they arrived, he read their hearts and their minds.

That same angel – the one back there on the ledge beneath the east window – watched us too as we arrived here this morning. He watched me come in. He watched you come in. And just as he read the heart and mind of Mary Magdalene, of the other Mary, of Salome and of Joanna, so too he read my heart and mind and he read yours. He knew why each of those four women had come to the garden tomb. And he knows why you and I have come here this morning.

Sh! Listen. Do you hear him? He is speaking. 'Do not be afraid', he is saying. 'For I know that you seek Jesus who was crucified.'

That is what he said to the women. That is what he has just said to us. Has he got it right? Has he read my heart correctly? Has he read your heart correctly? 'I know that you seek Jesus who was crucified.' *Is* that why we are here this morning? Oh, I know that Easter Sunday is a time when even some folk who do not normally come to church come because they feel it is right to do so, but I doubt that anyone comes *only* out of duty. And I know that some will have come today as they have come other Sundays: full of need. Some will be here feeling lost and confused, dismayed by the way the world is going. Some will be here fearful for tomorrow, anxious for what the future holds. Some will be here stooping under burdens that seem too great for them to bear. Some will be here grieving silently, full of pain. If asked, you might say 'I am here to try and gain direction. I am here to try and find comfort ... courage ... peace ... strength ... hope.' Yes – but if we only knew it (as the angel does), we are all, in our heart of hearts, seeking Jesus who was crucified. Look at the Table. Here, in this place, the cross is always at the centre of our seeking, whatever it is we might think that we are looking for.

And for all of us, as for the women at the tomb, the angel has a message. He has some news, some *good* news which sounds (but only sounds) like bad news. He says 'He is not here ... I know that you seek Jesus who was crucified, but he is not here.'

What can the angel mean? In what sense can what he says be true? I mean, it is Easter morning and *we* know it. His words were for the women in their ignorance but they are surely not for us. Or are they? Pause for a moment, and consider. Is it not possible, even today, for us to come seeking Jesus but, like those four unhappy women, to come looking for him in the wrong place and in the wrong way? I think so.

Is it not possible, for instance, for us, today, to seek him in the traditions of our Anglican church in this building ... in its stained glass and mosaics, its frontals, its flowers, its vestments, its silver and carpentry and stone, and its music and singing? These things are all lovely and good. They enrich our experience of worship. They give us something of permanence to hold on to in a throw-away world. But if we are seeking Jesus in these things, we need to know, even as we stand within them – he is not here.

Is it not possible for us, today, to seek Jesus in the liturgy ... in the familiar patterns of words in collects, responses, canticles, creeds? Mellifluous sounds? 'Not as mellifluous now as in the days of the Book of Common Prayer', some would say, but mellifluous anyway. A proper frame for proper worship? Yes, indeed. No one in here will disagree. But from within that liturgy, if that is where we are seeking Jesus, we have to say – he is not here.

Is it not possible for us, today, to seek Jesus in the sacrament of bread and wine ... in Christ's own most holy institution, in that awesome enactment of the last supper which we repeat Sunday by Sunday until his coming again? Yet – dare I say it? – in whatever sense it might be true to say that Jesus is 'in' the bread and the wine of Holy Communion, it is also true to say that he is *not* in it. He is not in the wafer. He is not in the wine. They are what they are and that is what they remain. To say otherwise is to be in error. We eat and drink 'in remembrance that Christ died for us ... that his blood was shed for us'. So even from within this service of Holy Communion, if that is where we are seeking Jesus, we have to say: he is not here.

I could go on. He is not here in the Bible, though it is the very Word of God. And he is not here in all or any of these things because he is risen! Because he, Jesus, is alive. And a living Jesus cannot be mounted in the glass case of tradition like a butterfly on a pin. He cannot be captured in liturgy like a fly in amber. He cannot be swallowed in a wafer and a drop of wine like some magic ingredient. He cannot be trapped between the pages of the Bible. He is alive. That is the good news in the seeming bad news that he is not here.

How the women's hearts must have leaped at such news! They had come to remember a Jesus who had died. Now they were being told that their much-loved Lord and Master was alive. 'Where is he? Where is he?'

'He is going before you', said the angel. 'To Galilee.'

Now we are told that, at this, the women departed with 'great joy' – but I wonder. I wonder if their joy at the news that he was risen was not somewhat dampened by those words, 'to Galilee'. As they hurried out of the garden and down the road, were they not saying to themselves: 'Galilee! But that's 70, 80 miles away in the north. Where in Galilee? Bethsaida, Capernaum, Bethany, Cana? When in Galilee? What day? What time? How will he meet with us? The angel was right – we did come here seeking Jesus and we thought our searching was over; but now, it seems, it has hardly begun'.

'It has both begun – and ended', says a familiar voice. The women turn, startled, and see, in the first light of that glorious new day, the one they have most longed to see, the one who has conquered death and is alive again. 'And, behold, Jesus met them and said, "Hail!" And they came up and took hold of his feet and worshipped him.'

What can I say? If you have come here this morning seeking Jesus, let those wonderful words travel straight to your heart: 'Jesus met them.'

Perhaps Jesus had fully intended to meet neither the women nor his disciples until they had all safely returned to Galilee. Perhaps it was not that the angel had got it wrong but that Jesus had undergone a sudden change of heart. Constrained by the longing of those four women, moved with compassion for them, he could not conceal himself from them a moment longer. 'And, behold, Jesus met them and said, "Hail!" '

I am not even going to attempt to prove the resurrection to you this morning. If you want the evidence and you have a couple of hours to spare, I will give it to you. It is formidable. So formidable that, as Bishop Westcott once said: 'There is no single historic incident better or more variously supported than the resurrection of Christ.' But the evidence alone will only convince your head. It cannot convince your heart. Indeed, there is only one thing that convinces hearts that the resurrection is true: it is meeting the one who has risen. It is meeting Jesus. 'And, behold, Jesus met them and said, "Hail!" ' Try talking to those women about proofs of the resurrection. 'Proofs of the resurrection?' they would say. 'Why would we need proofs of the resurrection? We've just met Jesus. We've just been talking to him!'

And that, of course, is as true today as it was then, for those of us who have had our own personal encounter with the risen Lord. The angel in the east window may be a figment of my imagination – *may* be – but the risen Jesus most certainly is not. There are any number of people here this morning, myself included, who live out their lives in the reality of his presence. He was with us before we set off for church. He is with us now. He will be with us as we sit down for Easter lunch.

This is the truth of the resurrection; that once you have met him, once Jesus has become *your* risen Lord, he is everywhere and he is in everything. He is even in all the things where he was not. 'He is not here' but, yes, suddenly, he *is* here. He *is* in the tradition, the hymns, the frontals, the flowers, the glass. He *is* in the liturgy, the responses, the canticles, the creeds. He *is* in the bread and in the wine. He *is* in the Scriptures. And more than that, he is in you and with you, morning, noon, and night, waking and sleeping, living and dying ... being to you your comfort, your power, your guidance, your strength, your peace ... now and for ever more.

How do you get to meet him and to know him in that kind of way? You open your heart and mind to his risen-ness. You pray in faith the silent prayer: 'Jesus crucified and risen – meet now with me.' And you open yourself up to experience his real presence, an experience that will surely follow even the most faltering step of faith.

Let us pray.

Lord Jesus ... risen Lord Jesus. Be suddenly among us now as you were among those women in the garden. Meet with us as you met with them. Surprise us with your real presence. Speak to us a word of greeting. And grant that there may be those here this morning for whom life will never be the same again: those whose eyes are even now being opened to see you and whose ears are being opened to hear you and whose hearts are being opened to receive you. Amen.

Comments

Margaret Brearley: *'Lyrical, well-written evocation of Easter angels and the Resurrection.'*

Jonathan Romain: *'A powerful affirmation of belief. It recognizes the limits of rational argument and that personal encounter with God is what carries the faith forward.'*

Remembering the Spiritual

SERMON PREACHED BY RABBI HOWARD COOPER AT FINCHLEY REFORM SYNAGOGUE ON ROSH HASHANAH, 21 SEPTEMBER 1998

Rabbi Howard Cooper, a member of the rabbinic team at Finchley Reform Synagogue with special responsibility for developing spirituality programmes, works most of the time in private practice as a psychoanalytic psychotherapist. He has a particular interest in the interface between religion and therapy, and Judaism and Christianity, and over the last twenty years has written books, articles and reviews about a variety of psychological and spiritual topics related to these interests. He has reviewed both for The Tablet *and, more regularly, for the* Jewish Chronicle.

Religiously, he sees himself as a rationalist with mystical inclinations. He views the psychotherapist's art as being like that of a novelist: a fictive endeavour, a way of telling stories that makes some people feel better, some of the time. What religion and therapy share, for him, is their attempts at articulating the truths of the imagination and of the heart.

Is there a place for preaching in the new millennium? Does it need to change? 'There will always be a place for forms of storytelling which map out regions of feeling and consciousness which may remain unexplored within the flux of our everyday lives and mundane concerns. A good sermon stimulates us to think again, think more carefully, about the purposes of our lives. A good sermon should give priority to questions over answers. A question which takes us deeper into ourselves is a religious act. A question which provokes us to re-think a cherished (but unexamined) view (or prejudice) is also a religious act. We need too to be reminded that we have a soul – and challenged to consider how we stifle its self-expression. At their best, sermons can help us with some of these human tasks. And if in doing so they can help us to establish a connection (or re-connection) to the well-springs of our religious heritage – to texts, rituals, ideas from within the tradition – so much the better.

'To see ourselves as but one link in the great chain of struggling, questioning human beings, searching for new meaning in each

generation, can enhance our spirituality by evoking in us some humility as a counterweight to our ingrained narcissism.

'The post-modern sermon eschews the three forms of sermon as traditionally delivered: the "be good", "do good" and "feel good" approaches of sermons each have their own appeal, but the over-zealous promotion of virtue forces us to be more good than we can bear to be. The acknowledgement that religion is now a voluntary exercise within a world shorn of external forms of authority is, to my mind, a great freedom. It marks the beginning of a more mature religiosity.

'The authority of a post-modern sermon derives from its self-questioning stance, its eclecticism, its reliance on (for want of a better phrase) Keats's "Negative Capability" – when we are "capable of being in uncertainties, mysteries, doubts, without any irritable reaching after fact and reason".'

The person I feel sorry for is Peter Mandelson. (Yes, I know it's hard to believe). Tony Blair's fixer, spin-doctor-in-chief and of course, Minister for the millennium. With the building of the Dome, he's presiding over the most lavish spending anywhere on the planet for this forthcoming year 2000. When asked to explain the Dome's purpose he was quoted as saying: 'It's a chance for people to think about their society and hopefully improve it.' And how would this noble aim be achieved? Well, he added, the chief attraction would be an interactive computer game called Surfball. O brave new world that has such people in't!

But let's not pause too long on the poverty of imagination, the lack of inspiration, here, for this is not to be the only delight. We are also promised the thrill of an enormous steel ball drawn to earth by a giant magnet. (This is indeed an intriguing prospect for those of us who had previously supposed that large metal objects were drawn to earth by gravity.)

But this is a serious project, an educational project: the original plans included visitors walking inside the model of a man, 150 feet high, learning how the body works – or most of the body, since the man was to have no genital organs. (Bill Clinton, eat your heart out!) The plan has been modified since: it will now recline, all 300 feet of it, although it hasn't been determined yet whether it will be male, female or genderless.

In spite of such unhappy symbolism, the business world has been queuing up to sponsor the Dome. Most of the different zones – Learning, Communications, Work – have their corporate backers. One exception, though, is the Spirit Zone, which was supposed to encapsulate the religious and spiritual life of Britain. By the sound of things, this part is going to have to be greatly scaled down. I suppose that in a secular age that is more interested in the Teletubbies than the Torah, or the Trinity, this is entirely fitting.

And yet there is something surprising here. Because there is something else going on in our culture, here in the West, over this last decade or so: a hugely increased interest in things spiritual, a search to find more in life than materialism and its undeniable comforts. And this is really what I want to talk about today. For these days between Rosh Hashanah and Yom Kippur are traditionally a period of reflection, the time of the year when we are called upon to judge (today, Rosh Hashanah, also has another name: *Yom Ha-din,* the Day of Judgement): to judge where we are in our lives, to assess what we value, what we believe, where we place our faith, time to pause for a while from the headlong rush of our lives – its joys and disappointments, its achievements and frustrations – and consider the values and beliefs which do guide us and inspire us; but a time, too, to ask ourselves about shallow values, fraudulent beliefs, which we might also subscribe to.

The question is, though, how do we judge? How do we learn to discriminate between values and beliefs that are deep and lasting, and beliefs that, like junk food, are cheap, omnipresent, tempting, but are empty of real nourishment, real sustenance? How do we gain enough perspective to see what is going on? We are immersed in our culture – is it possible to stand aside for a few moments and look at what goes on around us, and inside us, to look with a gaze which is both dispassionate and yet still compassionate?

Let me take you on a short tour of this contemporary quest for the spiritual, the yearning for belief, our deep human need to see more in the world than meets the naked eye. Some straws in the wind, from this last year:

Following her death, Diana (that sad and vulnerable woman) has appeared in dreams and visions to the sad and the lonely. There's the *X-Files* phenomenon, the cult TV programme now a 'major motion picture', in which our mundane world is suffused with the paranormal. The bestseller lists this year have been headed with books full of spurious scholarship about Bible Codes, and phoney prophecies about apocalyptic happenings in the new millennium. There was Hillary Clinton turning to a spirit medium and miraculously talking to Eleanor Roosevelt; and even that good Catholic girl Cherie Blair adding to her wardrobe a crystal pendant with supernatural powers. And of course we've had Glen Hoddle and his faith healer – though personally in the World Cup I would have put my faith in those players who'd actually taken penalty kicks before.

Now in bringing these very disparate phenomena together like this

I'm wanting to point to something which is increasingly underlying our culture: the huge disenchantment with a world governed by the rational, the scientific, by logic and reason. A disenchantment with a world that tries to explain everything but solves so little.

Take healing, which is increasingly becoming part of contemporary Jewish life. Although there is a longstanding Jewish folk belief in healing, particularly within the Hasidic communities, healing used to be associated predominately with certain strands of Christian spirituality. But we now have Jewish healers here in this community; the Reform Synagogues of Great Britain have workshops on it; there's a regular clinic at West London Synagogue. Or what about so-called 'alternative' medicine? I imagine that most of us here have at one time or another consulted an 'alternative health' practitioner in an effort to deal with some problem we have, as part of our elusive quest for a sense of personal well-being. Again, we have several people here in the community whose work this is. I was amazed to read recently that in Britain there are now more alternative health practitioners (homeopaths, naturopaths, reflexologists, herbalists, acupuncturists and so on) than GPs.

Interestingly, many of these practices claim to be based on forms of ancient wisdom, and a knowledge of how our bodies function, how we function, which orthodox medicine is said to have overridden or ignored, or even (in the more paranoid versions) suppressed. The language of complementary health is often spiritually tinged and quite seductive: the claim to work 'holistically' to treat the 'whole' person, to help us achieve 'balance' and 'harmony'. Even though orthodox medicine is the fruit of rigorous scientific research and methodology and something which has transformed the quality of our lives during this century, it is hard pressed to compete with the sub-religious appeal of harmony, balance and wholeness.

This disenchantment of ours with the rational and the scientific runs quite deep. At the end of the last century many well-informed people thought that science was virtually complete. Man – and it was predominately *man* – had uncovered almost all the secrets of nature, and now knew practically everything there was to be known. A hundred years later, our own perspective is rather different. We might today on Rosh Hashanah be celebrating the creation of the world, we even have a number for it, 5759, but we know this is poetic, mythic. We don't believe it literally. We know that the world has been around for two billion years – although we ourselves, *homo sapiens*, appeared only half a million years ago. It did take us a moment or two to find our feet (there being now only two of them). But just recently we managed to invent agriculture, the wheel, nuclear fission, microwave ovens, gas chambers.

Far from the work of science seeming near an end, at the end of this century we both observe and foresee dramatic changes ahead. But this creates in us quite an ambivalence. On the one hand there's an excitement at the potential opening up. But sometimes some of the consequences of science feel quite frightening. We know that one huge set of problems is environmental. Here in the synagogue we might use symbolic language, metaphors, of God as creator and ruler, in charge of the heavens and the earth, but how are the atmosphere and the ozone layer going to cope when a billion Chinese have cars and fridges? Although sometimes science appears to be on the verge of helping us gain greater control over the environment, technological advances are also seen as threatening it.

More intimately disturbing, perhaps, is our acquisition of godlike powers over the making and shaping of parts of nature: of plants, of animals, of human beings. Do we have the moral preparation to use these powers wisely, if indeed we should use them at all? There is plenty here to cause anxiety. Whether it's the assault on the environment, or biomedical/technological breakthroughs, or the insidious, demanding authority of new technologies (of which the Internet is a prime symbol), never before have we been faced on so many fronts at once with such potential transformations within society. And let's not forget economic globalization, where the power of technology to eliminate time and space means that financial insecurity that starts in one far-off part of the world like Thailand can sweep across the planet like a speeded-up contemporary version of a medieval plague from the East. The microchip-driven bacillus of economic instability can bring mighty nations to their knees. Is it not a fantasy to think that we can remain immune to this disease? We've come to believe that there's no problem big enough that decent marketing can't solve it. But the challenges of these four areas – biotechnology, environment, new technologies, economic globaliza-tion – are ones which cannot be met through the beguiling arts of marketing and spin-doctoring.

I think it's too easy, too convenient, to lump these phenomena together and say that the anxieties they do generate in us are all part of some pre-millennium fever. That precisely arbitrary moment, the arrival of the year 2000, will (as Auden once said of poetry) make nothing happen. We are going to have to learn how to live with the consequences of these scientific and technological revolutions regardless of which year our calendars say it is. Rather than the sense of something ending, we see vast new spaces opening up before us, and it is this vastness, that newness, that unknowness which in different ways excites us, and scares us.

But all this knowledge, all this information, all the achievements of the scientific and technological world, the triumph of our rational mental faculties, brings in its wake the disenchantment. In spite of it all, and the benefits we derive from it, we may still feel something's wrong, something's missing, something's been lost along the way. The spiritual – that mysterious and elusive dimension to existence that can't be measured, can't be created in a test-tube, can't be manufactured, can't be produced at will, that defies logic and rational explanation and all those tidy categories that reason loves to draw – the spiritual is what more and more seem to crave, to be drawn to in one form or another.

If we look into ourselves here today and ask why we've come to the service, I'm sure we could find a whole mixture of reasons: a sense of duty, or habit, or guilt; a wish to feel a sense of belonging, of connection to a community; to see friends; family reasons, maybe to do with parents, or partners, and if you have children, a wish to pass something on, a sense of responsibility to tradition, continuity; you probably don't feel particularly strongly 'This is what God wants me to do' though you may feel 'This is what Jews do' – or are supposed to do. Some permutation of these kinds of motives probably brings us here year by year. But I would suggest that underneath it all, whatever the conscious or half-thought-out reasons, there is something else which stirs, something else which may not have a name: something buried in you which has not yet quite given up hope that after all, after all you've had to bear through the years, after all we as Jews have borne though the ages, maybe there is something else, some intangible, concealed dimension to existence, beneath the rational, beneath the visible sheen of the material world – that the spiritual dimension to existence is real, is here and now and present and possible to touch, to feel, to know. That you could be moved, that you could experience, if only for a moment, the spirit, that nameless energy which our people have met and wrestled with through their history, that nameless One who has been called by so many names. Isn't this also why you are here? To remember and reawaken that hidden part of yourself. To recall your soul.

The problem is that traditional religion, synagogue religion, the religion of our services with their lofty words and tuneful melodies (or fairly tuneful), our services with their conventions and order and page numbers may kill the spirit, stifle the spirit, rather than liberate us to find the spirit – or be found by it. The problem is not confined just to Judaism: synagogue and church membership and attendance is falling throughout the Western world; but the vacuum which is then created in our souls, our souls still thirsting for contact with the unseen, with the spiritual, this vacuum is being filled with that myriad of alternatives that I began to speak of before. The trouble is that in the search for what goes beyond the rational, our neediness makes us susceptible to the irrational, to all manner of pseudo-substitutes for the reality of the spiritual, of the spirit of God. As the rigour of thought and the discriminating values of traditional religion wane, all manner of hocus-pocus, of the seemingly miraculous, of the supposedly supernatural, floods the market place. As the soul's hunger grows, the intellect is abandoned.

And this suspension of thinking means that people will believe in literally anything, from witchcraft to shamanism, alien abductions, the power of the stars, crystal balls, reincarnation, palmistry, Tarot cards, tea leaves. When you suspend your critical and rational thinking you can and will believe whatever you want to believe. Suspend the intellect and anything is possible: cancer can be cured by healing hands; God's name appears in vegetables; statues bleed; Jews murder Christian children and use their blood to bake matzot for Passover; killing Palestinians or your Prime Minister is religiously sanctioned; holiness resides in stones and walls and land, rather than what happens on the land between those who live there.

We, here, of course – we're a Reform community, intelligent, middle-class – probably pride ourselves on our lack of susceptibility to such deranged folly, our freedom from pre-Enlightenment super-stition and magical thinking. But I wonder what vestiges we do retain. How do we learn to discriminate, to use our God-given minds to sort out what is true from what might be wished for but is fantasy rather than reality? How do we learn how to discriminate between that spiritual dimension which is real, but beyond the rational, and all kinds of irrational phenomena? If we put that question in a traditional way, or rather using traditional language, we could ask: how do we learn to distinguish between the presence of God, *Adonai,* the One-Who-Is, and false gods, false beliefs? The battle between the God of Israel, the Holy One Blessed be He, our God who exists in our tradition with a myriad of names, one of which is Emet, Truth, the battle between that God of truth and justice, and the false gods – the idols we create and manufacture and conjure up and wish to put our faith in because they comfort us, they make us feel secure, because they give us what we want, which is hope, above all, hope – this ancient battle is far from over. We still fight it, inside ourselves. We need to fight it. This is our task, a holy task, as Jews, to learn to discriminate between what is true and what is false. Between God and idols. Between the pseudo-spiritual and the real, but enigmatic, Spirit of God.

Surrendering our intellects is a sacrifice we should not have to make in our search for food to nourish our souls. But it's not just all these substitute spiritual phenomena which ask us to suspend our capacities to think rationally. I said before that traditional religion is, and has been, declining in the West, but we know that all three of the monotheistic faiths have groupings within them, growing in popularity, who have adopted a fundamentalist, or better to call it a literalist, stance to their faith traditions. Judaism, Christianity and Islam all have growing numbers of adherents who are attracted to the feel-good certainties on offer from these sects. Based on a selective reading of their religious traditions, these groups claim to have the answers, the answers to all life's questions. What these groups share is an approach to faith which places more value on the emotional gratification of their followers than on developing their thinking capacities in relation to their faith. Of course it's wonderful to have a strong emotional attachment to one's religion, but when this attachment also requires the abandonment of historical and social and self-critical perspectives on one's own faith tradition in favour of uncritical devotion – then we need to stop and think. Because this discarding of history and scholarship is a failure of truthfulness, a failure to stand on that very narrow bridge of faith which risks facing uncertainties, paradoxes, ambiguities, a faith which acknowledges the mystery of being bound up with a God who is hidden, enigmatic, quixotic, a God of surprises, of hints, of allusions.

Nobody can tell you where your search for spiritual richness has to take place – it can take many forms: your search for moments of insight, moments of clarity, of well-being, of intimacy and connectedness, of a calm knowing, of quiet understanding, of seeing something you have been struggling with for so long suddenly appear quite differently; moments of seeing someone, or yourself, in a new way, moments where estrangement gives way to love, moments of illumination, moments of revelation.

Moments like those we will read about shortly in the Torah, when Abraham and Sarah's Egyptian handmaid Hagar, rejected and abandoned, wanders in the desert with her child, and as she sinks into a well of hopelessness, of despair, suddenly hears deep within herself a voice, a question, a whisper of a voice which asks *ma lach, hagar*, 'What is there for you, Hagar?' What is here, for you? A question we ask ourselves today. What is there here, for you? And she opens her eyes and sees a well of water. She sees what has always been there, but she was unable to see before reaching that low point, that point of nothingness, no hope, no belief, nothing. Then hearing in the silence of the desert, in the barrenness and bleakness of her situation in life, in the midst of that life which was no life at all, hearing a question, and opening her eyes, and seeing life bubbling up in front of her. And call it a miracle, if you want.

Nobody can tell you where the spiritual is going to be found. You may need to go to Tibet. But you might also find it closer to home. You may find it in your home. You might even find it in a synagogue. Of course we all want to be told where it can be found, how it can be found. But I have to disappoint you. The best I can do is what I am doing today: share some of my doubts about some of the places, some of the ways, where people with much conviction say it can be found, *know* it can be found.

The rabbis of old called today, Rosh Hashanah, *Yom Ha-Din*, the Day of Judging. But they also called it *Yom Ha-Zikkaron*, the Day of Remembering. Without memory there can be no judging. As the New Year begins we are engaged in a drama of individual and collective remembering. Life moves us on, but in our moving on we carry with us the remembrance of things past. When we hear the sound of the shofar we remember where we have come from historically, as Jews, as part of a covenanted community bound into a relationship with the divine. Through the liturgy we remember that we are a special part of creation, with a task and a responsibility: the struggle to bring the Spirit into our own lives and the lives of others. Through our own private memories we recall the unique contours of our own lives: what we have done well, what we have failed to do.

So this is the Day of Remembering. Without memory we become prey to anything that sounds convincing, feels good, seems plausible in the moment. Amnesia has its comforts. But our responsibility as Jews is to resist the encroachments of an Alzheimer society. Without memory we cannot give life the continuity it needs. Without memory the human spirit has no container for all it has experienced of value, no basis for judgement, no basis for discrimination. This is why the ritual of the New Year is still of significance for us, why we need it: whenever we touch into the world of ritual we sense that the thread of our own lives is part of a tapestry whose borders we do not see, a tapestry the picture of which we may only glimpse out of the corner of an eye, a tapestry which is still in the making after more than 3,000 years. The Jewish people have memories thousands of years old. Sometimes we are hated for it by those who wish to erase the past, but our destiny is to be the rememberers when others wish to forget.

I'm not talking, though, about false memories, memories which create comforting fictions which can provide a kind of pseudo-identity. I'm not talking about nostalgic, idealizing remembering, where memory, as Samuel Beckett said, 'is only another name for invention'. I'm not speaking of Jewish memory as Fiddler-on-the-Roof nostalgia, our very own Jewish false memory syndrome. We can use our simplified, sanitized, sentimentalized versions of the past as another country to inhabit, a mental space safe from the unsettling chaos of now. That kind of remembering is a way of avoiding living in the present, with its demands and problems and conflicts.

I'm speaking of a different kind of remembering, today on *Yom Ha-Zikkaron*, the New Year Day of Remembering. Our history, our traditions, our rituals, our texts help us remember that we are bound up within rhythms larger than our own individual lives. We remember that, like it or not, we have a task, a destiny. We remember that we have a soul. And we remember that disharmony and fragmentation, pain and loss, are as real as love and hope and cannot be airbrushed out of history, or personal lives, by wishful thinking or spiritual mumbo-jumbo.

We are the people of memory. Today, may the oil of memory feed the wick of life. May our judging and remembering be recorded in the Book of Life, for a good life, and a good year.

Comment

Peter Graves: '*The reality of the spiritual search and the importance of remembering clearly argued.*'

Does God Like Me?

Sermon preached by Mike Holdsworth at Ranelagh Road Christian Fellowship, Felixstowe, on Sunday 6 February 1999

Mike Holdsworth, 52, is married to Sue, and lives in Suffolk, where they are both members of their local Baptist church. Their two children are away from home at various stages of university education.

Their married life began in the RAF: ten homes in ten years, and nearly as many churches in almost as many denominations. 'Christian fellowship in the Armed Forces has wonderful qualities of warmth and immediacy because people often have no idea where they will be in a few weeks or months.' One lasting result has been his appreciation of different Christian traditions, which inspired a study of comparative religion as part of an Open University degree. Mike believes that any public-speaking skills he has stem from a mixture of staff training and observing others. His best critic is Sue, and his worst fear is to bore his listeners.

Another legacy from the Services has been his ongoing involvement with the use of hovercraft in developing countries. He was treasurer of the successful 1990 British Hovercraft Expedition to China, and as a director of The HoverAid Trust is currently planning to link communities by hovercraft on the Zambezi in western Zambia. 'Add to this a fulfilling career in facilities management and studying for a MBA, time for preaching is – at least currently – strictly limited. The one engagement I never turn down is to speak at our local Young Offenders Institution – one of the most stimulating environments for any preacher.'

Is there a place for preaching in the new millennium? 'Emphatically yes. The New Testament teaches that while time remains, preaching endures as a God-inspired method of sharing good news. At the heart of preaching we are dealing with relationships – broken, messy, restored and transformed ones. This seems to me to be one spiritual soap opera that will run and run. People and human nature are not about to change, and thankfully, neither is Jesus Christ.'

But he rejects the suggestion that preaching (and worship) don't therefore need to move with the times. 'The last twenty years have seen tremendous changes in worship patterns and evangelism. There have been real attempts to make the approach more culturally relevant. While traditionalists of every denomination will usually find their niche, mainstream churches ignore contemporary issues at their peril. Churches, like society, can suffer from information overload. One of the jobs of a preacher is to sift and distil all the conflicting messages in society with sensitivity and simplicity – even when he or she is only too aware they don't have all the answers.'

He feels strongly that one thing about a sermon can never change whatever millennium we are living in: it belongs to God, not the preacher. 'Without this recognition, it becomes little more than an academic lecture. Ability and technique are secondary to the preacher's role as the channel for God's message. In this sense, preachers merely need to deliver "more of the same". But in other areas, changes in congregations introduce new challenges for preachers and leaders.'

He says 'Churches, in my experience, are now far less complacent about the future, even though the millennium is a significant milestone and celebration. This is because many are waking up to the fact that they have been in a shrinking market for decades: attendances are down, buildings out-dated, leadership and cash are in short supply, and survival has become a real issue. This can concentrate the mind wonderfully, with the effect that some congregations are, as a consequence, more discerning of humbug in the pulpit; platitudes, worn phrases and clichés no longer work. The phenomenal success of the Alpha course is one evidence of the way many churches are moving their agenda from retrenchment to growth. Preaching, in a general sense, is embracing a far wider range of media, and through the Internet is acquiring a truly global dimension.'

He mentions two other discernible trends. Churches are becoming better organized. This is a spill-over from business methods and technology. Mission statements, five-year plans and management structures seem commonplace. Yes, there are benefits, but sometimes the 'professionalism' that treats a church more like a business sits uncomfortably alongside the 'creative informality' of the congregation. 'In our business processes at work we might challenge a prospective supplier to "Tell me something I don't know". The preacher often has the equivalent hard-nosed challenge of leading the congregation on a voyage of discovery and revelation.'

He finds congregations are far more eclectic than they used to be. 'In the open spaces of Suffolk, long-term changes in the rural economy have taken a heavy toll on village life and church congregations. As a result, some people think nothing of travelling

*twenty miles to attend a town church or fellowship considered to
have a more viable future. The quality and acceptability of the spoken
word is very often a deciding factor about where people will throw in
their lot – or move on to new pastures in a different fellowship or
denomination'*

Text: Ruth 1

Bible: New International Version

I recall hearing or reading some years ago about the way Christians
should witness to people around them. I can't remember the exact
words, or even who said them, but it was along the lines that you
don't have to like someone to love them. I suppose that subtle split
between loving someone or just simply liking them has always slightly
bothered me. I could always find plenty of people I liked, and
generally they happened to be the ones I loved, maybe because they
returned my love. It was hardly ever the other way round – people
that I didn't like, I didn't find much inspiration to love. Most likely
that the fault lay in me, not the theology. But this morning we are
asked to turn this question on its head, and put ourselves in God's
shoes. Not just: does God love me, but: does he actually like me?

Mike Yaconelli, the Christian teacher with what these days is
called 'attitude', has written

> I've always known God loves me, but I've wondered to myself
> whether God really likes me. Does he like my emotions and my
> ups and downs? Does he like my imperfections and my
> craziness? Does he like me? I don't want to hear that he loves
> me; I want him to say that he likes me and enjoys being around
> me. (Quotation from 'Does God like me?' from *All-Age Salt*
> material produced by Scripture Union for the first quarter of
> 1999)

Now, we are going to tackle this question through a case study. In
the book of Ruth, that little book tucked away in the early part of the
Old Testament between Judges and Samuel, we find the extraordinary story about the friendship between Naomi and her
daughter-in-law Ruth. This morning I want to think particularly
about Naomi, who in this first chapter we find returning home to
Bethlehem, totally disillusioned, from the land of Moab.

The land of Moab is that area east of the river Jordan and Dead
Sea. It's not often that the country of Moab is in the news, but if you
have read the newspapers or listened to the news this past week you

will realize Moab, or as it is called these days, the Kingdom of Jordan, has experienced great sadness with the terminal illness of King Hussein. And so is ending the latest volatile chapter in the history of Moab's relationship with Israel. Most of you will remember the 1967 and 1973 Arab–Israeli wars, and more recently the Camp David peace deal. Back in the 1960s and 1970s who would have expected an Arab to call an Israeli 'my friend' – but that was the tribute King Hussein gave the assassinated Israeli leader Yitzhak Rabin. And that is the way it was between Moab and Israel in Bible times. An unfriendliness and enmity, often breaking out into open warfare. Two neighbours who only wished each other ill. But here and there down history, Jew and Moabite came together in extraordinary acts of kindness and sacrifice, when they truly called each other 'my friend'.

The jewel of those friendships has to be the one we read of in the book of Ruth between Naomi and her daughter-in-law Ruth – a friendship that broke all the political and religious rules, but carried God's special blessing. But like the sadness in the land of Jordan today, the story of Ruth opens with a death in the family – in fact not one death, but three. We read the story of how famine forced a young family to flee from Bethlehem to Moab. But after a while the husband died, leaving the widow Naomi to care for their two sons: not an easy thing without a social security net to fall into. Fortunately, Naomi's sons were able to marry local girls, Orpah and Ruth. But earning a living was hard work, and after ten years, both sons also died, leaving three widows all alone, which in those times meant no money, no food, no livelihood.

Then Naomi heard that there was food again in Bethlehem, and decided to return home on her own, leaving her two daughters-in-law to find new husbands in Moab. But Ruth wasn't to be put off: where Naomi went, she would go. Naomi's people would be her people, Naomi's God, her God. And so the two friends journeyed to Bethlehem, where all of Naomi's pent-up grief and disillusionment spilled over. 'Don't call me Naomi [meaning "pleasant"], call me Marah [meaning "bitter"], for the Almighty has brought misfortune upon me.' It seemed obvious to Naomi that God didn't like her, or none of this misfortune would have occurred.

Have you ever felt like that? Have you? When it seems that despite all your best efforts, the cards in the deck of life are stacked against you? Just when you think you've cleared your debts, along comes another bill. The job-for-life suddenly folds. Serious illness strikes a loved one, or an accident threatens to mar the rest of your life – and we say cynically 'Someone up there doesn't like me! It isn't fair!'

The question whether God likes me is another matter that has also occupied the newspapers during the last couple of weeks. I'm sure it hasn't escaped you that last week the England football manager, Glen Hoddle, resigned over some ill-judged comments about disabled people. Whatever he meant to say, the impression he gave was that physical or mental disability is God's retribution, punishment for sin – and not just our own sins, but the sins of a previous life.

But how do you define disability? What do I say to someone who, as a policewoman, developed epilepsy after being attacked with an iron bar? Or a woman who is bent double with a hunchback, because as a child she contracted polio? Or the husband who loses his wife in a car accident, leaving him with two young children to rear? Aren't all these people really in the same category? And aren't we in danger of saying this is the way God judges us – all of us?

If we're rich and good-looking, without a care in the world, then God obviously loves us – and surely must like us. But if life is a struggle against the odds, if nasty things happen to me, then God might love me, but he doesn't really like me. But if we start to think about it, isn't that often the experience of most of us? That life *is* unfair. That things do go wrong without a reason – don't let's kid ourselves. There is nothing in the Bible I can think of that suggests fairness governs the universe – at least not until the end of time. But how often there's a nagging guilt in us that says 'I'm to blame – I deserve to be punished'. God is my judge, not my saviour. And unfortunately that is the theology of despair that Glen Hoddle has unwittingly presented to us, that has got up the nation's nose.

Sadly, that was also the belief of Naomi. I hope no one here believes that this is a Christian view of life – that when all is said and done, God really doesn't like me. Unfortunately, while this might not be Christian theology, it's often the picture we unwittingly paint. It's all too easy to suggest that Naomi was the author of her own problems, and that what happened to her was a form of divine judgement that turned her into an old and bitter woman – a very unattractive combination. I can imagine the approach some people might take to sorting things out for Naomi, and this is not hypothetical. I have heard similar approaches.

'Naomi, I'm your Christian counsellor. I'd just like encourage you in your faith. May I offer you my condolences for the sad loss of your husband and sons. But actually, it's all your fault for backsliding in the first place, covering up your mistakes, and trying to blame God. That's why you're a bitter old woman. So I suggest you snap out of it and get on with the rest of your life. Bless you, sister! I appreciate this opportunity to minister to your need.'

If that's Christianity, I resign now.

There was a riposte for Glen Hoddle in the 'Letters' column of *The*

Times last Friday, from the Chancellor of St Paul's Cathedral. Let me quote part of his letter:

> Millions today now do not believe in God because he did not come to the rescue of the victims of Auschwitz, nor does he seem to visit the torture camps of Latin America and beyond.
>
> It would appear that Hoddle has no theology of the God who suffers beside us, goes with us into the gas chamber, suffers with us in the prison yards of South America. His God is, apparently, not the Christ of Calvary, only the God who sits in judgement and condemns people for their weakness and indiscretions.
>
> Whom would your readers choose? The Christ of Calvary who loves the penitent thief, or the judge who condemns his victims in a wheel chair and tells them that it is their fault that they cannot walk. (Canon John Halliburton, letter published in *The Times*, 5 February 1999)

Of course there are times when we all get down, through circumstances. I do. I've been there and I know what a difficult journey it can be to get things back into proportion. Often things seem far worse in the night than in the light of dawn. How often it has needed the support of someone else, especially my wife, to help me count my blessings. I recall that one time when things were especially tough, she suggested we sit down and make a list of our blessings – to concentrate on the positive rather than the negative. So I remember listing things like:

- We have our home.
- We have our health.
- We have two lovely children.
- We have so many supportive friends.
- We have Christian fellowship.
- We have our Saviour, and he has us.
- We have a future and a hope.

I felt so good about doing that exercise – it just lifted my eyes from my problems. What if Naomi had gone through the same exercise? What could she have written?

I have life

Naomi had left three graves in Moab. But she was a survivor. Despite her griefs God, in His goodness, had kept her alive and allowed her to return home to Bethlehem. That in itself is a precious gift from God, that we can take for granted. Naomi thought that life had ended for her, but her trials were really a new beginning! Talking as I was of

Glen Hoddle, I was thinking about the analogy of a football match, where your side come in at half-time 3–0 down – at home. The heads are down, the fans are on your back, nothing to show for all the effort except a mouthful of criticism from the boss. But how often the manager's half-time pep-talk transforms a team of losers into winners. It is only half-time! Come on lads! And you go out and win 4–3. Doesn't always happen! But the point about Naomi is that when she arrived back in Bethlehem, it was only half-time. The match wasn't over, even though that was how she felt. All that has happened to her, all the trials, the test of her faith, is to bring her to this moment when God can use her for a very special purpose.

I have friends and family

She was surrounded by friends and family who cared about her. She may have felt that she was isolated from everything and everyone, but she couldn't say she was unwanted and unloved. She was home! She had security, something she had missed ever since her sons died. She had a God-given base from which she could move out and grasp the opportunities which were just around the corner – exciting events that fill the rest of the book of Ruth.

I have God

God had not forsaken her. Whether Naomi realized it or not, God was at work. When faced with trials we need to remember that God is in them and that He works through them to accomplish His purpose in our lives. Romans 8:28 reminds us that, 'In all things God works for the good of those who love him, who have been called according to his purpose', and verse 31 tell us that God is not only with us, but He is for us, He's on our side.

I have Ruth

Could any mother-in-law wish for a more loyal and loving daughter-in-law? What faith! What patience! What determination! Ruth wasn't of the same race, or even the same religion to begin with. But Ruth put up with Naomi's depression, she stuck like glue to her, offering all her commitment and encouragement, even prepared to surrender her own opportunities and journey to a foreign land with her. I think there is a true sense is which Ruth was heaven-sent for Naomi. Ruth was God's friendship in action. I think that's a good indicator of liking someone, that you support them through thick and thin. That's true friendship, that's truly liking someone.

Let's just think about this friendship issue a little more: what struck me is that we only learn about the power of friendship in the middle of life's circumstances, and in our everyday relationships. One of the telling criticisms of Jesus was that he liked all the wrong people: 'This man is a friend of publicans and sinners.' The ones who were on the edge of society, who probably, like Naomi, suffered from a poor self-image, received what was on offer to everyone, the friendship of Jesus. With Jesus, the one who knows us the best also likes us the most – humanly it's often the other way around: the more we see, the less we like. There was Zacchaeus the tax collector, one of Jerusalem's low-lifes. A man despised and friendless. Jesus knew all about his weaknesses, the cheating, the hand in the till, and in a simple act of befriending, went home to have tea with him. That man's life was transformed, but not only his life, also his own self-image. He began to take hold of his own future, to plan and take important decisions for himself, instead of drifting with the rabble. I don't want to look ahead in Ruth beyond chapter 1 today, but think about this when you read on. Naomi calls herself 'bitter'. But does she remain that way? Does she act like that – bitter? Like Zacchaeus, you'll find a very different person starting to emerge – the real Naomi, a confident and competent person, who is responding to the simple act of friendship from Ruth. Can I suggest that what Naomi in her heart of hearts is responding to is that God, after all, not only loves her, but likes her – because, in Ruth, she has sensed the true character of God: sacrificial love.

Recall the words of Jesus in John (15:12):

My command is this: love each other as I have loved you. Greater love has no one than this, that he lay down his life for his friends. You are my friends if you do what I command. I no longer call you servants, because a servant does not know his master's business. Instead, I have called you friends.

Are those the words of someone who doesn't like us? In the Old Testament, the highest compliment is paid to Abraham: he is called 'the friend of God'. Doesn't mean he was perfect – in fact Abraham did some very stupid things – but there was a heart relationship at work: growing, testing, developing and refining his character, as only true friendship can.

Hebrews 4:15:

For we do not have a high priest who is unable to sympathize with our weaknesses, but we have one who has been tempted in every way, just as we are – yet was without sin. Let us then approach the throne of grace with confidence, so that we may receive mercy and find grace to help in our time of need.

Just before Christmas there was an event to be treasured on TV: it was the screening of the venerable film made just after the war starring the great Jimmy Stewart, called, *It's a Wonderful Life*. Maybe you saw it, and like me, fell under its charming spell. It is the story of a modest, good man named George Bailey, who loses the will to live when his building society business fails apart after funds are accidentally mislaid. It seems that all he has worked for: his family, his community, his reputation, has come to nothing – the vision dies. But as he clambers on the bridge parapet to hurl himself to death, God steps in. He sends a bumbling old angel, Clarence, to save George Bailey. Clarence takes George back through his life, and to show him what things would have been like if he had never been born. The first thing George notices is that not only is he himself not present as part of his parent's family, neither is his younger brother. Then he remembers how, as a young boy, he had saved his brother's life, after his brother fell through ice while skating. But this time around, without George, there was no one to save his brother. Later, George, with Clarence, revisits his neighbourhood, and finds a selfish, ugly community at war with itself. The reason: without his building society as an influence for good in the community, encouraging people to save, to make their homes, raise their families, establish their businesses, realize their dreams, the community falls apart in greed and self-centredness. So the light dawns on George: his life hasn't been without influence, nor is he without friends and support in his darkest hour. He turns back from the bridge, and he discovers that the evil which was about to engulf him is swept away on a tide of love and generosity. You see, while his greatest enemy and creditor prepares to close him down, all those ordinary people, George's friends, that he has unwittingly helped all his life, rally round and raise the money to save his stricken company.

Does God like me? If he does, how do I know? To link our circumstances to whether we are liked or not is the route to despair. Our God is not one who watches from the touchline, to use the footballing analogy again, he's on the pitch, in the thick of it with us. He goes with us through life's darkest moments. We see his friendship supremely in the life of Jesus, and we understand that it's sacrificial – he went all the way to the cross to win our friendship back. Ruth's love for Naomi is a mirror held up to the character of God, reflecting love to where it was – just then – needed the most.

Just this past week, my wife, and other teacher friends in Ipswich and Felixstowe, have been going through what every teacher dreads: a school OFSTED inspection. I can't say whether it was coincidence, but in the middle of the week our minister had been invited to lead the school assembly. He invited half a dozen pupils onto the platform, and produced a shoe box, with a lid. 'In this box', he said, 'I've got something that God thinks is brilliant, fantastic, just the tops. You can each take a peek, but don't tell anyone until you've all had a look.' Then he asked what it was that so excited God. What was the answer? Each saw, in the box, themselves. Because our crafty minister had glued a mirror to the inside of the box! That was a simple message that God is our creator God, and he's pleased with what he has made – He really likes what he's done, and he wants us to know that!

Because God does indeed like us, the twofold challenge to each of us today is all to do with our relationships:

Have we first of all received his love – discovered for ourselves Christ's deep friendship. Maybe, like Naomi, we are going through a tough time, and we need a Ruth around us to show us practically the value of friendship with God.

The second challenge is that, having received it, how are we, like Ruth, reflecting that 'friendship of God' to the people around us, as evidence that God really does like each one of us?

Comments

Peter Graves: '*Makes real attempt to link story of Ruth with a positive approach to life. Perhaps too long, but contains some good insights.*'

William Beaver: '*In a sermon which darts between Naomi's thoughts and his views on matters several, the lesson comes home in surprising and delightful illustrations.*'

Jonathan Romain: '*I feel I know the Book of Ruth much better after reading this sermon. The 'This is Your Life Naomi' approach was very appealing.*'

Kieran Conry: '*Although rather long, this text is centred on God and gets right into the Scriptures, in this case a rather obscure book of the Old Testament. There is enough scholarship to make it interesting, but not too much to make it inaccessible.*'

Blessed Are the Meek

SERMON PREACHED BY ANDREW SAILS AT CENTRAL
HALL METHODIST CHURCH, WALSALL,
ON 18 OCTOBER 1998

The Sunday marked the beginning of One World Week. It was also
the Sunday following the award of the Nobel Peace Prize to John
Hume and David Trimble.

*The Reverend Andrew Sails, 50, and his wife Liz are both married for
the second time. Between them they have three sons, one daughter
and a grandson. Andrew entered the Methodist ministry in 1972, and
served in a variety of university chaplaincy churches, first as part of
the chaplaincy team at Hinde Street Methodist Church in the West
London Mission, then a circuit minister and Methodist chaplain at
Sussex, Liverpool and Bristol universities.*

*In the late 1980s he went through a period of personal crisis,
leading to his resignation from the Methodist ministry. He describes
this as a very dark and difficult time, when his faith and then his first
marriage collapsed. During this time he worked for the NHS Training
Division, eventually becoming its Director of Strategic Programmes.*

*By 1993 he had found his way back to the church pews. He began
to feel an increasingly strong call back to the presbyteral ministry.
Finally in 1996, to his very great and continuing joy, he rejoined the
ranks of the Methodist ministry.*

*Since 1996, Andrew has been the minister of four churches in
central Walsall. The largest of these is the Methodist Central Hall,
and over three years he has seen great changes there. 'Our
congregation has virtually doubled in size, and there is new vigour
and enthusiasm about the place. There may be many reasons for this,
but the major factor has undoubtedly been the way in which the
church community has addressed key questions about our role and
mission in the town centre. This has generated a sense of vision which
has made the worshipping congregation into a people with a purpose,
seeking strength for their journey.'*

*The church is now working on a £500,000 redevelopment scheme.
Andrew sees the development itself not as the end itself but as a
means to an end. 'We would not be spending this money on the*

property', he says, 'unless it liberated us to serve the local community and town centre more effectively.'

Andrew is also minister of the two smaller Methodist churches in Pleck and Caldmore, where he enjoys the opportunity of working alongside equal numbers of white and Afro-Caribbean Methodist families, and is also looking to develop dialogue with those of other faiths.

Andrew is, perhaps not surprisingly, a strong supporter of the preaching ministry, which he greatly values. 'The new millennium needs as much as ever to hear what God is saying to us', he says. 'Preaching is by no means the only way in which God confronts us, but I believe that it remains a unique and powerful medium for the proclaiming and hearing of the gospel.'

He believes effective preaching forges links between the Bible stories and the individual stories of people today. It only 'works' properly when the preacher can understand and identify with the situation and needs of his or her hearers, and also be open to the truths of the Scriptures, he says. 'In the Scriptures we hear the old, old story in a new way, and we recognize afresh what it means to us today. Only then does the preaching do what it is meant to do – take hold of us, mind and heart, and change our lives.'

He believes each generation shares and hears the gospel in different ways, according to the cultural context – be it through a mediaeval mystery play, a Renaissance painting or the latest computer software. 'Preaching has continued throughout the history of the Church, but the styles have changed. The sermon in coming years may well change to reflect our increasingly technological age – with, for example, greater use of multi-media sounds and images alongside the human word. But whether or not the technical components change, the underlying essence of preaching must hold firm. The sermon must retain its unique spirit-led fusing of biblical truth with contemporary concerns. In that way, the sermon avoids being mere opinion and rather does what sermons have always sought to do – represent the gospel for each new generation. Only then can the sermon help uncover God's word for today, comforting the troubled and troubling the comfortable.'

Text: Matthew 5:5

Blessed are the meek for they shall inherit the earth.

Bible: Revised Standard Version

H ere's an exciting subject for a sermon – meekness.
Did you hear of the church that had the notice outside saying
'The meek shall inherit the earth', and underneath someone had
scribbled 'as long as no one else minds'.

And that pretty well sums up how a lot of people think about
meekness.

In common usage, if you're meek you're a wimp, the fellow who
always gets sand kicked in his face. 'Oh', we say, 'he's quite a meek
and mild little man really – wouldn't say boo to a goose.'

We still have the hymn, 'Gentle Jesus meek and mild'. But it was
George Bernard Shaw who described it as 'a snivelling travesty' of
Christianity.

Meekness is not generally considered a virtue these days. Job
adverts tend to ask for self-confidence and assertiveness. I wonder if
you'd employ someone for a job if their reference described them as
extremely meek?

But all this is to misunderstand the Greek word which we normally
find translated as 'meek'. Interestingly, modern Bibles have tended to
look for a different translation. Rather than 'Blessed are the meek',
we often now find 'Happy are the gentle' or 'those of a gentle spirit'.

And immediately we begin to feel that this word has more strength
in it. When we say someone is really gentle, we are talking not about
weakness – indeed some of the gentlest people are very strong and
determined – it is just that their strength is controlled and sensitive to
others.

One commentator has come up with an expanded paraphrase of
'Blessed are the meek' which runs like this: 'O the bliss of the man
who is always angry at the right time, and never angry at the wrong
time, who has every instinct and impulse and passion under control
... He is a king among men' (William Barclay, *Daily Study Bible:
Gospel of St Matthew*, Edinburgh: St Andrews Press, 2nd edition,
1958, vol. 1, p. 93).

Someone who is gentle with others is someone to be trusted.
Pickfords produced a very positive advertising slogan when they
depicted themselves as the gentle giant – someone with caring yet
controlled strength and reliability.

And a truly gentle person has an inner security which means that
they are not striving for their own status or reward, but are genuinely
able to put others first, to stand by you, to stand up for you.

Blessed are the poor and the meek. Or as Bernard Miles puts it in a
rather more cheap and cheerful paraphrase, 'Jesus starts off telling
'em it's a darn sight better to be poor and humble than rich and
haughty, better to be hard up and happy than rich and miserable, any
day of the week'.

The quality of gentle meekness is something to do with being free from the constraints of self-importance and self-aggrandizement, free from the desire to be rich and powerful, happy rather to use our all to ensure the quality of others' lives.

The Bishop of Stepney once talked on the radio about going to take a confirmation in the East End. The girl being confirmed was called Sheila. She wore a white dress and veil and was the centre of attention. She was aged 40, and had Down's syndrome. Sheila was there with all her natural and quite unaffected and unselfconscious care and concern and love for others, said the Bishop. 'She made her promises with her friends and I laid hands on her and anointed her. We didn't need a sermon because Sheila was teaching us what we needed to know' (Bishop Jim Thompson, *Stepney Calling: Thoughts for Our Day*, London: Mowbray, 1991, p. 61).

And so we have read the Gospel appointed for today: 'Blessed are the meek for they shall inherit the earth. Blessed are the pure in heart for they shall see God.'

Blessed are the meek, for they shall *inherit the earth*.

Today is the beginning of One World Week when we think about the ways in which we as a human race share our one common world. This year's theme is 'Shaping our landscapes'. We are thinking about the different ways in which we use the landscape – some grab and control, others nurture and value.

It is interesting to compare the rich and aggressive, who seek to grab the landscape of the world for their private use, and the truly meek and gentle who seek to honour, nurture, preserve and share the landscape with and for others.

And Jesus says that it is not the aggressive grabbers who really have the precious prize, it is the meek who actually inherit the earth. Precisely those who seek to grab the world lose it. Or, as he says elsewhere, 'What good is it if you gain the world and lose your soul?' You have really gained nothing.

The troubles in Northern Ireland have so often come down to this – politicians, and sadly sometimes churchmen too, trying to bludgeon their way into the inheritance of the land, when really the victory can only come by gentleness and peace.

The new Irish President Mary McAleese spoke out powerfully earlier this year against the mutually hostile assumptions of Catholic Nationalists and Protestant Unionists. She recalled the Belfast of her youth. For her community, 'God was male, Irish and Catholic, his mother having presumably emigrated to Nazareth from Ireland after the famine. My Protestant friends meanwhile also understood God to be male, but Protestant and British. Reared between these two parochial gods, who carried their crosses like lances in a jousting tournament, we were all introduced to the Ya-Boo school of theology – the my-God-is-bigger-than-your-God school of theological bully-boys.'

How good therefore this week to witness another heartening development in the story of Ireland, as not only John Hume but also David Trimble – not so long ago very close to the Protestant paramilitaries – was awarded the Nobel Peace Prize.

The way to inherit the riches of the Emerald Isle, as of every promised land, is the way of gentle strength. Blessed are the poor, those who hunger and thirst for righteousness, blessed are the meek – they are the true peacemakers.

This One World Week we need to learn afresh what it means to be gentle and meek: gentle with each other and also gentle with our common earth if we would inherit it.

The meek inheriting the earth is nothing to do with opening a will and finding we have acquired a new piece of real estate. It is not putting up a fence around my garden with a big sign saying 'No admittance – I've got this and it's all mine'. Rather it is humbly standing on the mountain top and looking out to sea or perhaps over the promised land – and saying 'This is given to me and my sisters and brothers if we can but care for it'.

Do you know the famous passage from the American Indian Chief Seathl in 1855? The white American government wanted to buy the Indian land. The chief replies 'How can you buy or sell the sky, the warmth of the land? ... We do not own the freshness of the air or the sparkle of the water ... Every part of the earth is sacred to my people. Every shining pine needle, every sandy shore, every mist in the dark woods ... is holy in the memory and experience of my people.' But the chief knows he must sell the land, or the white man will take it by force, and so he says 'If we sell our land, love it as we've loved it. Care for it as we've cared for it. And with all your strength and all your might and with all your heart preserve it for your children and love it as God loves us all.'

Blessed are the meek, for they *shall* inherit the earth.

In one sense the meek already have their inheritance, their treasure. For those who put up the barricades do not really enjoy the earth: they destroy its value in hoarding and grabbing it. Whilst those who are truly meek and gentle find the way to honour and share with each other the good things of life in the midst of the ravages of the greedy and power hungry.

But in another very practical sense sometimes it seems that quite the opposite happens – the big guns of wherever seem to call the shots and they *do* take the land.

And that is where we need to realize that when Jesus says 'The meek shall ...', he is also talking of the end of time and the coming Kingdom of God. He is quoting a psalm about the return to the promised land, and reinterpreting it for the coming of God's Kingdom. In part we already see the riches of the meek and gentle – but we will only see fully at the end of time. It is then that those who think they have inherited the world by force will finally learn the error of their ways.

Mikhail Suslov was someone who tried hard to conquer the world by brute force. He was formerly the second most important person in the Soviet Politburo in the days when Russia was still a Stalinist dictatorship. When Suslov died, the Christian poet Steve Turner wrote a poem about his lying in state in Moscow:

> ... he lies in satin
> and flowers,
> All redness
> has gone.
> His skin has
> become neutral.
> At last
> he is one with
> Stalin's millions,
> At last he has
> climbed down into
> the people.
> His greatness has
> been mislaid
> through some
> mechanical fault.
> He can command
> only stares.
> He is meek.
> He will inherit earth.

> (*Up to Date Steve Turner, 1968–1982.*
> Reproduced by permission of Hodder and Stoughton Limited)

There is such ambiguity in that last line: the tyrant has lost his power, he seems now to inherit not *the* earth but merely *earth* – the earth of the grave. Though, perhaps the poet also invites us to ask, may even such as he – through God's grace – still inherit *the* earth, now God has shown him the true meekness of death?

We hope and trust to the power of God's love over *all* his children. But clearly Suslov, like Hitler and Napoleon, all the way back to

Ozymandias, could not ultimately inherit the earth by force and might.

And so finally, when *we* die, when we stand before God on judgement day, we will have to show him what we did with *our* lives, all the power and security and prestige and wealth and fame which we gathered to ourselves. And on that day, God will look at it all and say 'Burn it away – into the fire with it'. And we will find ourselves as part of a society of heaven where there are no barriers and no prestige and no wielding of power against others – only a community of strong and gentle trust.

And then at last may we finally understand what we have as yet seen but in a mirror dimly: 'Blessed are the poor for they shall know God, and blessed are the meek for they shall inherit the earth.'

Comments

William Beaver: *'By dissecting the well-worn phrase afresh, we soon see that what we thought it meant isn't what it really means.'*

Peter Graves: *'Full of useful insights on Scripture and meekness.'*

Kieran Conry: *'A good blend of not-too-heavy scholarship and lively illustration. It might seem as though an analysis of each word or phrase in a statement would not work, but it is put together well enough to relate each section happily to what goes before. There is a sense of the presence of God through it and a real note of hope and trust at the end. I think that hearing this, I would feel challenged in some way.'*

Remembrance Shabbat

SERMON PREACHED BY RABBI STEVEN KATZ AT HENDON REFORM SYNAGOGUE ON 7 NOVEMBER 1998

Rabbi Katz, 50, is married to Sandra, a dental practice manager, and they have two children. He went to Queen Mary College, London, to study history and then to Leo Baeck College in north London before being ordained in 1975. 'My father was a rabbi', he says. 'It is in the family.'

He believes preaching is essentially a teaching tool. 'Perhaps for many Jews it is the only time they have any exposure to Jewish teaching', he says. 'The rabbi's sermon is a chance to convey the relevance of this teaching to their lives. Preaching is therefore vital for the Jewish community. If we do not know how or why to maintain our Judaism, then it will quickly cease to have any sort of relevance or meaning to Jewish life. The sermon is a vehicle to show how and why Judaism can be a force for good. A sermon should show how Judaism can enhance their appreciation of aspects of daily life, whether it is at home with the family, at work or in the community at large. Of course, the first aim of any preacher is to wake them up. Every good sermon should contain humour, which is a great way of attracting attention. The point of a sermon is not to entertain, but there is no reason why a sermon should not be entertaining.'

He believes that Judaism possesses insights, often reaching back four millennia, on a whole range of issues which will challenge society in the new millennium, including God, family, war and peace, charity, work, medical ethics. 'For many Jews the sermon will be the only bridge of communication between tradition and today, past and present. Sadly, declining attendance at our synagogue services means that the tradition of Jewish insight and interpretation is reaching fewer Jewish minds and hearts, but if the sermon stimulates even one mind, activates even one conscience, warms even one heart then it will remain at integral part of the rabbi's work. The hope and prayer is that in researching his/her sermon the preacher's own mind will be stimulated, his/her conscience activated and his/her heart warmed.'

Religious worship in his synagogue has changed enormously in recent years, he says. 'In addition to the belated but welcome equality of opportunity granted to our ladies, conscious efforts have been made to introduce greater congregational participation in our services – the rabbi as prompter not actor, the congregation as actor not audience. To help encourage this trend the rabbi is dressed in less formal and forbidding clothing, more use is being made of modern musical compositions to encourage participation, more adult classes to help raise Hebrew literacy levels, so permitting more lay people to follow and, indeed, lead services.'

He has found that secular society has impinged on synagogue life in three important respects, each one embracing one of the three purposes and dimensions of a synagogue – House of Community, House of Study, House of Worship. 'The fragmentation and fracture of the family unit, added to the increasing workload of the GP and the social services, mean that those in society suffering the vulnerability of bereavement, marriage break-up and physical frailty have often no one to turn to for spiritual, physical and emotional support. The synagogue, through caring groups, job clubs and rabbinical counselling, is required and ready to offer community help.'

He also reports that assimilation is eroding both the numbers and the commitment of Diaspora Jewry. Consequently, more intensive efforts are being made to offer formal and informal Jewish education opportunities to children and adults, in an effort to equip the Jew with a knowledge, understanding and appreciation of Judaism.

'Third, the religious establishment is responding slowly and sometimes reluctantly to the equality of opportunity which women are being offered by secular society', he says. 'Reform Judaism has been quick to respond by granting women equality in all aspects of our synagogue's religious life.'

S ome British visitors to Normandy regard a Berlitz dictionary, a Michelin guide and an encyclopaedic list of cheap wine outlets as mandatory travelling companions. For my first visit to Normandy earlier this year, in addition to my wife and two daughters, I took Max Hastings' *Overlord – D Day and the Battle for Normandy 1944* as company. Moreover while many visitors regard trips to Bayeux, Rouen, Camembert and Calvados as *de rigueur* – testimony to the artistic, religious, architectural and gastronomic endeavours of northern France – I sat on the cross-Channel ferry to Caen thinking about Arromanches, White Omaha and Utah beaches, scenes of some of the most serious fighting during the Normandy landings. As our brand new Brittany Ferries ship neared the port of Caen 54 years later, almost to the day, I looked at the guide to the ferry: a choice of restaurants, bars, a playroom, TV room, cinema, duty-free shops. I tried to make the leap of imagination to what it must have been like to crouch in a crowded landing craft approaching these same shores on 6 June 1944. For those spared the threat of the ultimate self-sacrifice, death in military service of one's nation, it is impossible to feel the gripping fear, to sense the bewildering uncertainty, to hear the incessant pounding of the shore by naval guns, or to touch the enveloping darkness of the early hours of 6 June 1944. For my family in June 1998 there was no fear, no uncertainty, no darkness and the only noise was the monotonous drone of the one-armed bandits being kept fully occupied by a group of understimulated and overindulged schoolchildren. The smoothness of the crossing helped to ensure that we had travelled from Portsmouth to Caen without so much as feeling a drop of water. What was it like, though, 54 years ago to jump from a landing craft, wade through three, four feet of water, throw oneself, helmet, backpack, rifle and all, on to the sandy beach as, perhaps for the first time in one's life, one heard, in earnest, the ear-piercing fury of hostile artillery fire? During our week's stay in Normandy, enjoying the archaeological, religious, cultural and gastronomic delights of the area, I was always humbled, often haunted, by thoughts of how a previous generation of visitors had been forced to land in Normandy, thoughts intensified by some of the reminiscences included in Hastings' book. By the end of June 1944 more than a million men were pitted against each other on a front of scarcely more than ten miles. By August the number was more than two million.

As we drove through yesterday's killing fields of Normandy my car radio brought news of today's killing fields of one-time Yugoslavia. Why have we made so much technological progress, so much scientific progress, yet regressed morally so much? Perhaps part of the answer is contained in Caen's museum, Mémoire. It is an immensely impressive, innovative museum dedicated to commemorating the human cost and celebrating the human triumph of the struggle for Normandy which Hastings describes as the decisive western battle of the Second World War.

I expected the museum to focus upon the indignity and humiliation heaped upon the local population by the Nazi occupation and upon the loss of life, limb and property suffered when caught in the crossfire of the Normandy landings. The museum adopted a much broader perspective, embracing the causes of Nazism and also a refreshingly objective view of Vichy's relationship with Berlin. But the most expressive and eloquent aspect was to be found in the centre of the spacious entrance hall. It was a huge ceiling-high cylinder containing in chronological order of ascendancy the names of all those who had preached and promoted the causes of morality. There at the very base of the cylinder, holding up this roll call of moral giants, was Moses, then came prophets Isaiah, Jeremiah and Ezekiel, Talmudic rabbis Hillel and Akiva, followed by Jewish religious moralists Bachya, Ibn Pakuda and Moshe Chayim Luzzato. Their contribution to Judaism, to civilization, was not in the realm of law or liturgy; they devoted their life's work and energy to emphasizing that morality was the heart and soul of Judaism as it should be of civilization.

Sadly, though, through the centuries we have often shamefully neglected and sometimes contemptuously rejected the moral option, the moral mandate. Rather, we have assiduously built and wilfully worshipped a variety of hollow idols, the idols of material wealth, education, popularity – all for the purposes of vanity. All these idols of vanity are clearly visible: the size of our home and shape of our car are perceived to reflect material wealth; the name of school, the number and quality of GCSE passes are thought to portray the purity of parental genes; while the number of friends invited to a bar/batmitzva party or wedding is a public confirmation of popularity – all are idols and symbols of self-indulgence.

All carry the seeds of harm and hurt. The single-minded pursuit of material wealth can prompt a trail of transgression from an individual basis, family neglect and duplicity to theft and violence, while on a national basis violence and war are often a tragic consequence. Education is perceived by some to be a safety valve against the excesses of society, yet history shows that sometimes the most educated are in the forefront of brutality. The Nazi seats of power were peopled by brutes with university degrees and a love and knowledge of art and music. In our own time the Bosnian war crimes commission published some of its findings, printing the names of the dozens of men wanted for war crimes. In the village of Gacho, for example, accused executioners and rapists include a high school principal, a doctor, and an engineer. While neither material wealth nor education in itself is confirmation of morality, social status and popularity are the most fatuous of idols.

As parents we are giving our children the wrong signals. We are wrapped up in our self-indulgence, of how we look to the outside world. Because morality in childhood is practised largely behind closed family doors – whether one is a loving child, a caring sibling, a solicitous grandchild are not matters for public scrutiny – therefore morality is a low consideration on the agenda of parental priorities.

But the loving child, the caring sibling, the solicitous grandchild, is likely to grow into a loyal friend and responsible, contributing member of society. Morality, the cornerstone of Judaism, does not develop by itself. Children do not magically learn morality, kindness and decency any more than they learn maths, English or science. They mature into decent and responsible people by emulating adults who are examples and models for them. Schools can help children's minds to expand. However, it is up to parents to ensure that their hearts grow warmer, their eyes and ears more alert and sensitive to another's hurt and need.

The opening of our *Sidra*, the biblical portion read today, relates the birth of Jacob and Esau. They represent contrasting concepts of morality, indicated by their Hebrew names. The Hebrew letters of the name Esau may be read 'ASU' which means 'they have made' or 'they have completed'. This denotes that nothing can be done and that one should be satisfied with what one has already accomplished. The name Jacob, Yaakov, comes from the root which means 'heel of the foot', at the bottom. It implies that one is to grow, to develop, to look upward. Esau accepts the world as it is. But Jacob is not satisfied with the world as it is.

It is Jacob and not Esau who is to be the second patriarch, the second link in the chain of Jewish tradition. It is to Jacob, his name and his life, that civilization must look and aspire, always working, striving, for the betterment of society.

In 1939 Great Britain was in the vanguard of ensuring that Hitler's efforts to extinguish morality proved to be abortive, that Jacob would triumph over Esau. Today spring forth our heartfelt sentiments of tribute to the men and women whose valour and sacrifice secured the victory and salvaged our freedom: those who served in the Armed Forces, including the chaplains sustaining spirit and morale; the heroic resistance fighters in the underground and in the ghettos; the Allied leaders and commanders whose courage never flinched; and the millions who endured the sufferings of incarceration, oppression and bombardment, never losing faith that one day justice and freedom – the hallmarks of morality – will prevail. In humility and reverence we salute them all.

The scope and magnitude of Allied self-sacrifice in the Normandy landings, the quality of courage and heroism, was repeated again and again by Allied forces during the war, elsewhere in Europe, in Africa, in Asia; in the air, on the sea as well as on land, all in valiant search of justice and freedom. We must remember so that we always appreciate these supreme blessings and never take them for granted. We must remember too so that we remain ever vigilant, never tolerating the neglect or diminution of morality in family or in society.

Let the message ring out loud and clear from this service and from other commemorations of that time, that any infringement of human rights, any incitement of racial hatred, any effort to still or muffle the voice of Jacob with the cloying hands of Esau, must be resisted with every weapon we possess – moral, legal, economic and, if necessary, military. Failure on our part will only encourage a widespread decline in individual, family, national and international values. By the same token the fraying of individual and family morality, if unchecked, will percolate through the rest of society, tarnishing it, besmirching it.

Let us set to mind and heart the motto emblazoned on Caen's museum walls:

La douleur m'a frappé, la fraternité m'a enlevé, la liberté a sauté de ma blessure.

Pain broke me; brotherliness raised me up; liberty sprang from my wound.

Pain hurts, diminishes, destroys. In the last war the fraternity of Allied forces combined to remove the pain inflicted by Nazism and its surrogates. The reward: freedom.

Let us resolve to make Jacob not only our patriarch but our standard bearer. If we close our eyes, cover our ears, hold our tongue to injustice in our homes, in our country, in our world, we forfeit our vocation as Jews, our responsibility as members of civilization.

Let us resolve to ensure that these rewards of freedom and justice are appreciated, guarded, preserved, extended and passed on intact to the next generation and the next after that.

Comments

Margaret Brearley: 'Thoughtful, well-written ethical teaching for Remembrance Day drawn from the juxtaposition of personal reminiscences and interpretation of Jacob and Esau.'

Peter Graves: 'Very good sermon for Remembrance. Imaginative contrast between landing on beaches in war and going by ferry today. Clearly related to Kosovo.'

William Beaver: 'Vivid imagery and tightness of argument are the landmarks of this rapid-fire sermon well meeting the demands of a Remembrance Shabbat.'

Jonathan Romain: 'A sermon full of reasoned passion. And what a journey he takes us on: we start on board a ferry, full of noisy egocentric tourists, and end up resolving to be upholders of morality and liberty. We are in good hands.'

Kieran Conry: 'One of the strengths of this text is the wealth of illustration, a sense of being able to be with the author as he travels. But this may also be a weakness, because there seems to be more focus on recent history than on God. It is a good enough talk for some forum, but needs a little more to make it a better homily.'

A Sanctuary for God

SERMON PREACHED BY RABBI ANDREW GOLDSTEIN AT
NORTHWOOD AND PINNER LIBERAL SYNAGOGUE ON
SHABBAT TERUMAH 5759, 20 FEBRUARY 1999

Rabbi Andrew Goldstein has been the rabbi of Northwood and Pinner Liberal Synagogue for more than 30 years. Jewish education is one of his main interests and he has written a number of textbooks on Jewish subjects for both Jewish and secular schools.

Over twenty years ago he developed an interest in Czechoslovak Jewry that began with an investigation into the history of the Jewish communities that once used the Torah scrolls now used in Rabbi Goldstein's synagogue. These scrolls, together with other religious and secular objects, had been confiscated by the Nazis on sending the Jews to the concentration camps. The collection of Judaica now forms the Jewish Museum in Prague, but in 1964 over 1,500 Torah scrolls were brought to Britain. In Communist times only historical research was possible, but since the Velvet Revolution, Rabbi Goldstein has been going frequently to the Czech and Slovak Republics to take services and teach in the emerging Jewish communities. He is the consultant rabbi to the Liberal community in Prague. It is this connection that provided the background to Rabbi Goldstein's sermon.

Rabbi Goldstein's wife Sharon is active in the care provision and bereavement work in the congregation and is a magistrate. Their son Aaron is a rabbinic student at the Leo Baeck College in London, and their daughter Ruth is the Education Officer at the Wigmore Hall.

Dr Goldstein enjoys preaching and thinks his congregation expects a sermon, often two, per weekend. His sermons usually have an element of Jewish education, but also seek to give the congregation a feeling of God in their lives. The Czech connection and memories of the Holocaust make us feel it is our responsibility to rebuild Jewish life in Europe and in Britain.

Over the years Rabbi Goldstein's congregation has become more traditional, with more ritual, more Hebrew, and the reintroduction of many traditional ceremonies, but has also creatively added other new observances. Services need to blend the traditional with creative energy: more music, more participation and a good sermon are the ingredients to attract people.

Having said this, it is clear that worship gets lower down people's list of priorities year by year. We have to work hard to get the congregation to attend, we need to be welcoming, regularly explaining what is going on and involving the congregation in the ritual.

Synagogues will increasingly have a focus as places of social gathering, providers of care services, Jewish education and cultural expression, a community centre. But then the synagogue has always been a Bet ha-Midrash *(House of Study),* Bet ha-Teffilah *(house of Prayer) and* Bet ha-Knesset *(House of Meeting).*

Text: Exodus 28:8

Let them make Me a sanctuary and I will dwell amongst them.

'**W**here is the dwelling place of God?' asked Rabbi Mendel of Kotzk of some visiting scholars. They laughed at him, not really sure what to make of his question. 'What a thing to ask – is not the whole world full of God's glory?' Then he answered his own question: 'God dwells wherever we let God in.'

But can you find God if you have known only an atheist or godless background? Can you re-find God if you experienced God die, as did so many in the concentration camps?

I had answers to these questions and the two given in the story of the Kotzker last Shabbat, and the story I now tell could only be told by a very Liberal rabbi, because I spent much of last Saturday on a train. It left Bratislava at 5.50 in the morning, still dark, snowing hard. I had no Sabbath thoughts in mind for the first hour, just sleep, but once out in the Slovakian and then Czech countryside, covered in six inches or more of snow, the sun rising red and glorious, I got out my travelling prayer book and the early morning Psalms and prayers took on vibrant meaning. *Modeh Ani* – I thank you God for having awoken me to this sight – God needed no sanctuary: God was there to be experienced out of a train window, across the dawn of a winter landscape.

Onwards, past towns whose names told me stories of Jewish communities and Torah stories and more. Podivin, where Birmingham's Torah originates; Brno, where I might have been conducting a Shabbat service had the Orthodox Chief Rabbi in Prague not banned me. Better an Orthodox service with twenty elderly people than the 120 I got last time, young and old, for a Liberal service. God was not in such decrees.

A little country station flashed by and in the distance the hamlet of

Malin, the place whence came this Ark behind me: created in 1863 for the tiny prayer room in the tiny village, transferred to Kolin in 1922 when the Jewish community in Malin declined and died out. And twelve miles later, Kolin itself, the town where Jews once owned and read the Torah we used this morning.

Kolin, covered in snow and still snowing hard and soft. And there to meet me Hana Greenfield and her husband, by chance on a visit from Israel. Hana, born in Kolin, transported from there in 1942 to Terezin and then Auschwitz, one of only 28 survivors out of the 580 sent away by the Nazis. Saturday morning, we went up the synagogue street covered in snow, stood in front of the hidden synagogue, empty, cold, lonely. We three the only worshippers, though we could not enter. In the courtyard I said some more of the service and I found Hana joining in, a tear in her eye – I've never seen her cry before – too hard, suppressing her emotions to survive. I glanced up and there the Hebrew words, also on a board at the back of our sanctuary in Northwood, the words of Ezekiel, *And I will be to them as a small sanctuary in all the places of their dispersal.*

Our sanctuary, warm this Shabbat; Kolin, cold and empty. And yet as the three of us stood there in the snow I know I felt God's presence and I think that, despite herself, Hana felt God again in the place of her girlhood dreams. We visited the cemetery, no need to leave stones on the graves, just our footsteps on the virgin snow. Jews should not visit cemeteries on Shabbat as we did, and yet I know God was with us, so peaceful covered in snow. God to be found even there.

And on to Prague to conclude that long Shabbat – at Bejt Simcha, the Liberal congregation, for a lecture and Havdalah. All ages present, making it through the thick snow. A distinguished man of 77, Emeritus Professor of Physics at Charles University, another Auschwitz survivor, he told me, seeking again his Jewish roots abandoned as a boy in the inferno of the camp. He had tried the Orthodox synagogue and it left him cold. But my lecture clearly affected him and in the Havdalah candle's glow I saw here too a tear – and after the candle was extinguished he hugged me and I didn't ask but maybe God came back for him, for he clearly wanted to let God in.

As the Kotzka said, *God can be found wherever we let God in.* Last Shabbat, unorthodox indeed, I know I experienced a sense of God's presence across the 350 miles I travelled that day and I think I saw two people who had lost God find an intimation of God's presence. And the night before, as the Shabbat started and I my journey, in Bratislava, as the winter sun set through the falling snow, the quiet city greeted Shabbat. At the Orthodox synagogue, the only synagogue left standing by the Nazis and Communists in this once very Jewish town, there were just eight men to welcome the Sabbath. No *minyan* and therefore no proper service. The synagogue's 1920s functional concrete, empty and cold, a sanctuary devoid, I think, of God's presence that night. But round the corner at the Jewish community centre a different story. Here young Jews have gathered on a Friday night since the Velvet Revolution to meet other Jews and to decide which pub or club they would go off to spend the Sabbath Eve. That night a Jewish rock band was playing in a local club and most went there. But twenty of the older Jewish students, postgraduates who had invited me to Bratislava, godless raised, but now exploring their Jewish roots, singing lustily as we lit candles, drank wine, listened to my lecture on 'The Bible: myth or reality'. They sang Hebrew songs again, not yet ready for a service or prayers. I think they too found a sense of God in the friendship, in the joy of discovering the Jewish tradition. At least the signposts set up for their journey that might end in knowing God's presence.

Sunday I arrived home in England to see on the TV the mass demonstration in Jerusalem by the Haredim who wish the State of Israel to be Jewish only in their way. Let them have their way – but my journey, my very unorthodox journey, confirmed my view that there are many paths to God, many ways of experiencing God's presence, many ways of expressing one's Jewish identity, for God dwells wherever we search for Him, wherever we let Him in.

Let them make me a sanctuary ... and I think of the comment in the Midrash: *Wherever you find a human footprint, there God is before you.* And I think of those footprints in the snow in the cemetery in Kolin ... and yes, God can even be found in a cemetery if your intention is to let God in.

Comments

Ian Sweeney: '*If the reader believes that God is only to be found in certain sacred places of worship, Rabbi Goldstein will passionately shake your assumption into reality.*'

Peter Graves: '*Clear and concise.*'

Christmas, King Herod and Anarchist Football

SERMON PREACHED BY MIKE STARKEY AT A
CHRISTMAS CAROL SERVICE AT ST JOHN'S CHURCH,
FINSBURY PARK, ON 20 DECEMBER 1998

*The Reverend Mike Starkey, 36, and his wife Naomi, a commission-
ing editor at the Bible Reading Fellowship, have two children. A
finalist in the 1998* Times Preacher *of the Year Award, he has been at
his present church in Finsbury Park, north London, for four years
after serving as a curate in a large Evangelical parish in Ealing. He
was ordained in 1993 after working as a newsreader and reporter on a
commercial radio station in Cambridge, Q103.*

He was brought up in a Methodist home, but his faith did not
become meaningful to him until his mid-teens. It deepened during his
late teens and early twenties. But it was transformed when, during his
modern languages degree at Lady Margaret Hall in Oxford, he spent
a year teaching in the Loire valley in France. 'France is a very
secularized country', he says. 'It really knocked my faith for six and I
went through a real period of crisis, and of wondering whether my
faith was just based on my friendships, and on being in a church
youth group. After that, I went through a slow, painful process of
reassembling things.'

During his time at Oxford, he found most satisfaction in editing
college magazines. 'I always enjoyed communicating, and it is still the
part of my ministry that I find most fulfilling.' After leaving university
he worked for the music and religious press for a year, went to the
Jubilee Centre in Cambridge as press officer, campaigning against
Sunday trading, and from there to the radio station.

He was turned away from journalism and towards the priesthood
by a serious car crash. 'I was driving from home in a little village near
Newmarket to the radio station, where I was meant to be reading the
news on the breakfast show. I was late for work, and the road was
wet. I was skidding round some little country lanes when the car left
the road, bounced on its roof and ended up completely smashed in a
field after turning somersaults in the air. The car was a write-off, but
I emerged completely unhurt. Up until that point, even though I had a*

faith, I had never considered the ministry. That was something other people did. But after that accident, my sense of calling changed. From being a Christian working in the media, I felt called to use my journalism and communication skills within the Church. I suppose I felt that God had saved me for a purpose, like John Wesley felt when he had that experience of being pulled from a burning house.'

He also felt that reporting on other people's troubles was no longer enough. 'I wanted to be in the thick of it and to be there, offering people help.'

He regards preaching as a form of journalism. 'It is an extension of journalism, in that it is communicating with people at a very earthy level. I know we live in a multi-media age, but I think there is still an important role for the sermon as a teaching medium. I don't think the ways that sermons have been done in the past will necessarily continue, especially with regard to the long, expository sermon, where the shape of the text determines the shape of the sermon. I think that particular form of preaching may have had its day. The challenge for me is to write sermons in the same way that I write features for magazines. The homework needs to be done in the priest's study before the sermon can be written. The trick is to use arresting, short, punchy sentences and illuminating illustrations to bring a sermon alive.'

He is at the front line of the Church's ministry, reaching out to a parish which consists largely of the 'missing generation', young professionals in their twenties and thirties with little or no church-going background, living in converted flats in the large houses of north London. 'So the one thing I cannot be is boring', he says. In his book God, Sex and Generation X (SPCK, 1997) he discusses how the Church can make contact with this generation. His first book, Fashion and Style, discussed how Christians can dress more fashionably. His latest book, Restoring the Wonder (SPCK/Triangle), published in July 1999, explored the reasons for a loss of a sense of wonder in contemporary society, and looked in particular at the place of religious faith in rediscovering it. It is aimed largely at people on the fringes of faith. 'Wonder has become the major theme of my preaching and writing in recent months', he says, and argues that this must be addressed by preachers in the new millennium.

'Many people are aware that they have lost a sense of wonder in life. That twinkle in the eye, spring in the step and sense that life might constantly surprise and excite them has gone for many people. Preaching can be a primary place where wonder is restored. It can point people to realities beyond the mundane details of daily life. It can bring alive biblical scenes, so that people are enabled to stand face to face with the wonder of Christ, as the early Christians did. The *millennium is a kind of cultural "milestone" at which people are stopping and taking stock of their own lives and the state of society. Preaching can be the bridge between the profound questions people are asking and the answers offered by the historic Christian faith. It can point to the hope and experience of wonder restored.'*

But he believes change is needed. 'Preaching has been seen as essentially a way of dispensing information, and has often been done in the style of a lecture. That is, its appeal has been mainly cerebral. But we live in a society where reason and logic are losing their appeal, and where personal experience is becoming more important. In order to connect, sermons need to become earthed in stories, metaphors, everyday experiences. They need to tug at the emotions and lead to changed lives. In particular, I believe the old "expository sermon" has long passed its best-before date. Preachers can learn a great deal from journalists and broadcasters about creativity and artistry in communication.'

Historically, he says, people have tended to identify with one particular worship tradition: 'High Church Catholic, Low Church Evangelical, chandelier-swinging Pentecostal, and so on'. But, he says, 'That day is now passing. Young adults in particular are more interested in encounter with God, whatever the "label" on the packet. Our church, for example, blends High Church liturgy, an Evangelical focus on the Bible and teaching, with influences from Pentecostalism and the radical tradition of social concern. The different "strands" of worship are finally ending up bound together, which is where they should have been all along!'

One of my favourite stories from the *Hackney Gazette* this year was their report on the annual Anarchists' Five-a-Side Football Tournament. No, this is serious. Every year the local Anarchist community celebrates Hackney Anarchy Week. And the centrepiece of the week is a grand picnic in the park and football tournament.

Now, you might think the idea of Anarchist football is a contradiction in terms. After all, anarchy means the absence of order or rules. It comes from the Greek word *anarchos*, which means 'without a ruler'. And all my fears were confirmed when I read the *Gazette*'s account of the games. During the football matches, said the reporter, 'anarchy prevailed'. It all came to a great climax as the matches ended with the goalposts being symbolically ripped down. Presumably by way of protest against people dictating to them where they ought to be kicking, or drawing oppressive distinctions between real goals and missed goals. Far better, thought the Hackney Anarchists, to rip down the goals altogether so that everybody could do their own thing.

I enjoyed the report. This was partly due to some unintentional irony. The reporter informed us that all the Anarchists wore 'bright Mohican hairstyles' and 'trademark safety pins'. Now, I find it oddly heart-warming to think of Anarchists having a rigid dress code, or trademark *anything*. Anarchist uniform does rather seem like a contradiction in terms. I would have thought any consistent, self-respecting group of Anarchists might wear a chaotic mixture of pinstripe suits, cassocks, boiler suits and pyjamas – the only 'rule' being that there are no rules. If I were an Anarchist leader (which, of course, I couldn't be since they don't have leaders), I'd excommunicate as a heretic any member who dressed remotely like another one.

But there was a deeper irony afoot. Before the event, posters went up around Hackney promoting it. And on these posters the event in the park was billed as a 'celebration of subversion in East London'. The young anarchists were claiming to be subversives: in other words, challenging the basic values of our society, undermining all that the rest of us hold dear.

In fact, their soccer tournament turned out to embody, in miniature, all the central values of their generation. It was another utter act of conformity. Why do I say that? Well, we need to look at what these Anarchists were claiming: through their attitudes, their doctrines, and even the way they played football. They were claiming that no external authority should have power to determine people's lives. They were saying that there are no absolutes in life. They were saying that the only morality or rules are whatever we can piece together for ourselves.

And that's what you'd expect them to do – because that's what Anarchists have always stood for. The problem is, to say these things just isn't radical or subversive anymore. To most of today's young adults, the ideas behind Anarchism – that authority is oppressive, there are no absolutes, the only morality is what we concoct for ourselves – these are no longer subversive. They're simply the new 'common sense'. It's what practically all my contemporaries were brought up to believe. It's what most academics in our universities believe. It's what most of our media promotes. It's what most of our neighbours in Finsbury Park believe as well.

We live in a culture today where all the old certainties of the past are crumbling away. People no longer automatically trust the police, the monarchy, the judiciary, the social services, the Church. All the big authority structures of the past are being questioned. All the moralities of the past are questioned too.

Our culture works on a 'supermarket shelf' model of truth, where you simply cobble together whatever works for you, whatever happens to make you feel good. We like a personally-defined truth, which prefers words like 'relative' to words like 'absolute'. It prefers words like 'rights' over words like 'duty' or 'obligation'. And ours is a society whose favourite concept is freedom of choice.

So you see why it struck me that the Hackney Anarchists seem rather safe and predictable. They've chosen to make a political ideology of something that most of my contemporaries believe anyway. Where's the radicalism in that?

Let me suggest what a real celebration of subversion in East London might look like. How about this: an event which undercuts everything my generation has been brought up to believe, which challenges our most basic assumptions from the roots up. An event held in honour of a great King, who has supreme authority. An event which announces uncompromisingly that he alone is Lord, and that to him every knee should bow in service. It would be an event which tells us the only sure path to freedom is complete submission, putting yourself out of the picture and putting others first.

This radical, subversive event would insist that there are some firm guidelines beyond ourselves to which our behaviour ought to conform, that our freedom has strict limits. That our personal preferences have to be brought into line with a great and solid truth beyond ourselves. It would tell people that their rights were secondary to their duties and obligations, that freedom of choice is only meaningful if you make the *right* choices in life.

An event like that would be radical and scandalous to the mindset of my contemporaries. It would be utterly offensive. And of course, such an event does exist. It's called Christmas. Christmas tells that there is a King, and that the King has come to our earth to show us exactly what he's like. It tells us that the bottom line in life is not freedom of choice, it's making the right choices; bowing the knee before God's majesty; living our lives in accordance with his will. And it makes the scandalous, and frankly rather intolerant, claim that if you haven't met him, and offered your life to him as a living sacrifice, you really haven't lived at all.

Lots of people see the message of Christmas as something inoffensive and traditional, even predictable. Which is strange. Because in our culture of relativism and freedom of choice, our culture which mistrusts all authority, the message of Christmas is highly offensive. The message of Christmas is actually a declaration of war on the most cherished values of our age.

If you read the Christmas story again, you'll realize that at least one of the participants in the story seems to realize this. Perhaps the one figure who is most sensitive to the true meaning of Christmas. And his name is King Herod.

Herod understands very well that Christmas is an act of subversion. That if this baby lying in a food trough really is what the angels and the Magi and the shepherds say he is, the greatest King who ever lived, then that has to be a threat to his power and autonomy. And so his massacre of all the baby boys in the region is a natural response to this threat. He doesn't want any rivals to his absolute power, his absolute self-determination.

Herod sees with clarity and reacts with logic. He realizes that the song of the angels drowns out the feeble strains of 'My Way'. That the star over the stable means his own star has been eclipsed. That the seeking of the Magi makes self-seeking look rather pale in comparison. This new Lord alone has authority and might and deserves all honour and praise: 'Come and worship, Christ the new-born King.'

Our churches stand in our communities today, not as cosy huddles, conventional and unchallenging, but as revolutionary cells where, week after week, deeply subversive people meet to celebrate the overthrow of the current social order. Not by violent revolution, but by a revolution in the human heart. We meet to announce the coming of a new King. To relativize the relativizers. To assert that those who tell us with absolute certainty that there are no absolutes are absolutely wrong. To offer a different path to personal fulfilment than freedom of consumer choice, a different geography than the dreamscapes of materialism.

One of my great joys here at St John's has been to see a number of people coming into a deep Christian faith. Most of these people don't shout about it but week in, week out, it happens. And it's been interesting that almost all of them are people with no religious background at all. In fact, most of the people who come to start worshipping with us here at St John's have no religious background. They're by and large not people who had a Christian upbringing and are now returning to it (although that's certainly true of some). They're mostly people without any faith background at all.

Why is that? Why do non-religious people often respond in the most passionate way when they hear the Christian message? And get most excited about the Christmas story?

I wonder if maybe the reason is this.

Those of us who had a religious upbringing have learned to see Christmas as something safe and reassuring. Maybe it's people who hear the challenge of Christmas for the first time who can encounter it in all its dangerous and subversive glory. They come at it fresh, and can recognize that the sentimental old message of Christmas is actually a great pack of explosives placed at the base of all they've been brought up to believe in. And nothing short of wholehearted commitment and a re-orientation of their whole life will do justice to the size of the claims involved.

Of course conservative, conformist types like the Hackney Anarchists will carry on with their cosy, unchallenging systems of beliefs and values. They'll carry on consuming the undemanding fare of their culture and serving it up to others, with a bright sprig of Mohican garnish.

But radicals and risk-takers recognize that the real celebration of subversion is called Christmas. It's the announcement of the coming of the true King. And it tells us that all our schemes, all our rights, all our freedom to choose, must fall silent in wonder, adoration and praise.

Christmas undercuts almost everything our society believes in. And this Christmas, the challenge comes to each of us afresh. Will we choose the bland conformity of our culture, or the subversive gospel?

Comments

Ian Sweeney: 'A thought-provoking and, at times, humorous commentary on the place of Christmas and Christians in the world today.'

Margaret Brearley: 'A well-crafted, witty and markedly original approach to the traditional Christmas message: Christmas as a "real celebration of subversion" (pace the Hackney Anarchists).'

Peter Graves: 'Superb and challenging sermon that enables us to see Christians with new eyes.'

Jonathan Romain: 'A sermon that immediately intrigues us – what's the preacher on about? And he leads us gently but firmly to his central theme of the subversive gospel and gives a fresh angle to a traditional time of year.'

Kieran Conry: 'A good start promises well and the promise is met. A well-developed idea retains the interest through good illustration, effective use of humour and a balanced application to contemporary issues. It is an expression of faith and conviction and is focused on God. All the marks of a text that would be a delight to listen to.'

Unwanted Presents

SERMON PREACHED BY TREVOR HANCOCK AT
GRAINGER'S LANE METHODIST CHURCH ON
27 DECEMBER 1998, THE FIRST SUNDAY AFTER
CHRISTMAS

The Reverend Trevor Hancock, of Cradley Heath Methodist Church, was born in Lincoln in 1936. He says he has remained a 'yellowbelly' at heart, despite living in Germany as a boy, and then for periods in Singapore and Sarawak, Malaysia. He is looking forward to retiring to the Fens and the back of beyond, and being near his elder daughter who lives at New York, Lincolnshire – always a point of confusion!

He was also included in the Fourth Times Book of Best Sermons, *and wonders why it took almost 40 years before anyone (except his family – 'Shut up, Dad!') commented on his preaching.*

In serious moments he longs for a little more urgency about the ecumenical movement, and would love to see a re-union of Methodists and Anglicans in his lifetime, possibly as a prelude to the formation of a United Church in England. For some years he has been a member of the Ecumenical Society of the Blessed Virgin Mary and feels that both Protestants and Catholics have much to gain from each other spiritually. He is currently reading the late Cardinal Hume's little book To Be a Pilgrim.

He believes strongly that there will be a place for preaching in the new millennium, on the grounds that there will always be a place for preaching and that the new millennium is after all only a blip on the calendar. What St Paul wrote to first-century Christians remains true: 'I cannot help myself; it would be an agony not to preach' (1 Corinthians 9:16b).

But, he says, preaching, as it relates to liturgy and worship, needs to be shaped according to the culture of the times we live in. Consequently it may be shortened or lengthened or split into 'sound bite'-size chunks, or bathed in music or whatever, but essentially preaching remains the attempt to relate what is genuinely believed to be God's will to the everyday life of ordinary people. 'The Gospel is always Good News, but we have to convince people of it!'

The changes in society during the twentieth century have been so rapid and far-reaching that they have not yet been assimilated, he says. 'The change from Empire to Commonwealth and a series of independent nations has seen a vast migration of races and cultures and religions into Britain. This has brought religions which were once seen as "heathen" or "evil" into the High Street and into close proximity to the traditional churches. To this has been added the new secular Sunday, bringing so much choice that even our congregations are confused.

'The break-up of the family has also meant that children are taken to visit separated parents at weekends, so Sunday School does not get the priority that it once had. This leaves a generation gap which so far many churches have failed to bridge. The pattern is very marked in the Black Country, where the decline of the Sunday congregation is marked as the generations grow older. Sadly, preaching, however worthy, is by itself unable to alter this trend. One waits for the Holy Spirit to breathe some power back into our preaching.'

Bible: Revised English Bible

I went to Beatties in Dudley and bought myself a new raincoat. I can't go wrong; it was reduced in a pre-Christmas New Year sale, and Beatties claim that they will change or refund any unwanted or other miscued gifts. There's lots of them about! If you look in the newspaper small ads column you will probably see a number of similar ads which say, for example, 'Computer, boxed as new. Unwanted gift' and you could get a genuine bargain on the rebound.

A young lady, well known to me, attracted a string of suitors. One more ardent than the others showered her with gifts. The snag was that he wasn't Mr Right, but neither was he put off. His masterpiece of a present was a very expensive state-of-the-art wordprocessor with all the trimmings. But instead of making her fonder, it made her more angry, and when I offered to take the gift off her hands for free, she replied through clenched teeth 'You can't have it, Dad, it's going back!' However, I think her sister nipped in and saved her from wasting it, and they both married someone else.

To receive an unwanted gift, which in one sense is exactly what you want, but from an unexpected and undesired source, creates great personal problems. For example, the best-known verse in Scripture is probably John 3:16: 'God so loved the world that he gave his only Son, that everyone who has faith in him may not perish, but have eternal life.'

It follows on from the prologue of John's gospel, which says: 'So the Word became flesh; he made his home among us, and we saw his glory ...' (John 1:14a).

The problem here is that God, who doesn't always consult very widely, took it for granted that the young lady in question would be over the moon to get the present. After all, it was what every young Palestinian girl of the first century wanted. A baby boy! It marked her arrival in the community.

What he didn't expect was the after-Christmas small ad in the *Bethlehem Gazette* which might have said 'Baby, cradled as new. Unwanted gift. Genuine bargain. Don't come to my heart, Lord Jesus, there isn't room in my heart for thee!' Or in Mary's case, for 'heart' read 'womb'.

God, the Almighty Creator of the Universe and everything, is very good at giving presents, but they are not always predictable or respectable or readily acceptable. In the long run they may cause us more trouble than they seem to be worth. But he always sends them with his love.

Gold, frankincense and myrrh are all very well in their place, but not in a stable. Can you imagine Mary and Joseph waving the Three Wise Men off on their way after they'd presented their gifts, and as they disappeared down the road Mary might have turned to Joseph and said 'Be an angel, just nip down the road to Herod's Store and see if you can exchange the gold, frankincense and myrrh for some disposable nappies, baby food and talcum powder'. Well-meant gifts aren't always suitable.

A friendly neighbour once told us he was off sea fishing for the weekend, and would we like some fish? Not expecting much, we thanked him and forgot about it until a few days later when he called with a huge newspaper parcel. 'You're lucky', he said, 'we caught a giant conger eel. It should keep us all going for weeks. Put it in the freezer.' We were grateful then for such a gift, and after he'd gone we set about cutting it up to freeze.

It wasn't easy. The skin was as tough as leather and it wouldn't fillet because it consisted mainly of bones. We tried cooking it. It took ages and smelt awful. We gave our cat Dandelion some to try. He left in disgust, and when we tried it we realized why. If you don't like conger eel from birth, it tastes and smells dreadful. Eventually, because of the way the house began to smell, we took the remains – several pounds in weight – and buried it in the garden. The same night one of the visiting urban foxes dug it up and fled, not to be seen again for months. I can only say that we loved our neighbour, but we hated his gift. It would need a very strong stomach to appreciate it.

When God comes calling at Christmas, he bears no resemblance to old Santa Claus with his bag of goodies for all. You can rely on his love but you can't wheedle him into giving you what you want. Getting what you want and what you need are two very different things.

God's gift, like our conger eel, permeates the whole of life. It infiltrates your family, your finances, your moral behaviour, your relationships with other people, your daily work, indeed, your health, wealth, sexual preferences, and whatever else! To accept such a gift means making sacrifices to accommodate it, and it becomes too much of a bother. Easier to leave it on the doorstep.

Lots of marriages run into trouble when a baby comes. We really looked forward to having a baby. We treated the first one as though she was made of eggshell, but for such a small bundle – 6lb 8oz – she was unusually active. Birth can be a shock. Often the father (and sometimes the mother) hasn't taken into account the noise (there is no volume control on a baby) and mess and smell that babies create. Sleep patterns are altered and affections have to be shared. A whole way of life is disrupted and changed, and sometimes the house seems less of a home and more of a prison. If you can't accept that or adapt, then you're in trouble!

God's baby Jesus can have a similar effect on our lives. We love the Nativity scene and the manger and the angels, with Mary and Joseph showing off their infant to the shepherds and Wise Men and anybody else who turned up.

What we have difficulty with is reconciling the sweet cuddly little boy with the tortured bleeding man on the cross and the bit in between when the grown man calls for disciples to pick up their crosses and follow him. If only God had given us a choice when he sent his gift. Why couldn't we have watched a few TV adverts first to see what kind of present we wanted? But no, he just went ahead and did it.

The worst thing about God's gift is that you can't advertise it after Christmas. Like the cat that always came back, Jesus Christ lives on. Not in heaven or some mystical state, but all around us in human form. You see him when you least expect him, sometimes in the people you'd rather avoid. Jesus lives within the unsuitable, the inadequate, the inconsiderate, the incorrigible, the indolent, the ill-disposed; who are often so because the world has passed them by. He is there because God's gift is to the whole world with no strings attached, and oddly enough somewhere there is a label with your name on it and mine.

> How silently, how silently,
>   the wondrous gift is given!
> So God imparts to human hearts
>   the blessings of his heaven.
> No ear may hear his coming
>   but in this world of sin,

Where meek souls will receive him, still
the dear Christ enters in.

(Brooks Phillips (1835–93),
'O Little Town of Bethlehem', third verse)

Comments

Jonathan Romain: '*The real test of a sermon is not just the impact it makes at the moment but the images and message you carry away with you and take home. I shall think of Hancock struggling with his eel for some time to come!*'

Peter Graves: '*Good, clear, simple.*'

Ian Sweeney: '*It is the experiences of daily life that so effectively bring out the truths of Scripture. Who would have thought a conger eel could teach us anything about the birth of Christ?*'

Singing to God

SERMON PREACHED BY RABBI ALBERT FRIEDLANDER
AT WESTMINSTER SYNAGOGUE IN THE WINTER OF 1998

Rabbi Albert H. Friedlander, 72, has served as a congregational rabbi in American and British communities since his ordination as a Reform rabbi in 1952.

He has had many books published in the fields of theology and history, and has written songs (including a wedding hymn text for the Prince of Wales and the late Diana, Princess of Wales, with the music composed by the Master of the Queen's Music Malcolm Williamson), as well as a cantata with Donald Swann.

He and his wife Evelyn have three daughters, who between them work as a rabbi, a Jewish museum director, and a journalist.

Rabbi Friedlander believes that religious leaders must participate in fighting social wrongs, and once marched alongside Martin Luther in a civil rights march from Selma to Montgomery, Alabama. Together with Canon Paul Oestreicher of Coventry Cathedral, he participated in civil rights demonstrations in Trafalgar Square and in Berlin, and he is active in the interfaith dialogue. For the past twelve years, he has given opening sermons at the German Protestant Kirchentage and at the Katholikentage. Dr Friedlander has served as a counsellor to students at Columbia University in New York, is the Dean of the Leo Baeck College in London, training Reform and Liberal rabbis, and has served as a visiting professor in many universities. Nevertheless, he still feels most comfort in a pulpit. 'Rabbi means teacher, and the pulpit remains the place where young and old can be addressed and taught', he says. 'It is my basic conviction that this is central to religious life, particularly as we pass the year 2000.'

Nevertheless, he feels he must note the changes which have taken place in religious life. 'The houses of worship often stand empty, and congregants feel that their needs are not addressed in the sanctuaries. Why? For many Jews, the Holocaust has caused them to wonder whether a compassionate God still controls the universe, and whether the prayers of ancient times speak the language of today.' In his work in Germany, Rabbi Friedlander tries to deal with the problems of guilt, suspicions between the generations, and the failure of the

Church to confront the heritage of a dark past. The burden of history is hard to bear, and is carried over into the next century.

Rabbi Friedlander feels that the next generation is maimed and scarred by the parents' past, and that all who live after the Holocaust have to receive comfort from their religious leaders. This is why religion, worship and rituals have to change, he says. He himself, together with the Nobel Peace Prize winner Elie Wiesel, composed a new liturgy for Christians and Jews, to be used on appropriate occasions. There must always be new prayers, often written by congregants, to make them share in worship. Prayer also takes place at home, perhaps more often now, and Judaism has many home rituals which are basic to our religious survival today. 'Our society has become far more secular – but Judaism lives within secularity. We must beware of fundamentalism, and ultra-traditional approaches which could create new ghettos.'

His congregation has survived and doubled within the last fifteen years. He says this is because of its openness and participation in various causes of social justice. Having recently retired, Rabbi Friedlander is confident that this will continue with its new, younger, able and caring rabbi.

Looking to the new millennium, Rabbi Friedlander believes the sermon must fulfil many functions. 'It must be a teaching medium. All religions have become distanced from the Bible and other revealed texts. Preachers throw passages at their listeners without commentaries, assuming that a biblical verse is its own authority and must be accepted as such. Yet all these texts have moved through thousands of years, acquiring new surfaces, new meanings – and new prejudices – travelling to us through the centuries. "Deicide", women's duties to "obey" and the "authority" of the preacher are built into these texts and sermons. In the next century, the preacher must point out how much of the original text has been misinterpreted, and how much of our life today must be added to make these texts relevant. Religion is no longer opposed to science; the sermon must be aware of new insights, both in physics and in psychiatry.'

He believes the sermon of tomorrow must also perform a 'counselling' or 'healing' service for the listener. 'Preachers tend to go on ego trips, supporting their role as "leaders". But they have to learn to listen to the congregation. If we are fortunate enough to find worshippers in our pews, we must learn that tomorrow's congregation wants to take part in the quest for meaning. I believe that many of the sermons in the next century must be open. They should include a question period which must be more than a period for information. It must be a time for congregants to challenge the preacher, to give their own views – even to come up to the pulpit. The preacher need *not surrender his role, but must learn that any sermon can and should be a door to dialogue. If that happens, this key aspect of tomorrow's services will remain totally relevant, and the preacher will also benefit.'*

Text: Exodus 15 (the Song of Moses)

On Shabbat Shira, we read the 'Song of Moses', which gives us the opportunity to consider the impact of music in our lives. According to tradition, expounding the Torah should be preceded by a text found later in the Bible. Psalm 96 begins*: Shiru ladonai shir chadash: O, sing unto the Lord a new song; sing unto the Lord, all the earth* (Psalm 96:1).

W hy do we need *new* songs when the Bible is filled with the great songs of our ancestors? In our prayers today we sang a part of our Torah portion: *Mi chamocha ba elim, adonai: Who is like unto Thee, O Lord among the mighty? Who is like unto Thee, glorious in holiness?* Our liturgy builds upon 3,000 years of tradition, a secure foundation of three millennia during which we sang unto God. And the psalm reminded us that the earth itself has sung to God from the moment of creation; the music of the spheres fills the universe. Surely, music itself belongs to the first moments of Creation. The astrophysicist Steven Weinberg, looking at the first moment of creation, claims that a faint static still reverberates through the cosmic ether from one end of the universe to the other: the final echo of the Great Bang. If that is so, why should we not see this as part of the Song of Creation? Job speaks of the beginning of creation *when the morning stars sang together* (Job 38:7); and sanctuary music should mirror the songs of heaven.

But we are no angelic choir: our songs are not *that* good. Music should enhance worship; but it can also destroy it. Even the greatest music presents us with problems. This morning, we must also consider the misuses of music in our world. It can distract us from our work, which can be a good thing. The great critic George Steiner once quoted Lenin: 'I must never again listen to Beethoven's *Appassionata*, because when I do I feel like stroking the heads of children instead of smashing the heads of my enemies.' Yes, music has charms to soothe the savage beast; and David played for Saul to drive away his darkest moods. But music can also inflame us and send us into wars. The Song of Moses praises *Adonai ish milchama, Adonai sh'mo: the Lord is a man of War, the Lord is His name.* Now, I do have pacifist leanings; and I worry about martial music which inflames us to go into battle. But I grew up in Nazi Germany, and learned that one must fight evil, must wage war against it. Every once in a while, one of the great films of our century re-appears on television: *Casablanca*, where music plays a central role in one of its great moments: The scene, of course, is Rick's Bar Américain. Some loutish German officers are singing their national songs. Then Paul Henreid, leader of the French underground (and husband of Ingrid Bergman), rises and directs the other guests in singing 'La Marseillaise'. And the Nazi leader realizes that *that* man, and *that* music, have to be silenced. The joint appeal to emotion and to ethics is too dangerous.

A different dimension comes into play here: is it the music itself which takes hold of us, or is it the connection between music and the occasion, whether in the sanctuary or on the battlefield? Some view the music of *Parsifal* as the greatest music ever written, regardless of the character of Wagner or the contents of the *Ring* cycle. Beethoven's Ninth Symphony will stand on its own, without the text of the final movement, Schiller's 'Ode to Joy' which proclaims universal brotherhood. Can we not just surrender to great music and thank God that we have the capacity to hear it?

It remains a problem in the sanctuary. Plato's *Laws* rejects music for supporting emotion against reason. But we know, both in our lives and in our prayers, emotion and reason are joined in battle. The most emotional prayer in the synagogue is the Kol Nidrei, read and sung on the eve of the Day of Atonement, a confession of sins and a plea to God to forgive it. From its very beginning, most rabbis opposed it bitterly. In a world where the Jews were so often accused of not fulfilling their promises, here was a prayer which *seemed* to say that their promises were annulled before they were even made! The fact that the prayer only related to promises made to God, and that all promises to humans had to be kept was ignored: we cannot give false impressions! And so the rabbis banned the prayer. The ban was useless. Over the centuries, the beautiful, haunting melody which attached itself to the prayer meant that the congregation refused to abandon it. Even Jews who rarely come to synagogue insist upon coming that night, if only to hear that prayer with its music. In the end, it was the music which matters and still inspires our congregations.

I must confess that I cannot be objective in this matter. During the last seven years of her life, I visited Jacqueline du Pré almost every week. Often, since she was confined to the wheelchair and hindered in her speech, we listened to some of her recordings. Always, on the day before Yom Kippur, I would come and we would listen to her recording of Max Bruch's *Kol Nidrei*. We would hold hands, and I would cry. Jackie did not and could not cry, but the music was a prayer for us which led us to the High Holy Days. On the day of her death, two hours before her death, I sat next to her bed, listening to that recording and still holding her hand. She was in a coma; but I was convinced that the music somehow entered into her soul. Music was her religion. After I had officiated at her funeral, I received a present: the actual score of the Bruch piece from which she played. It is filled with her hand-written annotations: 'animato' over a tremolo; 'praestoso' at another place; 'peaceful contrabile' under a *un poco più animato*, or an extra 'serene'. We understand the Torah better because the medieval scholar Rashi reverently annotated every sentence. Jackie's annotations of the musical score contained a similar piety where an authentic text is enhanced with new insights. In her genius, she did create a new song.

We return to the beginning of our meditations here: *Shiru ladonai shir chadash: sing unto the Lord a new song.* This happens in every generation, and in every individual at prayer. Something within us responds to the music of the universe, to the songs which reach towards God. In our prayers we draw closer to each other and assert the visions of the Bible and of all the centuries through which we have wandered with our ancestors. The music of Bach and Bruch, of Lewandowski and Milhaud, accompanies us through our prayers. Within our sanctuary, we have walked through dark valleys and have been exalted, standing upon the mountain tops of life. In the end, having received support from our community at prayer, we also learn that we stand for ourselves. Every individual is unique, has been touched by the song of the morning stars. Now, we must find the divine which has been placed into all humanity and into our heart. Our hymns and prayers give us strength for the lonely quest into our innermost selves. We ourselves are the new song, the new praise of God.

In November 1998, I listened to a memorial lecture given by Lord Justice Konrad Schiemann, given on the 60th anniversary of the call to the Bar of Helmuth James, Count von Moltke. He quoted from a letter von Moltke wrote to his wife Freya shortly before the Nazis executed him for his fight against their injustices. In it, von Moltke confirms the freedom of the individual against the forces around him. He wrote:

Suddenly one feels that all these forces are holding their breath, that the gigantic orchestra that has played so far has fallen silent for one or two bars, to let the soloist set the tone for the next movement. It is only one heartbeat at a time, but the one note, which will sound out alone and solitary, will establish the next movement for the whole orchestra. And all await that tone.

There comes a time when we all have a solo role, and when our voice is heard. Here, in the sanctuary, we may not be the heavenly choir heard by Isaiah as they sang: *Kadosh, Kadosh, Kadosh: Holy, Holy, Holy is the Lord of Hosts*. But we still sing; and human actions also proclaim the divine in the world. All of us can make our lives a song unto God.

In *Casablanca* Claude Rains rounds up the 'usual suspects'; and then he and Humphrey Bogart, arm in arm, march forwards into an uncertain but perhaps glorious future. Why should this not happen to us? We have our own heartbeat of time, our solo moment. At any point in our lives, we may be called upon to sing a new song to God. Let us be ready for that moment. Amen.

Comments

Margaret Brearley: '*A meditation on singing to God: gentle, reflective, poetic, inspiring.*'

William Beaver: '*With music and riches of allusion, this joyful sermon is about praise, whether in harmony or as the soloist.*'

Jonathan Romain: '*A sermon by someone who knows his congregation well and is sure of the cultural vocabulary that they share – in this case, classical music – and who uses it to develop his theme. The advantage of preaching to a 'home crowd' is that the minister has a real sense of who they are and can speak directly to them.*'

It's the Thought That Counts

THE WINNING SERMON OF THE 1998 *TIMES* PREACHER
OF THE YEAR AWARD, PREACHED BY PASTOR IAN
SWEENEY AT METHODIST CENTRAL HALL,
WESTMINSTER, ON FRIDAY 27 NOVEMBER 1998

*Pastor Ian Sweeney, aged 34, and his wife Jennifer, a nurse who also
teaches sewing part-time, have three children. Mr Sweeney's father
was an engineer, and both parents, who came to Britain from Antigua
in the 1950s, were Seventh-day Adventists in Leicester.*

'Being a minister was always what I wanted to do. I was brought
up in a Christian home but, all credit to my parents, I was never
forced to go to church. At the age of about ten I felt a deep conviction
that my life should be spent sharing the word of God. From that age, I
never had any inclination to do anything else.'

*He has three congregations, with about 150 worshippers in
Carterknowle, Sheffield, 110 in Burngreave, Sheffield and about 25 in
Chesterfield, Derbyshire. The largest two are predominantly Afro-
Caribbean, with the smallest being mainly indigenous English. Mr
Sweeney was ordained in 1994 after studying for BA and MA degrees
in theology at Newbold College, Berks.*

'The value of preaching as I see it is that I am trying to help people
come to a closer encounter with God, or a clearer understanding of
the reality of who God is and what God desires for their life. I try to
make God a reality for people by being as relevant as possible to
where they are in their life. I do that by trying to make my sermons as
applicable to their experiences as possible. So I will try to make a
spiritual point by using illustrations people can relate to because they
have been there in their lives.'

*He says that a good sermon must have an aim, a purpose or an
object. 'I have to be going somewhere with a sermon. There might be
one point, two points or three points I want to convey. They have to
be points that are relevant and applicable to people's other lives right
now. The sermon needs to be illustrated as much as possible, because
people remember the illustration more than anything else. Humour
helps because it engages people. People have to engage with the
message. We live in a time when entertainment is so fast, immediate
and colourful that if you stand up in front of people for 20, 30 or 35*

minutes and are not creative, they will go to sleep on you. That is a fact.'

As a child, he recalls listening to a fiery sermon when the preacher's false teeth flew out halfway through. 'He was going hammer and tongs in the pulpit. He was an old West Indian and was really giving it. But he clearly must have played cricket. Because as his dentures flew through the air, he caught them with one hand and whipped them back in as fast as they came out. It happened so fast most people missed it, but us youngsters at the back nearly died. The preacher was as cool as anything.'

He has not seen The Full Monty. *'But I find Sheffield tremendously warm. The people are characteristically Yorkshire, in that they call a spade a spade. Even though Sheffield is a large town, there is still a strong sense of dignity. While I would be lying to say that words do not hurt me, my parents taught me that ignorance will always seek to attack that which it does not understand. I accept that the world does have a number of ignorant people in it. That is a reality of life. I don't allow things to hurt too much.'*

He believes strongly that the millennium is primarily a Christian festival. 'It is set around a time period. My hope is that it will bring people to a sense of the reality of Jesus Christ. Like Christmas, there is a danger it will be too easily hijacked and understood in terms of everything other than its original purpose.'

Winning the contest last year had more impact than he could have imagined on his life. 'Both within the church in which I serve, and in the wider community and other denominations, it has brought a wider ecumenism to my ministry. It has granted me an exposure I could not possibly have envisaged. It has been great.'

He adds: 'I really do think there is a future for preaching. Folk always look to be inspired, to be challenged. Sometimes people need to have their comfort zones challenged. Preaching helps give a greater sense of meaning to life.'

Text: John 3:16

For God so loved the world that he gave his one and only Son, that whoever believes in him shall not perish but have eternal life.

I am sure that we have all had the following experience. We tear open a neatly wrapped gift given to us by one of our nearest and dearest. We hope beyond all hope that it contains that special thing that we have been dropping hints about for the past twelve months. As the wrapping paper comes off the anticipation rises – yes, yes, yes, it is, what I've always wanted ... a pair of socks!

With joyful anticipation crushed by the reality of this boring gift, we are then counselled with the words 'NEVER MIND IT'S THE THOUGHT THAT COUNTS!' So it's the THOUGHT that counts, is it?

Well if it is, part of humanity's problem is that we don't always sufficiently apply THOUGHT before we GIVE, like the motorists who did not think through enough what they were giving as the mitigating circumstances for their accidents. Here's what they wrote on their car insurance claim forms:

'I pulled away from the side of the road, glanced at my mother-in-law and headed over the embankment.'

Or how about 'I was on my way to the doctor's with rear end trouble, when my universal joints gave way causing me to have an accident.' Or even 'To avoid hitting the bumper of the car in front, I hit the pedestrian instead.'

I know from experience that in ministry, in seeking to do God's work, we do not always sufficiently give THOUGHT before we GIVE. Picture with me the happy band of Christians who went to a prison to lift the spirits of the inmates with the good news of the gospel. Could a song more appropriate for this situation be sung than the following? Here's what they sang:

> Bless this house, O Lord, we pray,
> Make it safe by night and day.
> Bless these walls so firm and stout,
> Keeping want and trouble out.
> Bless the roof and chimneys tall
> Let Thy peace lie over all.
> Bless this door that it may prove
> Ever open to joy and love.
> Bless these windows shining bright,
> Letting in God's heavenly light.
> Bless the hearth a-blazing there
> With smoke ascending like a prayer.
> Bless the people here within,
> Keep them pure and free from sin.
>
> (Helen Taylor, 'Bless This House', © Copyright 1927
> by Boosey & Co. Ltd. Reprinted by permission of
> Boosey & Hawkes Music Publishers Ltd)

But if there were ever a case where it could justifiably be said that 'IT IS THE THOUGHT THAT COUNTS', then surely John 3:16 is it, for as Jesus said: 'Because God so loved the world he gave his one and only Son, that whoever believes in him shall not perish but have eternal life.' John 3:16 reveals the extent to which God THOUGHT before He GAVE the gift of His Son to humanity. John 3:16 reveals a number of important lessons, but to highlight two, the first of which is: THOUGHT WITHOUT ACTION IS MEANINGLESS!

Let us consider. Hurricane Mitch, which has caused so much devastation in South America. News reports have focused on small villages and communities which serve to illustrate the desperation of the situation millions of people now face. In watching those gruesome scenes it may have been that our sympathy has reached out to our brothers and sisters over there. However, if we do nothing practical to help, while capable to do so, we have said, in our inactivity, 'Never mind, it's the thought that counts.'

We all know it to be true that all of our thoughts, sympathy, and sorrow will do nothing to relieve their misery. Thought does not count for anything unless it is translated into meaningful ACTION. God thought through the needs of humanity and then He acted in sending His Son.

Now I have to admit that, having given thought, at times I wish I did not have to act. A colleague was running a series of meetings in his church focusing on family matters. He invited me to speak and address the subject of sexuality. 'Hey, no problem', I thought. I have a sermon entitled 'Let's talk about sex, baby' which is geared to a youth audience and is a frank exploration of sexuality. I had given the sermon much thought but when I stood up to preach, however, the congregation was full of old age pensioners – where were the youth?! And sitting right on the front row were two grey-haired octogenarian ladies looking expectantly into my face ... my silent prayer was 'Lord, for what they are about to receive, may they be truly thankful. Amen.' Even when you have given thought to something, you don't always want to act on it.

John 3:16 tells us that God gave thought to the needs of humanity and then put into place practical action in sending His Son.

A second and potentially troubling lesson of John 3:16 is this: THE GIFT GIVEN OFTEN REFLECTS THE VALUE PLACED UPON THE RECIPIENT. I do not want to put doubt into anyone's mind, but, husbands, what value has your wife placed on you by giving a pair of socks? 'Come to think about it, what did my wife give me last Christmas?'

THE GIFT GIVEN OFTEN REFLECTS THE VALUE PLACED UPON THE RECIPIENT. Parents, our children understand this lesson. When our children see that we do not give them quality time and attention, preferring to give our time to career, work, leisure etc, they understand all too well the value we have placed upon them.

Believe me, there are great rewards to be found in giving quality time to our children, I think of the father who was explaining the facts of life to his daughter. She listened very attentively for a while and then said 'Daddy, does God know about this?'

If anyone here today doubts the value which God has placed on us, permit me to share a true story which ever helps us to understand the value God has placed upon me as reflected in His gift.

One summer day in 1937 John Griffith, controller of a railroad drawbridge across the Mississippi, took Greg, his eight-year-old son, with him to work. About noon, John raised the bridge to let some ships pass while he and Greg ate their lunch on the observation deck. At 1:07 p.m. John heard the distant whistle of the Memphis Express. He had just reached for the master lever to lower the bridge for the train, when he looked around for his son Greg. What he saw made his heart freeze. Greg had left the observation tower, slipped and fallen into the massive gears that operated the bridge. His left leg was caught in the cogs of the two main gears.

With the Memphis Express steaming closer, fear and anxiety gripped John as his mind searched for options, but there were only two. He must either sacrifice his son and spare the passengers on the Memphis Express, or sacrifice them to spare his son.

Burying his face in his left arm, John, with an anguished cry, pulled the master switch with his right hand to lower the bridge into place.

Lord knows what anguish John Griffith had to go through, whichever decision he made.

But I know this, God values us enough to sacrifice His Son that we might live.

'For God so loved the world that he gave his one and only Son, that whoever believes in him shall not perish but have eternal life.' Most certainly in God's case, IT IS THE THOUGHT THAT COUNTS.

The Judges

Panel chairman Peter Graves

The Reverend Dr Peter Graves comes from Blackheath in south-east London. On leaving Eltham Green school, he served for a time as a library assistant and then as an Executive Officer in the Civil Service. He spent four years at Handsworth College, Birmingham, training for the Methodist ministry, and then received a scholarship from the World Council of Churches to do postgraduate studies at Union Theological Seminary in Virginia. He later trained at London University to be a teacher.

Peter Graves served Methodist churches in the Enfield and Highgate Circuits before becoming Chaplain and a lecturer at the Middlesex Polytechnic (now University), where he spent ten years and eventually became Head of Student Welfare.

He then returned to work in the local church. For ten years he was at Epsom and then moved to the North East for six years to serve in Cullercoats Methodist Church near Newcastle upon Tyne; these are two of the largest churches in Methodism. In September 1995, he became the Superintendent Minister of the Central Hall, Westminster, which is the central church of British Methodism. As such, he served as leader of the Methodist Parliamentary Fellowship, which meets in the House of Commons.

A regular writer of daily devotional notes for the Bible Reading Fellowship, he has also published articles for numerous theological and church journals, and is a frequent broadcaster. He became Vice President of the Bible Society in 1997 and was Chairman of the Judges for *The Time*'s Preacher of the Year Award for 1998.

Dr Graves is deeply interested in church growth, popular apologetics, evangelism and the use of the Bible in the local church. He is widely travelled and internationally known as a preacher and lecturer. He is married to Tricia and the couple have three children: Matthew (21), Luke (19) and Eleanor (17). He lists his interests as travel, theatre, reading and current affairs.

William Beaver

The Reverend Dr William Beaver is Director of Communications for the Church of England and the Archbishops' Council.

Prior to his appointment in 1997 he held senior communications posts at the Industrial Society, NatWest, AGB Research and Barnardo's. His doctorate is from Oxford, where he was a research fellow at the same time as preparing for holy orders at St Stephen's House.

Priested in 1983, he was a curate at St John the Divine in Brixton for fifteen years before becoming priest in charge of St Andrew's, Avonmouth. He is currently junior curate on the staff of St Mary Redcliffe, Bristol. In each post he has been recognized for the quality of his preaching.

Margaret Brearley

Dr Margaret Brearley, an Anglican, is married to Stephen, a general and vascular consultant surgeon, and they have two sons. After studying at Oxford, Münster and Cambridge, she became lecturer in mediaeval, Renaissance and Reformation literature and history of ideas in the German Department of Birmingham University, during which time she set up a day centre for the mentally ill. Dr Brearley took early retirement after thirteen years in order to found and direct the West Midlands Israel Information Centre, based in Singer's Hall Synagogue. In 1987 she became Senior Fellow at the Centre for Judaism and Jewish–Christian Relations at the Selly Oak Colleges, and from 1992 to 1996 was part-time Research Fellow in Christian–Jewish relations at the Institute of Jewish Affairs in London. Since her youngest son's serious illness, maternal commitments have prevailed over academic ones. She has lectured widely in Britain, Germany, Israel, Finland and the USA, and has published many articles, most recently a research report for the Institute for Jewish Policy Research on 'The Roma/Gypsies of Europe: a persecuted people'. She is also the author of the Foreword to this book.

Kieran Conry

A native of Coventry in the West Midlands, Monsignor Kieran Conry has been Director of the Catholic Media Office for the past five years.

Ordained a Catholic priest in 1975, Kieran spent the first four years of his ministry teaching in north Staffordshire, before being sent down to London to serve as Secretary to the Apostolic Nuncio, the Pope's representative to England and Wales. He worked with two Nuncios, Archbishops Heim and Barbarito, and then returned to his own archdiocese of Birmingham, and then to the Cathedral parish in the heart of Birmingham.

Kieran lives in the parish house of St Thomas à Becket in Wandsworth, south-west London.

Peter Kerridge

Peter, 38, is a Baptist minister. He trained at Regent's Park College, Oxford University, and has an MA in theology. Peter is married to Karen and has a four-year-old son called Jonathan, and is a keen supporter of Newcastle United.

Peter's life in radio began when he was 17. He worked as a presenter at Metro Radio in the North East and then at BBC Oxford. Peter went on to work for the Essex Radio Group, first as a presenter, then as Religious and Community Affairs Manager. He worked for Ten 17 as Managing Director and Group Director responsible for Business Development. Peter joined Premier Christian Radio on October 1996 as Programme Director, and has been its Managing Director since October 1997.

Jonathan Romain

Born in 1954, Jonathan Romain is rabbi, writer and broadcaster. He took his first degree at University College, London and then gained his PhD in Anglo-Jewish history. He studied for the rabbinate at Leo Baeck College and was ordained in 1980. As minister of Maidenhead Synagogue, his parish covers much of Berkshire and Buckingham-shire, but also allows time for writing, which includes regular articles in the religious press and, to date, six books. These include *The Jews of England* (Jewish Chronicle Publications) and *Faith and Practice: A Guide to Reform Judaism Today* (RSGB); his recent book on mixed-faith marriages, *Till Faith Us Do Part* (HarperCollins), has helped pioneer a more welcoming attitude to couples who fall in love across the religious divide. He is currently preparing a book for SCM on religious conversion in modern Britain. He is a member of the National Board of the Council of Christians and Jews, and is a trustee of the Family Policy Studies Centre. He is also the Director of the Jewish Information and Media Service, and appears regularly on the radio and television. He is married with four sons.

Pastor Ian Sweeney

(see page 201.)